PRAISE FOR
Reclaiming Calliope

"*Reclaiming Calliope* is both a finely wrought, intimate artistic memoir and a triumphant journal of a lifelong quest for the authentic, liberated female voice in face of historical and present-day patriarchal disdain."

—GABOR MATÉ, MD, author of *When the Body Says No* and *In the Realm of Hungry Ghosts*

"*Reclaiming Calliope* is many things at once. It is a memoir of such honesty and insight that it illuminates all our individual lives. It is an unflinching assessment of how the authentic female voice is systematically deprecated and silenced in our culture, exiled from the body's deep wisdom. It is a keening, outraged lament for that violence—and at the same time a patient, nurturing methodology to help women, especially, reconnect. It is a fresh, story-filled, life-affirming, beautifully calibrated message of hope."

—PHILIP SHEPHERD, author of *Radical Wholeness* and *New Self, New World* and coauthor of *Deep Fitness*

"Fides Krucker's personal and prismatic reflection on womanhood, art, the voice, patriarchy, the body, and history offers various brilliant methods of unshackling our most primal and most free selves.... It is a revelation, a freewheeling compendium of insight and great depth."

—PATRICIA ROZEMA, filmmaker, *Into the Forest*, *Mansfield Park*, *Mouthpiece*, and *I've Heard the Mermaids Singing*

"With a consummate understanding of human anatomy and physiology and with immeasurable compassion for the body's intuition, Fides plumbs the depths of the human voice, weaving its flesh and spirit together in order to unleash its true potential. This deep dive into the siren call left me digging the mermaid and brought tender tears to my eyes. Just listen. This is a love song to the human voice."

—PAUL DE JONG, voice teacher and coach/cohead of coaching, Stratford Festival

"Krucker courageously and candidly shares knowledge hard-won by experience and deep, clear-eyed examination of the damage inflicted on the human voice, especially a woman's voice, by society, cultural norms, and music (popular as well as classical) that have forced the voice into an 'acceptable' box devoid of integration with the whole self. Through personal stories, illuminative exercises, and raw truth, *Reclaiming Calliope* presents an engrossing invitation to self-discovery for singers, actors, and anyone interested in the voice."

—GRACE ZANDARSKI, head of voice and text, associate professor adjunct at David Geffen School of Drama at Yale

"In language that is as imaginatively wrought as it is deeply intelligent, Fides Krucker creates an unforgettable reading experience for anyone who has ever felt the power of song. Fearless, committed, passionate, and wise, the author is utterly frank about her own life and experiences as a woman, mother, and successful professional singer. However, the very core of this richly varied book is her innovative approach to deeply visceral and authentic singing. Interleaving revelations of her own life with penetrating insights into iconic singers, she also, and most importantly, fully immerses her readers in her own challenging—but nurturing—voice classes."

—THEO DOMBROWSKI, author, artist, and illustrator

"An utterly unique and groundbreaking exploration of voice. Weaving together personal, political, and historical anecdotes about singing, opera, and female agency, Krucker reminds us of the honesty of our bodies. You will fall in love with gravity and with the truth of the raw voice. You will fall in love with this book."

—TESSA MCWATT, author of *Shame on Me*

"To understand the imbalances in our global ecology, we desperately need to understand women and their voices. Historically, women and voice are not spoken about from the lens of the body and, when they are, emotion is amputated. As a disabled woman, artist, somatic specialist, and advocate of intimate access in the arts and all sectors, I cannot tell you how dangerous that is to our health, and how refreshing it is to relate to the climactic discoveries that Krucker shares about women."

—TRACI FOSTER, founder and artistic director, Listen to Dis' Community Arts Organization and somatic artist, Fitzmaurice Voicework and Somatic Experiencing

"This remarkable book takes the reader into its exploration of voice as a means of recovering the wholeness of being human.... 'Undomesticated singing' becomes the means for rediscovery of the authentic self and, consequently, for the ability to live authentically in relation with others.... I defy anyone, whether male, female, or nonbinary, to read this book without undergoing their own journey of transformation. *Reclaiming Calliope* can help us all reclaim our full humanity and thereby be able to find the joy of true mutuality."

—STEPHEN K. LEVINE, professor emeritus, York University, Canada; Paul Celan Professor of Philosophy and Poetics, European Graduate School; and author of *Philosophy of Expressive Arts Therapy*

"With a radical mission in a gentle tone, Fides weaves together elements of wellness that often stay apart—the nervous system, our anatomical components, and our most primal urges and desires…. This book is a personal and professional gem that explores and restores our individual and shared human landscape. There is no-body that won't benefit from reading this."

> —JILL BODAK, M.OMSc, clinical osteopath and anatomy
> educator

"*Reclaiming Calliope* is an eloquent and practical gift for the beginner vocalist to the consummate singing professional. It is also an exciting read for those simply curious about the compelling life of a brave singer who has generously, extensively, and uniquely shared their ever-growing knowledge."

> —ERIKA BATDORF, MFA graduate program director,
> Department of Theatre, York University, Canada

"Fides manages to combine an intensely personal narrative that includes intimate and family relationships with a deep knowledge of how our stories affect vocal presence, range, and the ability to assert ourselves whilst still communicating from the heart…. An essential contribution to the practice of voice within a holistic vision. Krucker's courage is exemplary in shining a path toward recognition of the intrinsic value and uniqueness in every voice, beyond cultural and societal constraints."

> —KEVIN CRAWFORD, voice teacher; founding member of
> the Roy Hart Theatre; former MFA program director at
> Accademia dell'Arte, Arezzo; and coauthor of *Roy Hart*

Reclaiming Calliope

*Freeing the Female Voice through
Undomesticated Singing*

fides krucker

North Atlantic Books
Huichin, unceded Ohlone land
aka Berkeley, California

Published by
North Atlantic Books
Huichin, unceded Ohlone land
aka Berkeley, California

Cover art: *Willow Corsets* by Kathleen Doody, photographed by Jeremy Mimnagh
Cover design by Jasmine Hromjak
Book design by Happenstance Type-O-Rama

Printed in the United States of America

Reclaiming Calliope: Freeing the Female Voice through Undomesticated Singing is sponsored and published by North Atlantic Books, an educational nonprofit based in the unceded Ohlone land Huichin (*aka* Berkeley, CA) that collaborates with partners to develop cross-cultural perspectives; nurture holistic views of art, science, the humanities, and healing; and seed personal and global transformation by publishing work on the relationship of body, spirit, and nature.

North Atlantic Books' publications are distributed to the US trade and internationally by Penguin Random House Publisher Services. For further information, visit our website at www.northatlanticbooks.com.

Library of Congress Cataloging-in-Publication Data

Names: Krucker, Fides, author.
Title: Reclaiming Calliope : freeing the female voice through
    undomesticated singing / Fides Krucker.
Description: Berkeley : North Atlantic Books, 2022. | Includes index. |
    Summary: "An exploration of the practice and politics of singing with
    the uninhibited, authentic female voice"— Provided by publisher.
Identifiers: LCCN 2021057484 (print) | LCCN 2021057485 (ebook) | ISBN
    9781623177065 (trade paperback) | ISBN 9781623177072 (ebook)
Subjects: LCSH: Women singers—Canada. | Voice teachers—Canada. |
    Singing—Instruction and study. | Women in opera.
Classification: LCC ML82 .K88 2022 (print) | LCC ML82 (ebook) | DDC
    780.92/520971—dc23/eng/20220301
LC record available at https://lccn.loc.gov/2021057484
LC ebook record available at https://lccn.loc.gov/2021057485

1 2 3 4 5 6 7 8 9 KPC 27 26 25 24 23 22

I would like to dedicate this book to my mother, Mary Krucker (1931–2021), and my daughters, Magda and Oksana Sokoloski.

They are the bench/mark where I set down body and soul to catch my breath.

Land Acknowledgment:
A Place to Begin

In Canada a growing understanding of and respect for the traditional Indigenous caretaking of territories and waterways is now formalized through spoken or printed land acknowledgments.

Throughout the summer of 2021 more than a thousand remains of Indigenous children were found on the grounds of former residential schools. The light shed on this history of assimilation and abuse demands that I face and absorb my country's shameful colonial actions.

Overt, insidious, and enduring genocidal practices codified into government legislation and commonplace attitudes have attempted to eradicate the physical presence and cultural wealth of this land's Indigenous peoples.

The more I learn about these First Nations the more unbounded my respect and gratitude.

We are all treaty people: relationship based on covenant. The Truth and Reconciliation Commission's 94 *Calls to Action*—released in 2015—outlines first steps to rectify systemic imbalances experienced by Indigenous peoples: medical care, access to education, social services, self-governance, and more. This requires consideration and engagement from non-Indigenous people as well as First Nations.

On July 1, 2021—Canada Day—I made a list of the places where I have lived and worked—places that have nourished my growth.

Tiohtià:ke/Montréal, Québec, is on the unceded* Indigenous lands of the Kanien'kehá:ka/Mohawk Nation.

Québec City, Québec, is on unceded Huron-Wendat lands.

North Bay, Ontario, is situated in traditional Anishinabek territory, on lands occupied by the peoples of Nipissing and Dokis First Nations whose aboriginal and treaty rights are recognized by the Robinson Huron Treaty of 1850 and affirmed by Section 35 (1) of the Constitution Act of Canada, 1982.

Lester B. Pearson College of the Pacific, Metchosin, British Columbia acknowledges that its community lives, learns, and works on the unceded territory of the Sc'ianew First Nation.

Banff Centre, Banff, Alberta, stands on the traditional territories of the people of the Treaty 7 region, the Stoney Nakoda, the Blackfoot Confederacy, and the Dene Tsuut'ina. It is also home to the Métis Nation of Alberta, Region III.

Vancouver, British Columbia, is on the traditional, ancestral, and unceded territory of the Coast Salish peoples: Sḵwx̱wú7mesh (Squamish), Stó:lō and səlílwətaʔɬ/Selilwitulh (Tsleil-Waututh), and xʷməθkʷəy̓əm (Musqueam) Nations.

Iqaluit is in **Nunavut**—Inuktitut for "our land." This traditional Inuit territory has been increasingly governed by its original inhabitants in a consensus-based, nonpartisan style since April 9, 1999. The process of devolution—relinquishing of federal powers—is a work in progress.

Regina, Saskatchewan, is on the traditional lands of the Treaty 4 territory. Treaty 4 was signed with thirty-five First Nations from Southern Saskatchewan and parts of Alberta and Manitoba. These

---

* *Unceded* refers to land never signed away to the Crown or Canada.

original territories of the Cree, Saulteaux, Dakota, Nakota, and Lakota are also the homeland of the Métis Nation.

Whitehorse, Yukon, is on the traditional territory of the Kwanlin Dün First Nation and the Ta'an Kwäch'än Council.

Toronto/Tkaronto, Ontario, is in the "Dish With One Spoon Territory," established by a treaty between the Anishinaabe, Mississaugas, and Haudenosaunee that bound them to share the territory and protect the land. We all eat out of the dish and there is only one spoon, meaning everyone is to ensure that the dish is never empty. Toronto is also covered by Treaty 13 signed between the Crown and the Mississaugas of the Credit First Nation, and the Williams Treaties signed with multiple Mississauga and Chippewa bands.

My home this last thirty years, Tkaronto, is diverse: a multiplicity of Indigenous nations and peoples—including the Métis and the Inuit—as well as Europeans like myself, and newcomers from around the world. The "Dish With One Spoon" treaty was based on the inviolability of peace, friendship, and respect, and it is up to me to honor this as an instruction, not just an invitation.

What can I do to replenish the dish?

How should I listen?

Contents

PART III: **Women and Voice**   **233**

Poem for My Ribs

Un-sticky but grasped around me
like a wrapped squid and hard hard
hardly a building. But such architecture
and arch and texture. I know what you're
thinking: this is beautiful, oddly.

Dear bone cage dear hard corset,
I've counted you up and down,
twelve twins and measures. No,
this is odd, beautifully. It's all bone
play and octaves, a dozen pair
of reaching arms.

Dear birdcage dear dirty corset,
inside you is a chair where no one
sits. Make me love this chair, love
the things I cannot see: my xylophone,
fishtail, musical bars and scales. A ladder
to all things so true and false and floating.

—Kimberly Grey

PART I

Unfettered
Female* Sound

---

* The words male, female, man, and woman are used throughout this book. I have felt their specific weight within my life experience and have countered their limitations through trusting what I feel in my body and recalibrating what has been constructed internally and externally in relation to gender. As much as they are necessary to the unfolding of my story I invite the reader to adapt or play with these terms in ways that resonate authentically for them... that welcome wholeness within identity and relationship.

I

"Hope" Is the Thing with Feathers

FEBRUARY 2014. THE HUMAN VOICE floats freely through the fresh spring air. There is no traffic, no hum of tall buildings. I hear women and children calling out to each other, men singing fragments of song. A community in conversation, competing with nothing but the birds and the wind and the occasional dog or cow. I yawn, mouth and arms twisting wide, eyes drifting away from the computer screen, ranging up to the sky.

I am staying at a retreat center on the edge of a small village in northern India. Its modest azure and apricot houses perch beside the deep gash and spill of a recent landslide. The waterline at the slide's foot is low, but it will soon rise, filling Pong Dam Lake to the brim with the coming monsoons.

This renowned bird sanctuary's already lush foliage floods with new color as multiple winged species return in springtime waves. The birds look and sound glorious—call-and-response, subtle acoustic triggers, and not-so-subtle showing off between males vying for females. Their orchestra swells section by section, each song's motif adding to a symphonic richness Mahler would have appreciated.

I am a singer. For thirty-five years I have performed concert repertoire with European orchestras; interpreted just-hatched contemporary opera in Canada, the United States, and Italy; created interdisciplinary work at home in Toronto. Now in my fifties, I teach professionals from all walks of life and create vocal material for younger performers—nurturing others while maturing my personal vocal passions.

Even before India, birds were on my mind. For artist Sara Angelucci's performance project *A Mourning Chorus,* six other Toronto-based singers and I used our voices to bring endangered and extinct birdcalls to life in the Art Gallery of Ontario's Walker Court. In Chicago the cries of pigeons, kinglets, and grosbeaks inspired my "vocalography" for Erica Mott and Ryan Ingebritsen's opera-installation, *3 Singers,* protesting the garment industry's deadly work conditions. A year immersed in birdsong has left me trying to make sense of every avian fragment within earshot. Practicing solitary yoga on one of the retreat's marble rooftops, I reproduce the garden's range of feathered calls just under my breath. Birds have permeated me.

Earlier this morning a throng of expansively winged, blue-black birds flew overhead. Reaching up from my second-floor balcony as if to touch their white tummies I hear gasps and "Oh, looks!" from Bella and her father, Dave. Along with Bella's mum, Izzy, and Bella's fiancé, Jono, they run the Basunti retreat center, combining intelligence, beauty, brawn, and good humor so that yoga practitioners—and occasionally, artists—can get away and, in my case, become comfortably unsettled. Bella and her dad—even Jono, when pressed—are bird fanatics; they have never seen a flock so large fly so low. I share my exhilaration with my close friend Tessa over lunch. We are both here to write, she a novel set in India and I this book on voice. Between meadow walks and simple vegetarian meals, we bow our heads to the keyboards of our respective laptops.

A few days later, I find myself tapping away against a backdrop of full-on human song. It is coming from the village. I ask Izzy what occasion is being celebrated. She tells me that Holi, the Festival of Colors, is a short festival by Indian standards, lasting only the weekend, and this is the last morning of ritual. The women have been singing and drumming for hours. I have just finished my morning's work and need a little foot stomping before lunch to clear my mind. It is hardly three minutes to the village, and the women's insistent voices draw me straight to the bright blue bungalow where they are assembled in song. I can't help myself; I wave.

The women excitedly call me into the courtyard and motion me toward a brown plastic lawn chair. They remain seated on the ground around a young drummer who looks no more than ten. Her ebullient pace tethers schoolgirl to grandmother through shared rhythm. They sing hard and loud for another ten minutes, the same eight lines, an A section followed by a B section, and then the A again. The song circles incessantly, gathering energy. Their voices are fervent, nasal, strident ... fantastically invigorating ... full of shared intention. The potency of their singing strikes me as "real."

They stop for a moment and one of the young women asks me if I would dance. I blush—I don't dance. But I feel I should offer something. I tell them I sing, and would they like that? Could I sing them a song? The young woman translates and as their heads gently wobble *yes,* I summon up a beloved Armenian folk song "Loosin Yelav." I ask my impromptu translator to explain that it is about the moon and that I am singing it in honor of last night's full one. I launch in.

Seconds later several doors fling open around the courtyard and three men dash out to see what is going on. The women laugh and I want to as well, but instead force my way to the end of the chorus. My voice's loudness stuffs my ears till I can no longer hear. My heart is pounding. *Why am I so nervous?* When the song ends we all grin at each other. I excuse myself and hightail it back to Basunti for lunch.

Why did I force myself to finish the song? Why did I rush home? Why didn't I laugh or linger? Was it necessary to be so loud? Is singing solely about performance for me? I twist and turn through these thoughts while writing, while walking, while talking to Tessa over afternoon tea on the wraparound veranda.

I wanted to thank the village's women for their voices and their lovely invitation to participate, but the dose of *fight or flight* I felt throughout my body while sharing my song has left me with a funny feeling about being a "singer." The encounter revealed the artificial within my art-making, the defense within my performance. I am disappointed that, even without a contract in hand, my offering was about something I added on to myself. Their singing appeared to be a part of life, held within the seasonal cycle of belief, ritual, food, and play—shared vibrations, more like the birds. And it looked like so much fun.

As a teacher I believe that everyone can sing. The sounds and impulses needed to express ourselves in this way come from the human autonomic nervous system, the system that gives us butterflies or tells us when we are safe, the one that moans and groans and giggles. Here in India, far from the everyday bustle of teaching, performance, and family, I am tying word to page to describe how to reconstitute emotion through breath and sound—voice integrating flesh and spirit. The truthful fine-tuning of self leading to inner harmony—an accord between heart and mind—as well as the ability to "get onstage." Expert and amateur alive within one body.

Late that afternoon Bella and I head up to the marble rooftop where I have been practicing yoga. Our mission is to sing like birds before the supper bell rings. From our perch we can see the Himalayas suspended above the far-off mouth of the reservoir. A pink haze accompanies the setting sun as Bella and I start to make sounds that are anything but polite, our big bodies translating the birds' caws and shrieks into patterns we can repeat. We practice for about an hour, throats squeezing like genteel heavy metal singers, noses channeling some Janis Joplin–esque screams, belly-laughing in our own wilderness.

That evening Izzy tells me that she and Dave were stopped dead in their tracks by sounds from above. She asked him about the "new birds" in the garden—had he ever heard this particular noise before?

2

Room to Breathe

IF YOU WANTED to join my vocal studio, I would ask you to take an introductory private lesson. In that first session you would learn that air wants you to thrive, that it does not discriminate between individuals, that it is not out of reach. As our first hour progressed I would focus on your body and its breath patterns. I would weave in some of my personal story while asking about yours.

"How do you describe your relationship to your voice?"

You answer and I listen. Empathy toddles between us.

"Sit beside me." I indicate a cushion on the floor of my studio. "I'm going to demonstrate an exercise known as the *dark breath*, originally taught to me in the late '80s by my mentor, Richard Armstrong."

I lie down on my daughter's faded blue yoga mat, nestle the back of my body into its thin rubber skin. Opening my mouth, I invite air to flow all the way into my lower torso, swelling right where my belly displays and betrays ... where Buddha softens. Falling in love with gravity, I softly release muscle past pubic bone to vagina, perineum, and anal sphincter. Each inhale silent, gentle, expansive. The work of it does not look or feel like work—it is pure pleasure.

Receiving air encourages me to stay present to myself, stay true to today's challenges and gifts. My goal is not to impress you but to allow you to see me in process; no "measuring up" under the microscope of someone else's gaze. Follow your hunches with regard to what you see in my body, what you feel responding in yours. If my sound is sad, mad, or glad, you are allowed to note and name it. I am not the emotional expert ... *we are.*

I ease my sacrum into the mat with each exhale, melting further into earth. My legs and pelvis come to life. With each "out-hale" soft undulations sluice toward toes. I feel a ripple up my spine as well and allow my head to move as it wishes, skull loosely weighted to the floor. The slow wiggle through my neck bones is a more recent development, led by my body's gentle intuition as it accounts for the remains of a frozen shoulder. Arms release wider still as I turn into a single-celled creature in love with primordial ooze. For the moment, a persistent tendency to take on too much slips away. I swim in what is current.

Exhaled breaths tumble out smoky-audible: unvoiced sighs from behind my sternum, birthed at the base of my trachea. I ask my body, "What's up? *Now ... and now ... and now.*" My inner animal awakes, responds with a touch of phonation, vocal cord on vocal cord, sound within the smoke. Preverbal exploration further loosens breath, allowing my voice to fall in more deeply with gravity ... to darken.

I think of earth, of where my food comes from. I picture my youngest brother's organic farm, the dirt on our boots when we return from a visit. Chris and his wife, Denise, practice permaculture—a cooperative, indigenous agricultural tradition that returns the land to itself, invites plant and animal species to be true to their nature and to collaborate with one another. This appeals to my mind and heart, but it is the taste of the food and the feeling of deep well-being after a walk on the uneven trails in the woods behind his barn that leave my diaphragm freer. This memory of wholeness encourages me to follow my body, hear what it has to say here on the mat.

Lying in front of you, I am both specimen and breath whisperer. Besides today's earthy memories, I learn that I have been defending myself under the covers. Clutching my ribcage through the night "from the inside out" has left me with a painful ache where floating ribs and diaphragm meet. I note that the opera I recently produced and sang is over, but much as I can let those responsibilities go, I seem to be dragging my feet when it comes to releasing my character's trauma. (She suffered a brain injury and then killed her ex-lover ... not the most relaxing of times.) I am also holding on to the less operatic, but equally epic, stresses within which my real-life partner and I have been mired for longer than I'd like to admit. Getting out of bed anything but refreshed, our impasse clings to my early-morning body. Allowing my diaphragm to pull wide "involuntarily" as I demonstrate for this new student has clarified where my current physical and emotional stories meet while reminding me of breath's capacity to renew and heal.

Please take your turn on my daughter's yoga mat.

I will talk you through.

Surrender. Receive. Swell. Soften. Release.

This is Annette's* first lesson. She has just taken her place on the mat. The quiet gurgles coming from her tummy let me know that she is ready. Before she takes this first foray into the wilderness of breath, I ask her what secret wish brought her here. Her lower lip trembles. "My digestion has been bad for almost a year now. It would be wonderful if that improved."

Annette has only a few months to delve into her voice. She is a dancer, and like many dancers, she is a gentle soul with abs of steel. She is about to begin a new project with a choreographer who will push her to her edge. Annette tells me this with glee, but all I can think is *I remember that feeling ...* and *that is hard to sustain.* I ask her how her autonomic nervous system figures into her dancing. Her response is swift and accurate; she needs to encourage *rest and digest* functions because she is tightly strung. I see her attachment to her autonomic nervous system's sympathetic responses in the certainty of her belly. Annette also confesses that the adrenaline of *fight or flight* can get the better of

---

* In order to include studio stories I obtained written permission from my students; some granted the use of their actual name, and some chose an alias. I am grateful to each one for the courage and self-awareness it takes to invite readers to eavesdrop on their transformations.

her nerves in performance. I note that her upper chest is doing all the work when breathing and her lower torso appears girded for battle … nothing betrayed.

As well as dancing, Annette teaches Pilates, originally called Contrology. The codified "working" breath within that discipline, and many other physical practices, can become an armed diaphragmatic breath if it supplants *rest and digest*'s intrinsically replenishing breath. When an even slightly gripped diaphragm takes over from one that remembers how to expand into time and space, shallow breathing can become that body's pernicious default mode … and, in consort with the mind, can create a tale of perpetual, low-grade anxiety.

I don't reveal these thoughts. As a teacher I try to be diplomatic around breath. Because we breathe to survive, we are justifiably possessive of habitual tension. I tell Annette that all breath has purpose, and that what we work on here might be different from how she breathes elsewhere. Mostly I tell her that her body needs to be listened to in order to lead. It is more than willing to tell her what is gorgeous about being alive and with enough time can teach the conscious mind about balanced breath.

Seated on the floor beside Annette I guide her through the *dark breath* exercise, quietly witnessing and encouraging her journey. My hands occasionally touch her belly, lower back, or upper and lower ribs, subtly suggesting more—or less—work. Annette gradually stops drawing air in through her nose, stops directing its inward flow to her upper chest. As she softens into her belly, the sounds coming from her mouth deepen as well. They tell the intimate story of her body—some disgust, some pain, some comfort, some pleasure. I witness her as a lover might. No need to explain or justify the body's sounds.

I draw the exercise to an end and ask Annette what she experienced in her body, how it feels now. She tells me that she has increased sensation in her vagina, which makes it feel less defended … her jaw too … and even the top of her ribcage has become soft. These things surprise her. I am delighted by Annette's sensitivity and clarity when recounting this fully in-the-moment story of her body.

If you were lying on my daughter's faded blue yoga mat I would ask you how your body had responded to the *dark breath*—what it told you. I would encourage you to recount its story, beginning with something you enjoyed, or something your body taught you. Something brand-new or accidentally tucked away. I would hope that—just like Annette giving in to her body's tale—you had been able to release into your flesh, breath, and blood story … maybe even start a new narrative line.

One that is yours.

3

Night after Night

I CAME ACROSS a *New York Times* review of minimalist composer John Adams's new violin concerto while sharing writing time with my friend Julie Trimingham at her Lummi Island home in the Pacific Northwest. Anthony Tommasini's March 27, 2015, article is titled "John Adams Unveils 'Scheherazade.2,' an Answer to Male Brutality." As conjured by Adams and embodied by the brilliant violinist Leila Josefowicz, Scheherazade is "commanding and vulnerable, slashing and sensual." The last of the concerto's four movements is called "Escape, Flight, Sanctuary." I am hungry to know more about Scheherazade and scavenge online. The bones of her story are easy to find, nestled within one of the world's greatest folkloric treasures.

The Arabian Nights is a collection of individual tales culled from a wide geographic swath that includes India, Iran, Iraq, Egypt, Turkey, and possibly Greece and China. They began to coalesce around the same time that Islamic architects discovered that an imam's voice projected more easily into the courtyard when a mosque's ceiling was clad in hard materials. Also known as *The One Thousand and One Nights*, the collection preserved a rich tapestry of Indo-Persian culture for ten centuries before Antoine Galland's 1717 French translation titillated European audiences, in part, through its original scaffolding device. This narrative frame introduces the young, beautiful, and intelligent

Scheherazade and marries her to King Shahryar of Persia. Night after night, for close to three years, she tells her husband bedtime stories … perfects the serial cliff-hanger. I imagine them on the edge of the royal bed—her breath baiting his—he, edgy with bated breath. But why?

Long before marrying Scheherazade, Shahryar was betrayed by his first wife. Like his brother's spouse, she'd been sexually unfaithful. Both men were enraged. The king sought revenge by marrying virgin after virgin, killing each one in turn after a single night of wedded bliss. What a mental file of 3-D centerfolds! What a way to guarantee fidelity! The shame of cuckoldry must be worse than that of killing a woman.

Other works of art promote the idea that women have a hard time staying true. In Mozart's 1790 opera *Così fan tutte** the story's moral guide, Don Alfonso, explains to his young male charges that all women are fickle and will cheat! Without this key suspicion there would be no opera, no fiancés disguising themselves as Albanians, no young women swooning over dark strangers, no shenanigans or broken hearts.… But that's another story …

Back in Persia, Scheherazade's paterfamilias—the king's vizier—was charged with finding marriageable girls for Shahryar, and, in some versions of the tales, with beheading them too. When the kingdom ran out of virgins, Scheherazade offered herself up in marriage, wanting to help her father, who was in a really tight spot. Sounds reckless, stupid, silly—but a girl often loves her dad enough to try to fix a bad situation, make up for his shortcomings.

Fortunately Scheherazade was well educated and well spoken and, well, charming! She was convinced that she could keep herself alive if her sister, Dunyazad, "kept six" on the other side of the matrimonial bed's curtain by requesting yet another tale. Scheherazade's careful dropping of narrative crumbs led the couple through that first night and into the promise of another day.

Fear makes us hold our breath. It tightens hips and diaphragm. Did Scheherazade hold her breath ever so slightly while privately

---

* This opera will be exposed more fully in a later chapter.

entertaining her husband and king? If she was afraid, could he tell, or was she confident in her ability to spin tales of epic proportion? Whose narratives kept them preoccupied? I look over the list: Aladdin, Sinbad, Ali Baba, The Bull and the Ass ... lusty trysts, crime, and horror ... science fiction (yes, science fiction in the tenth century), philosophy, and Islamic discourse. Did she reveal anything about herself? Not really; her story is about telling other people's stories. One woman keeping herself alive by recounting almost exclusively male stories. How precarious. Dangerous for us all. And what a pity for a man not to learn more about the woman with whom he shares the intimacy of his bed.

Despite all the sites devoted to this couple's bedtime ritual, I don't learn anything about Shahryar's earlier wives. Were these brides not clever or inspiring enough? What were their stories? Thankfully for a bunch of virgins the king never got to, Scheherazade was a canny survivor who knew how to guarantee her own breath—phrase after phrase after phrase, tale after tale, puff after fragile little puff. Inspire, expire ... inspire again.

Stories can keep us alive: they are persuasive, they reveal, and they teach. Besides appreciating the extraordinary range of fables that Scheherazade told from Islam's Golden Age, and the thrill we experience when she escapes death, we can ask, what else happened, and what is ours to learn? There are many different endings. In some she bears him three sons over those three years, which warms his heart toward her. In others he is simply distracted from his original purpose, that of beheading her. And in another version she asks for pardon, and it is granted. *Pardon from what exactly?*

My female friends get a happy look on their faces when I mention Scheherazade's name. We see her as a heroine—well known and good at what she does—and yet very few have registered the ramifications of her awkward, personal position, despite *The Arabian Nights* becoming so public, so famous (so viral, so YouTubed, so tweeted, so selfied, so Instagrammed ... so Kim Kardashianed ...). We have missed the fact that its framing device is essentially and insidiously violent, and, instead, have internalized a story that teaches us that a woman must

15

learn to entertain extremely well—strategically, even—through telling primarily male stories, night after night. And, if she does a good job, she gets to live. And, if she does not, she will be killed. Maybe this is exactly what celebrity Kim Kardashian is still doing and why she has such a wide reach. Balancing a martini glass on your ass might be just as survival-based as Scheherazade's spellbinding storytelling over one millennium before. Both women living off the compromise. *But what kind of living is this?*

Just this morning a young woman came for a first lesson. After demonstrating the opening breath and voice exercise, I spoke of the connection between the mouth on my face and the mouths of the pelvic floor, both anus and vagina. I saw her shift a little, her face tighten slightly. I invited her to share her thoughts, whether she imagined I'd like them or not. She took a deep breath and said that she felt uncomfortable seeing my mouth so open while making such rich, unfettered female sound—sound unbound by anyone else's storytelling. "This may sound crazy ... I shouldn't even say it, it's so dark ... but I am worried that if I were to open my mouth that wide I would be raped."

4

Old Stories

IT IS 1965. I am smack dab in the middle of a picnic blanket, surrounded by my mum, my Aunt Fides, and my younger brother Andrew. Behind us an enormous tree stands guard over the late summer's yellowing grass.

My young Swiss aunt is glamorous in her dark sunglasses. Next to her, Andrew, freckled and toddler-chubby, squints at the camera. Mum's hair burns deep russet, and mine—chestnut—is gathered into one long braid that dangles the length of my spine. Knees bent, head thrown back, mouth wide open, eyes sweetly closed. Four-year-old features fully surrendered to song.

Dad must have taken the shot but I can't imagine him with us. When I show the picture to Mum neither of us can figure out where my littlest brother is either. Maybe Dad is juggling baby and camera?

As a young man my father applied his good eye and manual dexterity to pastry-making, becoming a baker like his father and grandfather before him. After a four-year apprenticeship in Sion, Switzerland, he turned his back on his family's wood-burning ovens and the tightness of the Alps. One week on a boat crossing the Atlantic, followed by a long train ride north through miles of bush, landed him at a state-of-the-art paper mill in Témiscaming, on the border of Ontario and Québec. Trading cold Alpine rock for even colder Canadian shield, he baked bread and Black Forest cakes for international businessmen staying at the White Oaks Inn.

My mother met my father the following summer at a Muskoka resort where she was salad girl to his much higher status European pastry chef. The chemistry between them is visible in the few black-and-white snapshots we have from that time. Mum and Dad married in Montréal two years later, once he had left the Roman Catholic Church to join the Anglicans. My mother is quite clear that he did not do this for her, though I can't help but note that her father was a charismatic evangelical Anglican minister, suspicious of Catholics. One of my dad's sisters recounts how, on the other side of the Atlantic, their father railed up and down the streets of their little town at the thought of his son marrying *eine Reformierte* woman.

This reformed woman, a Protestant, stayed home and raised three children. She kept a clean house with minimum time spent on daily chores; a favorite trick was to leave the vacuum cleaner running in the middle of a room, exit, and then close the door on it! She volunteered at Sunday school and was a substitute teacher off and on in primary and middle schools.

We started moving after I finished Grade One, changing house, school, and city often over the following years. My father's abilities were in high demand and his ambition meant that he was willing to uproot the family. By the time I entered Grade Twelve I'd been to twelve schools—first in French, and then when we left Québec for Ontario, in English. Mum was willing to do whatever it took to make our lives stable, smoothly setting up home while finding a suitable church. We kids knew that Dad's daily disappearance to "go to work" was import-ant, and although I felt distressed when he went away on a business trip, none of us questioned the value of his job. At home Mum held the fort so well that what she did didn't seem like "work."

Now having parented two daughters and three stepsons, I want to know more about my mother's inner experience during those years. Mum often reminds me that her mother wore a corset as a young woman, replacing it during her childbearing years with a full girdle. The invention of the washing machine was a really big deal for Grandma, as was flying in an airplane. She once whispered to me in the backseat of a car that *she liked eating pizza!* I expect similar stories from my mother.

But she takes me down a darker path. When Mum was still single in the mid-1950s, she was hired to work with high school students in Montréal for an interdenominational Christian group—she has always had a keen interest in young people. When she and my father decided to get married, they chose a date during March break for the wedding so as not to disturb the school calendar. When she alerted her employer, he told her she would have to leave her job; once married, her husband would be able to provide and they would likely be starting a family. Dad's work was sanctioned and Mum's was not. Mum's eyes soften helplessly and the back of her neck takes on a tiny side-to-side shake as she confesses her story, hurt and shock resonating through her usually robust and cheerful being. Mum's deeper body truth is news to me.

Remembering the faded photo of our happy picnic, I realize that my twenty-six-year-old aunt, visiting from Switzerland, wouldn't have had the right to vote federally in her homeland for another six years. On both sides of my family, beliefs about women, their value and their agency, have been stuffed into the bodies of my forebears through lived female experience. This legacy has shaped me—body, voice, and spirit. It has also shaped my brothers.

Cultural tales, absorbed through bouncy rhythms, seductive arrangements, and catchy melodies, become deeply incorporated. Children love to belt out a favorite school song, or borrow a hook from their parents' playlist. They are good at *lalala-ing* their way through a glad, sad, or mad moment. The tunes that looped on the family car eight-track tape deck still wind through my mind … *Michelle, ma belle, Trailers for sale or rent, Is that all there is?* … even a little Swiss yodeling. The hymns we sang in church also return unbidden. Square my shoulders.

When I pulled on my grandmother's mandarin-collared emerald silk dress this past Christmas, it curved perfectly over my breasts and hips. The polished gleam of her silver tea service and the soprano sheen she and my mother shared when singing—never quite spilling over into our own sadness—are also mine.

5

"This Is a Man's World!"

AFTER TWO YEARS of intensive study at Lester B. Pearson College of the Pacific,* I sat for my International Baccalaureate exams in May 1979 and, after saying goodbye to dear friends through shared tears, headed to my parents' temporary home in Seattle, Washington, for the summer. I was nineteen, knew no one in the city, and to make the months before our planned return to Burlington, Ontario, less lonely I took piano, harpsichord, and singing lessons at Seattle Pacific University. In September I followed several of my Pearson friends to the registrar's office at Trinity College and was accepted as a second-year Bachelor of Arts student at the University of Toronto. My courses included anthropology, psychology, psycholinguistics, Italian, and German. Striding the six-minute length of Philosopher's Walk to the Royal Conservatory of Music, I found a singing teacher and was soon slipping into practice

---

* Pearson College, founded in 1974 near Victoria, British Columbia, was the second United World College to be established; there are now eighteen such schools, on four continents, with the aim of uniting cultures and countries around the world through international understanding. When I arrived in 1977, the student body was two hundred strong, from fifty nations, and each of us was on full scholarship. The campus is nestled in the woods next to the ocean, on the unceded territory of the Sc'ianew First Nation.

rooms between classes to work on Bach arias and lieder by Schumann and Schubert. At the end of the year, disillusioned by the size of my psychology classes and the department's behaviorist approach, I decided to take a break from academic study.

I announced to my parents that I was going to study harpsichord in Switzerland and started to pack my trunk. Two weeks before my planned departure, my father asked me to stay. He needed someone to run his new business, a large industrial bakery specializing in croissants. I was surprised that he wanted to fold me into his work life and thought it an unusual opportunity for a young woman more aligned with musical lines than assembly lines. Despite a dusting of flour in my dark curls, I did not find the bakery remotely romantic; it was grueling. After two years of hard work I'd had enough, but I didn't know how to say *no* to my father. To avoid confrontation—and to have what, for my mother, would have counted as legitimized sex—I got engaged. My fiancé, a favorite cousin's roommate, was a theater major who had spent his early adolescence in Sicily. Lino looked like a young Frank Sinatra, had a great sense of humor … and he liked my cheesecake.

The day of our wedding my father bundled me into his vintage red Corvette and drove at breakneck speed to the white clapboard Anglican church he and my mother attended. An uncontrollable case of giggles helped me relax; I even forgot that morning's fruitless search for the wedding bands Lino and I had had engraved. By the end of the reception, held in Hamilton Place's velvet-draped Studio Theatre, my cheeks ached from smiling. That day's drama marked my move away from German lieder's elegant agony toward the chaotic wrestle of Italian aria. I loved the emotional pitch of Sunday lunch at my in-laws' home and wanted to set up camp forever in their unreserved, easy-to-read climate. Faces were animated; voices rose in chorus. Joy, sorrow, and passion resonated freely, careening past a 3-D plaster image of the Colosseum, down to the pale-blue velvet chesterfield below, and back again to our linguine-trailing forks.

After the wedding I majored in Italian literature at McMaster University while continuing to work part time for my father as he moved his business into an even larger plant. So much for escaping the bakery. I found time to study with two voice teachers, but in doing so broke a sacred vocal rule. It takes trust to make over the inside of the breath canal, devotion to balance resonance within chest, mouth, and sinuses. Differing pedagogical approaches are confusing for a young singer. Maria Pellegrini, a sensuous *spinto* soprano—*spinto* meaning lyrical, yet capable of pushing dramatically—was at the height of her expressive powers and modeled a glimmering *bel canto* technique that reflected her Italian roots. Wayne Strongman—intellectual and progressive—used his determined, Germanic vocal pedagogy to dive into the creation of new opera. One teacher spoke to my instinct and sensuality, the other to my drive and curiosity. Though it sounds like a great educational cocktail, their differing values were hard to reconcile in one body.

For the next two years I performed small roles with Opera Hamilton, became a soloist at Central Presbyterian Church, and sang lieder and arias in concert. When my husband went to work full time for my father, I practically ran off to the Banff Centre to perform in Benjamin Britten's opera *A Midsummer Night's Dream*. Against an enchanted backdrop of magical flower juice, mixed-up lovers, and some of the twentieth century's most glorious classical music, my marriage to Lino came to an abrupt end. This was not entirely surprising; our rings, invisible to me before the ceremony, had been located post-honeymoon right below the bathroom mirror where I had checked my hair and makeup before heading to church to assume the role of "wife."

Lino kept the condo and I stayed in Banff to attend the Centre's two-year cutting-edge Music Theatre Studio Ensemble (MUTSE) program along with eleven performers from Canada, the United States, and the United Kingdom. The Centre's resources were ample in the '80s and we were all on full scholarship—tuition plus room and board. MUTSE, the brainchild of Michael Bawtree,* was entering its fourth year of existence the fall our cohort arrived. I breathed in the program's freshness along with the bracing mountain air.

Six days a week we arrived in the studio at 8:30 a.m. to train in movement, acting, singing technique, and Pochinko-based clowning.† The physical practice of maverick movement and clown pedagogue David MacMurray Smith and individual coaching with beloved speech instructor and healer Colin Bernhardt were pedagogical building blocks. Renowned voice teachers, feted composers-in-residence, inventive librettists, and provocative directors came and went as we workshopped a variety of new operas: excerpts and whole pieces. Experiencing multiple drafts of words and melody allowed us to tinker with the engine of lyric storytelling, and, even though what came across our music stands wasn't always good, there was much to learn from trying to sing and act emergent material under the eyes of an experienced, international faculty.

Studio time led into ongoing arguments in the hallways or over a pint of early Alberta craft beer in the Sally Borden building: What should we call the art form we were engaged in? Should it be "opera" or "music theater"? "Musical theater" was not an option, as we looked down our noses at "musicals," thinking them popular entertainment. We were "classical singers," proud of our superior vocal athletics and refined aesthetic tastes.

Opera can turn both singer and listener inside out. Epic voices ride sound waves, set flesh vibrating, trigger emotion. One audience

---

* Michael, an actor, writer, and director, was born in Australia in 1937 and educated in England. He immigrated to Canada in the early '60s and held many important roles at the Stratford and Shaw Festivals before founding COMUS Music Theatre in Toronto with the Canadian contralto Maureen Forrester. After taking over as director of the Banff School of Fine Arts summer performance program he established MUTSE as a full-time winter program to modernize opera creation and performance.

† Richard Pochinko was a revered Canadian clown pedagogue through the '70s and '80s. His unique, rigorous, and expansive style of clowning drew from both First Nations and European traditions.

member's chest feels ripped apart; another's eyes and sinuses sting and flood; a third gets clammy hands, then starts to fidget. Held by the theater's darkness, we are riled, soothed, seduced, inspired. Music and emotion are birthed under the skin.

The term *opera* originates from the Latin word for work or labor. "Grand opera" is considered "whole," as it uses the human voice, an orchestra, full-blown staging, and often dance to bring the music and text to life. Michael Bawtree's pioneering program sought to balance a libretto's story within the challenge of New Music. Its risk-taking productions demanded we give equal interpretive value to both sing- ing *and* acting. Each week's still-wet handwritten scores had char- acters and situations that were contemporary, with music that was much less of a foregone melodic, rhythmic, or harmonic conclusion. This adventuring made the traditional operas that had been part of our previous undergraduate training programs seem predictable and out of date. But despite the newness of what we were attempting, our "music theater" was not free of opera's limiting relationship dynamics.

I cannot recall a single libretto that did not carry stale beliefs about how men and women should behave with one another and what a woman's place was in the world. I am not surprised. Our "radical" new opera program was as cloistered by institutional hierarchies as the Centre is by snowcapped mountain peaks: it was run by men, had a predominantly male faculty, and supported pieces created, for the most part, by men. Pieces that promoted tragic female arche- types, ignored second-wave feminism, and left me trying to get things "right" under the gaze of male directors and conductors. Our rehearsal hall conversations did not consider gender inequality—nor invite a range of unfettered sound from the female voice—either of which could have ushered in a new sense of operatic "wholeness." These omissions encouraged the development of a vocal "self" utterly out of step with social progress.

At the end of my second year I was invited by one of my favorite teachers, and Bawtree's life partner, Colin Bernhardt, to perform the

1958 monodrama *La voix humaine* (*The Human Voice*) by French composer Francis Poulenc. For forty minutes a woman's last desperate phone call with her ex-lover is wrought larger than life. Jean Cocteau's text has her plead with him for affection, remind him of their former happiness, and reveal that she has attempted suicide. Colin's production was lavish. Wearing a silk teddy and jewel-toned turban, I paced the raked set, antique phone in hand. The show was an unusual double bill; before I sang the opera in French, Colin had me act the entire play in English. Each evening I went through Elle's emotional torture twice.

The production's monthlong rehearsal process held an additional layer of stress for me due to our pianist's expansive, sensual nature and his relentless talk about sex and creativity during our one-on-one music rehearsals. He was one of the younger faculty members and friends with my boyfriend and me. The lines he crossed verbally left me feeling pressured, confused, and exhausted. I managed the coaching room dynamics through deflection and humor, much as I would throughout my career, and because nothing tangible happened, I never voiced my discomfort. I didn't want to lose out on Colin's sensitive, mystical stage direction, which was encouraging me to grow as an actress, and the pianist was a brilliant musician. But, despite giving the production my all, I can now see that I missed the point of the story. Elle's tragedy is not that she is betrayed by her lover; it is that she must act out being an unnamed, secondary character even when she is the only person onstage.

Acting and singing Elle taught me to long for an unavailable man while suffering beautifully under performative duress, on and off the stage. I wonder if her creators, Cocteau and Poulenc, as well as my director, Colin—all of whom identified as gay before homosexuality was legalized—were invested in this story because of Elle's unrequited longing, her behind-closed-doors pain, and the shame that unsanctioned desire engenders. In hindsight I believe that our music rehearsals' coupling of muddy sexual waters with artistic process hobbled my ability to speak up, while further inuring me to my profession's gender inequalities.

During my final year at Banff, the great late-twentieth-century composer Luciano Berio* was invited to be the music program's composer-in-residence. The second I knew he was coming I begged to sing his *Folk Songs*. The year before, at British director Richard Jones's suggestion, I had listened to Cathy Berberian's extraordinary recording of this song cycle. She was not only Berio's ex-wife; she had collected a number of the songs. Through listening obsessively to Cathy's artistry, accompanied by the gentle hiss of needle on vinyl, I began to imagine vocal sounds not condoned by the classical world. I sequestered myself nightly in a practice booth, and, following her lead, took on the breath, chest, and sinus patterns of "real" women from eight different cultures. It felt like coming home.

Berio's arrival at the Calgary airport was met with heavy snowfall. During the nerve-racking trip into the mountains, he asked Daniel Janke—a fellow student doubling as rehearsal conductor and van driver—about the three singers who would be performing the *Folk Songs*. When Daniel told him that there was only one, Berio countered angrily: since Berberian's death he had not allowed any one singer to handle the cycle alone, and had instead split the eleven songs among three singers according to each woman's timbral quality. At our first rehearsal Berio underlined his displeasure by reaching over my music stand to take away my score. In silence, he lifted his baton. My heart plunged; I hadn't consciously memorized the songs. Riding my own racing heart, I transformed myself from the inside out, grateful for the hours I'd spent identifying with his ex-wife as she voiced a wide range of emotion, culture, and story. I passed Berio's test and over the following years received phone calls from various European orchestras inviting me to sing the

---

* Luciano Berio, Cavaliere di Gran Croce OMRI, was a third-generation Italian composer who began his studies with his father and grandfather. From the early '50s he made a name for himself as an authoritative practitioner of the avant-garde. Prompted by his wife Cathy Berberian, he expanded the expressive use of the female voice in his compositions. He focused on music theater to further research his poetics and the balance between tradition and new forms. He established Italy's first electronic studio.

Folk Songs, at his request, with conductors such as Myung-whun Chung and Peter Eötvös.

During those early post-Banff years, I also toured Paul Dresher's two-hander *Slow Fire* throughout the States and performed a staged *Pierrot lunaire* in the United Kingdom and Middle East. I didn't feel balanced, but I was stimulated. To deal with the pre-show terror and excitement that ping-ponged through my adrenalized being, I prayed to the gods while stretching out my hips on hard dressing room floors. In Europe, Berio was often present at rehearsals of his *Folk Songs;* sometimes he conducted. During those sessions I learned to hide behind pillars during breaks to avoid his attempts to kiss and grope me. I had been shown his letter of recommendation by the Opéra de Lyon's artistic director and knew that my vocal adventuring reminded him of his ex-wife. He reminded me of my father due to his age, European charm, and high standards. After a few years of embrace-dodging, I'd had enough and rented a car post-concert. I fled down the coast to Sicily, seeking refuge with an older female friend, singer Petra Malakova. I stopped at phone booths along the way to explain to Berio that I couldn't sing for him anymore. His voice's thick texture made me suspect that my flight was just as intriguing to him as the pillar game.

My rejection of Berio's selfish, greedy behavior affected my career. I returned to Canada and, instead of taking time to process what I'd experienced, threw myself into interdisciplinary and New Music creation. Work provided a rough and humble path that consumed my creative passion, but Berio's conflation of my sexuality with my voice left me with a complex emotional residue that would take decades to wash away. Would I ever be a good enough singer?

6

Death by Traditional Opera

LIKE SCHEHERAZADE IN *The Arabian Nights,* opera uses a woman's voice to convey men's stories. Carmen, Tosca, and Violetta are three of the better-known female characters incarnated through melody to suit their male composers. They tell us their fictional stories at the tops of their lungs. Bizet's Carmen, a cigar factory worker who moonlights as a smuggler, is murdered by the "nice guy" when she tries to maintain her sexual freedom. Puccini's Tosca sings that she "lives for art" while trying to save the life of the artist she loves; in the final act, unable to prevent his execution at the hands of the authorities, she jumps to her death. Verdi's Violetta is a high-society courtesan who falls in love with a respectable young man. His father asks her to break it off for social reasons and she does. Violetta becomes ill and dies of tuberculosis.

———

In Chinese medicine the lungs are home to grief.
In opera women's lungs spew grief.

A soprano uses her cultivated skills and vocal prowess to illustrate the deep suffering of the operatic character she is embodying, so that when listening to an aria we think we are hearing how the feminine is *feeling*. But opera actually reinforces how we *treat* women—without ever letting collective female truth out of the bag. The out-of-this-world breath control a "solo" singer employs to express her character's situation, combined with society's resistance to women fully expressing their dilemma, results in irrefutable punishment. Often the courtesan, smuggler, or "girlfriend of" knows that death is on its way, can feel it in the accompanying orchestral undertow, but no amount of intelligence, emotional sensitivity, or loyalty will avert the playing out of her tragic end.

A domesticated woman (even a partially domesticated woman) does not a good opera heroine make. The role she plays is much too foundational to everyone's daily existence. Today's partner and/or mother (who usually has a job) does not have the time or space to sing about how fucking happy or utterly unbalanced she feels. A courtesan, a bohemian artist, or a smuggler from the eighteenth or nineteenth century singing about how fucking happy or out-of-bounds she feels is much less threatening. Her exotic role excuses her extreme feelings and behavior while explaining the over-the-top actions and reactions of everyone else onstage. More importantly, when she dies, her place at the edge of society protects us from feelings of guilt or responsibility over her treatment. Ironically, the beautiful vocal contours a singer gives her doomed character's anguish relieve each man or woman listening of their own pain: manageable personal catharsis without tearing down social constructs.

My mother, listening to the Saturday afternoon Metropolitan Opera broadcast while lying on our chesterfield, could take a well-deserved three-hour break from caring for my brothers and me. The singers' vocal bodies might have reunited her with her sensate self, but their luxurious sounds didn't provoke fundamental change.

The opera that hooked me when I was nineteen, and had only taken a few singing lessons at the conservatory, was Viennese composer Alban Berg's *Lulu*. Written between 1929 and 1935, it is a hallucinogenic cocktail of sex, betrayal, murder, and blackmail. In the prologue the owner of a small circus menagerie introduces Lulu, the opera's sexually liberated central character, as an evil snake who has been tamed by human reason. The ensuing three acts reveal Lulu's desperate quest for love. At a dizzying pace, she mistakes passion for connection, sharing her body first with her physician husband, followed by an artist, then a newspaper editor and his composer son, after them an athlete, then a schoolboy—and finally an African prince. Sometimes Lulu is manipulated, and sometimes she does the seducing. Either way each sordid encounter spawns disaster.

Lulu is married three times during the opera, shooting her last husband partway through Act Two. This lands her in prison, where she intentionally contracts cholera in order to escape with the help of the much older, lesbian Countess Geschwitz, who is in cahoots with the athlete and Lulu's father—an asthmatic beggar who denies his parental role by stating that *no one* has fathered her yet. By Act Three, her finances crumbling, Lulu resorts to prostitution. She is drawn to a mysterious client and offers her body for nothing. Meanwhile, the countess resolves to become a lawyer to fight for women's rights. Lulu's mysterious client is Jack the Ripper; he kills her. The countess declares her undying love for Lulu and dies as well. What a pell-mell story.

Berg worked on *Lulu* for six years before dying at fifty of sepsis, leaving Act Three unfinished. It premiered, incomplete, in 1937 and was not performed again for decades. In 1979 it was published with a full instrumentation for the third act by Austrian composer and Berg disciple Friedrich Cerha. This version was conducted by the renowned composer Pierre Boulez in Paris with the great Canadian singing actress Teresa Stratas playing Lulu. I saw the Canadian Opera Company's production the following year while studying at the University of Toronto.

The opera is based on the free-spirited, sexually potent protagonist of Frank Wedekind's (1864–1918) two *Lulu* plays, in which he criticizes bourgeois Viennese attitudes toward sex. His central character's story and Berg's atonal music combine for a thrilling, destabilizing, and violent ride. The nightmarish intensity of Lulu's situation and her refusal to shut down right to her last breath intoxicated me. In my twenties I did not analyze why this was so, but, like the opera, I had little time for quiet feeling or reflection.

Wedekind's personal life story included early sexual promiscuity, syphilis contracted from frequenting prostitutes, a child out of wedlock, repressed homosexuality, and a sadistic streak held in check. In his forties he married an actress twenty-two years his junior, developed a fiercely jealous nature, became creatively and sexually neurotic trying to please her, and died at fifty-three from medical complications resulting from the hernia operation he insisted upon in order to return to his marital bed obligations. His own pell-mell life is a heartbreaking backdrop to the hell he fabricated for Lulu.

Wedekind gives Lulu a father who can't breathe, has no resources, and won't acknowledge fathering her, except in the rare moments she is of use to him. Under this sick, unengaged patriarchal shadow, Wedekind flings Lulu from one man to the next, and for this *she* is deemed untrustworthy and a liar—like Carmen, Violetta, and the sisters in *Così*. Lulu does not own her own body, despite appearing to have sexual freedom. Lack of real agency makes her so reactive that she commits mariticide. This failed psychic escape only lands her in prison, and to get out of that incarceration, in what might be a psychosomatic twist, she makes herself sick. When a woman who loves women declares her feelings, Lulu turns away to offer herself to an actual lady killer. Although Wedekind championed women's rights in real life, he fails, like the unrequited Geschwitz, to save Lulu. Lulu can't seem to spot affection, nor does she know how to say *no*, or simply walk away, when none is there.

Today I have a hard time swallowing Wedekind's cruelty. If *Lulu* is a cautionary tale, I wish he had recompensed his central character's impossible psychic workload by giving her a glimmer of useful power. In light of the historical period, his own chaotic life, and how utterly humans have relied on women as possessions, I shouldn't be surprised. In a climate of inequality and repression, it is difficult to know and own one's self. Under these circumstances most relationships will be compromised ... will struggle to mature.

Women should not have to experience physical or emotional isolation or abuse ... but we still do. In the early '80s, when I fell in love with *Lulu* and got married for the first time, marital rape was still legal in Canada. Today, much as I try to value the opera's potential to illuminate a desperate need for change in how we look at women and sex, I would not want to subject my voice to her story by singing her arias. It is not enough for opera to provide window dressing for how women are treated. It needs to offer new stories, new ways of hearing the female voice. None of us should have to sing beautifully when the going is impossible.

7

First Cries of the Feminine

I HAVE PLAYED out many surreal operatic moments by inhabiting stories that reinforce what we believe about women without actually mining the intelligence of our bodies. I've worked hard to recognize myself and the women I know in each role, frequently sneaking in personal needs and vocal preoccupations: private undertones that acted as counterpoint to the story's surface layer. I appreciate why I took on each job—the gist of a story, the artistic team, its national or international location—but it is my long-term growth as a woman and artist, forged through the "fleshing in" of each female character, that I value most today.

In the summer of 1986, immediately after completing Banff's two-year MUTSE program, I threw myself into the development of a "two-hander" by Berkeley, California–based composer Paul Dresher and writer/performer Rinde Eckert. *Slow Fire* centered around the rabid and rapid corporatization of farm practice in the American Midwest and followed the central character's descent as he armed himself to avenge the loss of the family farm. As his sister, I represented the natural world. I spent the first act cocooned in plastic under the stage before emerging to sing about our mother letting her hair down under the potato moon.

During my late teens and twenties, like many young women in North America, I had an eating disorder. I used that disenfranchised corporeal experience to delve into and interpret the heart of this "sister of." Books by the Canadian mythopoetic analyst Marion Woodman supported me. Though I found her writing transformational, I kept my inner, subtextual research secret. At the time I believed that my bulimia was linked to a dearth of forward-looking female role models in both my family of origin and the wider culture. Today I see that the trouble I had being well in my body also came from the lack of value and agency afforded women in both private and public space—a deficit that is still experienced in my daughters' generation.

Slow Fire toured wonderfully grungy venues like the Painted Bride in Philadelphia and Seattle's On the Boards, and I enjoyed the excitement that results from working well on the cutting edge of an art form. Unfortunately, less than a month before going on the road for a second season, Paul called me in the United Kingdom to tell me that the sister was no longer needed. He and Rinde had decided that the show worked best as a "one-man" narrative; the sister neither amplified the man's descent, nor saved him from it.

What would have happened if I had made my story known? Years before the organic movement took firm root as an alternative to chemically enhanced and genetically modified agriculture, my struggles with eating might have brought to light our undervaluing of women, the human body, and whole food nourishment. But I was ashamed of my compulsive behavior, and at twenty-six didn't know how to link my creative impulses to what I couldn't stomach in our culture. I now know that the intimate struggle of a binging and purging sister could have stood in for the plundering of Mother Earth, could have become a potent catalyst within *Slow Fire*'s narrative. Her corporeal dis-ease might have offered poignant relief to the brother's vengeful, mercenary stance ... and a "real" way into the story.

At the end of 1987 I returned to Banff to workshop Michael Wilcox and John Metcalf's opera *Tornrak*. I played the central character, Milak, a young Inuk woman who is stolen from the Arctic in the late 1800s and put on display in Great Britain. The opera, based on historical events, juxtaposes Inuit and British value systems in scenes that explore the worth of an individual, the importance of community, and how nature fosters spirit.

The opera's heart and plotlines center around a missing and murdered Indigenous woman. In the late 1980s, three decades before *The Final Report of the National Inquiry into Missing and Murdered Indigenous Women and Girls,* our creative conversations did not contextualize Milak's death as part of a centuries-long genocide. I am certain that all of us thought of Milak as a brave young woman—a Joan of Arctic—and did not connect her tragic end to the immediate world around us. Her punishable crime is rabbit poaching but her deeper offense is that she refuses to be owned. We might not have acknowledged that her death sentence resulted from stepping outside of patriarchal, colonial structures, but it did.

Milak's exoticism is as seductive as her independence—making her perfect operatic fodder, like Carmen, Violetta, and Puccini's Madama Butterfly. Unwittingly, I added to Milak's otherness through asking if I could throat sing in parts of the opera. I thought vocal authenticity might help her push back against the enduring colonialism that allowed British men to create a piece about Indigenous people. My ignorance is humbling. We were all appropriating from Inuit culture.

Historically, Inuit lived in nomadic groups of about fifty in the High Arctic. In this harsh northern climate, caribou, seal, and whales are still carefully tracked and hunted for food and clothing. Nothing is wasted. After an animal is skinned, and its meat, organs, tendons, bones, and fur distributed, the community thanks that creature's spirit for what it has provided. This cultural practice respects the complex dependence of hunter on prey, locates men and women within nature, animates animal and human alike. This relationship between human and animal was deepened by the traditional practice of bestowing a *tornrak*—Inuktitut for spirit animal—on each new baby, to guide and protect them through life.

Despite the opera's Inuktitut title, the libretto was completely in English. After intense debate I persuaded the creators, Michael and John, and director Keith Turnbull that my character's text should be in

Inuktitut for the first act when Milak is still in the Arctic. I approached one of my Pearson College friends, Blandina Makkik, to see if she would translate Milak's words. She agreed and invited me to her home in Iqaluit. Sitting together at her kitchen table, we transformed Milak's sentences from oh-so-practical English constructions into Inuktitut's image-based compound words. It was a once-in-a-lifetime experience. Though I don't regret paying for the cost of my journey, I am not sure that the work Blandina did was remunerated. Rereading the program, I note that her name is misspelled and wonder why her translation is not mentioned as a key part of the artistic process.

Inuktitut is an intimate language that lives far back in the throat; it is articulated within a narrower pitch range than English. When I pointed these things out to John, he composed my character's first-act melodies so they would span no more than an octave. In Act Two, after Milak is taken to England and learns English, her arias widen to an operatic two-and-a-half octaves. Deciphering my penciled notes in the original score, I recall that I sang her fractured, poetic second-act English with a subtle Inuktitut accent to amplify her outsider status in scenes where she meets the queen, is displayed in a circus, escapes and is arrested for rabbit poaching, and then is tried in court and sentenced to death.

John is a lyrical composer; the arias he writes are tonally pleasing. Complexity emerges through his meticulous—and often difficult-to-learn—rhythmic setting of text. In Milak's final sung line, form and content fuse emotionally. In response to the death sentence handed down by a heartless British judge, John has her crash through gnarly melodic terrain, using widely arpeggiated, descending intervals to tell the court, "You have no spirits—no *tornrait*.* You are not men." The vigor of this vocal plunge and the treacherous angular path of its pitches rely on a singer's mental clarity for accuracy, as well as an intact core to inhabit its quickly shifting resonances. I loved wrapping my mouth around Milak's last words because despite how far she is from her motherland, she doesn't shy away from flesh, bone, and nerve to speak her truth.

---

* *Tornrait* is the plural of *tornrak.*

To prepare for the role, I began with Inuit *katajjaq*, or "throat sing-ing." I had taken a first-year ethnomusicology course a decade earlier and remembered that when a hunter was paired with another as "broth-ers," their wives became sisters-in-song, often using this breath game to pass time in the camp while the men were out on the land. Reading further I discovered that throat singing was used to resolve disagree-ments between men through their wives' playful competition, and, from another source, that wives may have used the shamanistic sounds of their singing to keep their husbands safe when far from home.

For months before the first workshop I listened to vinyl UNESCO recordings from the '60s and '70s until I could mimic the organic in-and-out breath of this oral tradition. Twice I went north to learn it first-hand. While working on the opera's text, Blandina introduced me to Elisha Kilabuk, the youngest son of a throat singer who lived in Apex, just outside of Iqaluit. It was extremely unusual for a man to sing, but as his sisters weren't interested this inheritance fell on his shoulders. He was accomplished, passionate, and tactful—a good teacher. We'd sing for hours, my ribs aching by the end of it and my head as light as the expanse of late April snow still blanketing the ground.

Throat singing is drawn from the natural world of the Arctic and the many practical activities that are a part of everyday Inuit life. Sounds based on animal calls, the mundane swish of icing *qamutik* (sled) blades, vocables from Inuktitut, even a scrap of infant lullaby make up the rich vocal palette used in this nonnarrative musical form. Each song's repeated pattern is based on the circularity of the breath cycle: a sigh length, voiced exhale followed by an audible inhale. The inhale is part of the musical pattern and provides an aspirated, percussive kick—or reset—making it unnecessary to stop for breath.

Typically two singers face one another, hands placed lightly on each other's shoulders or forearms, offsetting their patterns so that halfway through one woman's exhale—or as she begins her inhale—the second one breathes out her version of the same rhythmic vocal block. The tex-ture is throaty, often using the false vocal folds to thicken the sound of the airflow. The effect is a dense, rolling wash of breath, growl, and groan. Tonal variations include high nasal honking—the geese!—and a wide variety of specific and virtuosic guttural sounds that gain complexity as patterns progress. Sometimes the entwined, offset voices make it sound like a third singer has joined. Even without this acoustic side effect *katajjaq* is exuberant, carnal, and profoundly moving.

I recorded my sessions with Elisha on my Walkman, editing a how-to for ten patterns, and brought that back with me to Banff. John included several fragments of this vocal technique in the opera as a way to deepen the work's cultural context; it became a common musical language for Richard Armstrong's two bear characters and me to share. I taught several patterns to Richard, and he coached me in the "extended" vocal sounds that became Milak's musical tapestry after her death. For this final scene I sat on Richard's shoulders, spread my fifteen-foot fabric wings, and delicately accessed an owl's ascending peeps and throaty coos to express Milak's spirit animal, her *tornrak*. These "extended" sounds felt like natural partners to the throat singing.

After the opera ended I went north a second time to study throat singing, this time with an older female singer in Igloolik. I was introduced to Annie through Francis Piugattuk, a young man who had been recommended by Blandina to serve as a cultural consultant for our production. Francis had spent several months at the Banff Centre teaching the men of the chorus how to tie spears and walk on the set as if it were snow, and me how to pronounce Milak's Inuktitut text. Francis's mother and her sister, Annie—whom he referred to affectionately as "my fat aunt"—had been singing partners. After Francis's mother's death, Annie had no one to sing with and stopped. One morning as she taught me in her living room, her grandchildren ran from their bedrooms down the hall to join us, jumping in freely with their voices and laughter; they had never heard her sing before. These young women took so naturally to throat singing, its vocal template completely in sync with their language, landscape, and cultural values.

From the time of European contact, Inuit throat singing was vilified by the church as the sound of the devil. The form was almost lost by the 1980s. Only moments before it would have been too late, Inuit women reclaimed this part of their heritage, and through the '90s and early 2000s throat singing experienced a revitalization, thanks to young duos across Alaska and Nunavut. Currently, solo artists, including Tanya Tagaq, Taqralik Partridge, and Kathleen Merritt, are marrying its sound palette and inherently layerable, looping form with improvisation, spoken word, and folk traditions. In 2014 throat singing became the first cultural "object" to be given UNESCO's intangible cultural designation by the government of Québec.

Three decades after *Tornrak*'s premiere, I visited Blandina at the Toronto art shop where she had curated the Inuit gallery for more than a decade. She greeted me warmly and commented on how "bold" I had been when we worked together on the opera's translation in the '80s. She even wondered if it might tour the north today. I felt such relief at her open, generous response. Before reconnecting with Blandina I had experienced shame in relation to my involvement in the development of *Tornrak*. Even though I had successfully encouraged the opera's creators to include Inuit artists and consultants in our process, I did not have a true understanding of colonial power dynamics or the lived experience of how Inuit were treated after European contact. It was not my story to tell, and how much better if it had been told by Inuit creators and Milak sung by an Inuk woman.

Crawling creatively into what I imagined as Milak's skin changed me. Shortly after the opera closed, I had an owl tattooed onto my right ankle to acknowledge her animal spirit, her protective *tornrak,* her various gifts to me. I remain profoundly grateful that learning to throat sing tangibly invited the embodied feminine into my process—that its "transgressive" sounds cradled my own nascent transformations, personal and professional.

Tornrak and *Slow Fire* illuminate that how we value and treat women hasn't changed much since the time of Carmen, Violetta, or Tosca. But there is something useful in how these contemporary pieces include and expose our relationship to land. The connections between *woman* and *body* and *land* are actual, which is why we can so quickly link them symbolically. But when we don't understand nature as a fully functioning main-character ecosystem—to which we belong—it is very difficult to value the fullness of a "human-just-being," or the nuanced continuum of identity, or the important interdependence that is community.

———

For two years after playing Milak, I split my time between Vancouver and Banff. I toured with the Burnaby-based dance-theater company JumpStart Performance Society, singing and dancing in *Berlin Angels* through Canada, the United States, and Germany. I premiered roles for Vancouver's New Music Society by Canadian composers such as Owen Underhill and Claude Vivier. I continued to workshop a variety of pieces in Banff, learning all the while how music and story accompany and strengthen one another. I loved moving around.

At the end of 1991 I landed in Toronto long enough to meet and marry Thom Sokoloski. Thom was known in Toronto's burgeoning premillennial theater scene for producing and directing composer R. Murray Schafer's large-scale, site-specific Patria cycle, as well as devising his own shows through his company, Autumn Leaf Performance. We spoke for the first time one week before an October 1 arts grant due date—I needed advice—and got married November 1—the same day Disney's *Fantasia* was released on VHS. I was on tour for two of those five weeks and had barely enough time to make sure that both our divorce papers from previous marriages were in order. My decision to marry Thom was impetuous, reactive, and risky. Luluesque. The best part of it remains our two daughters, Magda and Oksana, and my stepson, Sacha; and the shows we birthed were pretty unique, too.

Thom and I worked on one of his projects for each of the seven years we were together: *Hermes Trismegistos* inside Toronto's Union Station; *Archeology of the Female Voice* at the Royal Ontario Museum; *Zürich 1916* in Banff; *Artaud's Cane* at the old Music Gallery on Richmond Street; *Down Here on Earth* at the du Maurier Theatre, at Factory Theatre, and in Montréal; *Pierrot lunaire* in Belgium with family in tow (the show was remounted in Toronto after our breakup); and several concerts for CBC's *Two New Hours*. Staying close to home made sense for me while raising kids.

Thom loved the irreverence and potency of extended sound, and I am grateful for the opportunities that came out of this. The summer after our wedding he directed R. Murray Schafer's *Hermes Trismegistos*, the fourth opera in the Patria cycle. Each night the Great Hall of Union Station was transformed into a theater right after the last train had pulled out: seating was rolled in from the SkyDome, cherry pickers put in place for two of the soloists, and ticket booths transformed into stages—there were even T-shirts for sale. Mezzo-soprano Jean Stilwell was to sing Melusina, and when she canceled last minute to perform a *Carmen* in Japan, I auditioned for Murray and got the part.

Melusina is *prima materia* ... original feminine substance within Jungian thinking. I asked Murray if he would listen to me sing through her arias before we went into rehearsal, as I wanted to use a variety of textures. He was excited by what I was offering and allowed me to stray well beyond *bel canto* propriety while staying true to his pitches and rhythms. I was ecstatic. It wasn't a stretch to inhabit a woman's generative power as the performances coincided with the early weeks of my pregnancy with Magda. After our last show a chorus member pulled me aside to explain that whenever I sang using "extended techniques," one of his hands flailed erratically for no apparent reason. At first he hated this loss of control, but as the run progressed he began to place a positive value on the effects of my character's out-of-the-ordinary female sounds, and by closing he was won over. But not every project Thom and I did together allowed women to thrive.

Zürich 1916 was co-commissioned by Thom—through his company, Autumn Leaf Performance—along with Keith Turnbull, the head of the winter program at the Banff Centre in the '90s. The libretto is by the late John Bentley Mays, and the music is by iconoclast composer Christopher Butterfield. For its 1994 workshop, Thom and I went to Banff and brought Magda, not yet two, with us. I was going to sing whatever mezzo part was on offer.

The two main rehearsal studios in Banff's Laszlo Funtek Teaching Wing are massive, with extremely high ceilings. The view from their windows inspires and distracts: full-bodied conifers sway in the foreground; rugged, stark mountains crash up behind. Working day after day on the music for *Zürich 1916*, I found myself becoming more and more agitated. Was it the size of my role—was I bothered that it was smaller than what I was used to? Not really; small was good given I was also a full-time mum. Was it being at Banff with my husband: the challenge of being perceived as the producer's wife; the complexity of not feeling as independent as I had been at the Centre before marriage? Maybe, but we were still in the honeymoon phase, and this was a chance to travel as a family. Did I not like the music? I had performed and recorded another of Christopher's works in Vancouver and loved how his idiosyncratic intelligence and droll humor transferred into melody and rhythm—and I considered him a friend. I struggled with my feelings the full two weeks.

At the end of the workshop we debriefed our experience: singers, director, creators, and producers ringing a table set far from the studio windows. The sunlight streaming through their thermal panes remained just out of reach. I raised my hand. "I think it is awful that the female characters in your Dada opera are simply there to support the men's story, give it a little sparkle. Men *do* and women *decorate*." Heart pounding, I broke into tears ... and then we moved on.

I tried to continue the conversation later in the hallway, asking John, the librettist, if he could see what I meant. I had read his recent memoir about his struggle with depression and was in awe that he could remain married to his daughter's mother after coming out as gay. I thought he might understand my feelings of being minimized, and I pointed out, once again, that the place of women in the narrative was limited, and, in that, choking. The surprised look on his face was entirely lacking in compassion; the opera had numerous female characters! Both John and Christopher's interest in Dada centered on the male characters' through-lines; they couldn't see past the agency of the masculine to where a woman's might lie. My husband couldn't empathize with my distress, either. The whole incoherent episode left me embarrassed and apologetic.

When the Dada movement popped up in Zurich, suffragism had gained serious ground in the United Kingdom, the United States, and Canada. But Zurich is in Switzerland, and Swiss women had to wait sixty more years for their men to grant them—through direct, democratic plebiscite—the right to vote. Maybe John and Christopher were correct to sideline *Zürich 1916*'s women. The Dada movement intended to uproot bourgeois nationalism and domestic materialism, but when women's voices rise only to support men's needs, deep systemic change cannot happen. It's a good thing that I'd had enough of the same old operatic same-old, hardly ten years into my career. Defying Dada fast-tracked the undoing of my Lulu.

8

Seeking Creative Voice

A CLASSICAL SINGER continues to study during the early part of their career, and so, after finishing Banff's MUTSE program, I returned frequently to the Centre to access ongoing training while workshopping new pieces. In 1987 I had the good fortune of meeting Richard Armstrong. Richard is tall and handsome—leonine. An enigmatic mystique surrounds him and his vocal methods. He asks things of his students that are radically different from the usual classical approach, and singers emerge from his classes feeling emotionally connected and vocally freed.

Flutters—from nerves, as well as a small crush—coursed through me as I headed up the Laszlo Funtek backstairs for my first private lesson. In a windowless classroom, I reticently revealed to Richard the gravelly strain that had begun to show in my singing voice after a particularly strenuous year of creation, rehearsal, and touring in the United States. My D, D-sharp, and E crackled, preventing clean singing in the *lower passaggio,* the range of notes that embrace the female speaking voice. Nor could I rely on my G, G-sharp, or A. Those pitches, so close in timbre to a woman's cry, sometimes failed to sound. Eyes rooted to the drab linoleum floor, I explained that I was still reverberating from my recent divorce, which had been finalized while working in Berkeley, California, far from friends and family. I was desperate to fix my vocal troubles by covering things up, but Richard wanted me to dig in, deepen my connection with the mess, splash around in what was fragmenting. My back hardened against his proposition; it seemed anything but right—terrifying, in fact.

The sound that had first drawn me to opera singing was akin to the perfect, unattainable beauty of a *Vogue* cover. When I was twenty-one this seemed like a good thing to aspire to; its gloss was exotic and blameless, suiting the conflicting mix of escape and certitude that I had looked for in my first marriage. I was twenty-six when Richard asked me to shine a light on the cracks in my voice, and the resulting sounds gave me a glimpse of just how wide each person's timbral range can be. The vocal "stepping out" that he encouraged built on what I had begun exploring through Berio's *Folk Songs.* It deepened my belief that the regularity of the *bel canto* sound was not only restrictive physically and emotionally for me; it would never go far enough to express what I wanted to reveal as a woman.

Richard's suggestions risked exposure and the unknown. The roars, peeps, and shrieks that emerged from my body—which he insisted were simply human sound—spoke to my imaginal, feminist self through legitimizing all sorts of raw feeling. The vibratory chaos breaking my surface felt revolutionary, and even though I had no language to contextualize these vocalizations, their cathartic nature began to liberate me from my need to sound perfect. If opera had seduced me into making sound, Richard's Roy Hart lineage encouraged me to do it with less disguise. I jumped at the chance to rebel by trying to forge a classical career that would include "extended voice," but this was not as easy as I had hoped.

In contemporary opera the male voice has been asked to "transgress" more often than the female. Richard's teacher Roy howled and chorded his way through an extraordinary array of extended sound for composer Peter Maxwell Davies to use in the creation of his monodrama *Eight Songs for a Mad King.* Its companion piece for mezzo-soprano, *Miss Donnithorne's Maggot,* was written five years later, yet asks for nothing beyond clean female sound to express the central character's dilemma.

Miss Donnithorne's vocal line restricts itself to the death-defying rolls and runs of nineteenth-century coloratura ornamentation, moving quickly and virtuosically over an endless stream of notes. The cerebral angularity of its twentieth-century intervals makes her line sound contemporary but it is only the melody that challenges. Rehearsing her arias at the Banff Centre for a tour that included both the Edmonton Fringe and the Stratford Festivals I longed for the full vocal transformations that Maxwell Davies asks for from his baritone in *Eight Songs*. Impressive, pretty singing represents only a fraction of what a woman has to say and I was ready for sound that would allow a woman's body to step beyond polite, upper-resonator timbral changes; in other words, out from under good vocal behavior.

My disappointment in contemporary opera fed a craving for nonhierarchical, feminine ways of telling. After a particularly enjoyable time performing with soprano Cathy Fern Lewis* in Vancouver New Music's production of Claude Vivier's *Kopernikus*, she and I gathered together an all-female collective of creators and performers. We thought that an interdisciplinary process—fairly new in 1991— would provide space for the full female voice. Based on my professional experiences to date, I thought life would be simpler in more ways than just the creative with no men in the studio. What stories might arise given half a chance?

The invited artists were accomplished and unique: dancer/choreographer Marie-Josée Chartier, clarinetist Lori Freedman, percussionist Beverley Johnston, singer/composer Lisa Karrer, and composer Linda Catlin Smith. Each of us brought a mature art form, sophisticated craft, and personal history, and these became the tools for shared daily training during the development phase of each new work. Aesthetically we hoped to start from scratch.

---

* Cathy participated in our group's first voice workshop, led by Richard Armstrong. Our two- to three-week creation periods were also going to be in Toronto due to everyone else's home base, and Cathy lived in Victoria, British Columbia. She made the difficult decision not to continue with the project to prioritize a healthy balance for her family.

To get our creative juices flowing, we researched three female artists who also happened to be muses for male artists—Georgia O'Keeffe, Tina Modotti, and Frida Kahlo. The first piece we made never went beyond a rehearsal hall, midday showing, but the comments from that audience supported our shift away from being the object of someone else's vision to the subject of our own. It also revealed that we needed an outside eye.

Joanna McIntyre joined us as facilitating director for our first full-evening work. From its title, *I Had an URGE to Write You*, we culled our ensemble's name, URGE. It was the collective mandate of URGE that each woman bring in what was most current in her life. Joanna's expertise encouraged us to stray from what we thought we knew into places that were uncomfortable and, through that undertaking, meaningful. Fresh and surprising impulses became elements for improvisation and creation: the repetition of a daily chore; the unusual use of mundane and sacred objects; the darker tones of life-chafing and life-changing events or situations; and the unfolding landscape of a night's dream. An important aspect of the work in URGE was the structuring of "improvised play" into the fabric of each public performance, ensuring an ever-changing, evolving landscape of sound and image within the parameters of a show that was contained by precisely called lighting cues. We became well knit as well as wild and woolly.

An example of the currency of our work and the ribald inclusion of the feminine was a scene based on my first home birth. Partway through *I Had an URGE to Write You* I walked onto the stage in full diva garb, found my stage light, and took in an imagined, adoring audience. In an abrupt change of mood and lighting, I fell back into the arms of my all-female chorus, who stripped me of my gown so that, half-naked, I could crawl the stage while accessing the carnal state that laboring demands. The words *sweeeeet baby* tore from my lungs, sang me down a path of improvised vocal sound that musicalized the deeply autonomic journey of childbirth. My animal memory of that uncompromised state, prompted by the audiotape I had made of Magda's birth, fed the creation of this aria, as did the unconditional support of the other women in tandem with Joanna's theatrical spurring.

URGE lasted thirteen years and resulted in four full-length pieces that explored the wilderness of the feminine through music-driven, nonnarrative storytelling. It was undeniably organic and interdisciplinary from the bottom up. In 1995 *She Promised She'd Bake a Pie* brought in pianist Eve Egoyan, actor/flamenco dancer Anita La Selva, and performance artist and eventual core member Katherine Duncanson to join Linda, Marie-Josée, and me. In 1999 *Trousseau/True Nature*—our second show to tour to Calgary's High Performance Rodeo—folded actor Gabi Epstein into our process.

URGE's exploratory path—for me, concurrent with birthing and raising two daughters—began a period of creativity during which my allegiance to my voice became increasingly grounded in the feminine. As my career careened down two differing paths—that of interpreter and that of creator—my marriage to Thom tugged apart. We separated just before the new millennium dawned. I made a resolution on New Year's Eve to only sing work that my voice wanted to sing, and bit by bit this became my reality. I formed a company to create and produce lyric theater. Its mandate is to explore the fragile cracks of what it means to be human; I called the company Good Hair Day Productions because who doesn't want a good hair day!

GHDP's first full-length show was a gathering of electroacoustic gems: the sumptuously beautiful *White Lodge* by Gavin Bryars; Rainer Wiens's *Mercy Suite*, a solo song cycle culled from his opera for three characters and five prepared guitars; and a brand-new monodrama commissioned from Wende Bartley with Anne Carson's writing. The text was selected from five of Anne's books and, once the excerpts were ordered, I called the piece *The Girl with No Door on Her Mouth* after her poem about the nymph Echo, as named by Sophocles.

Anne Carson is a brilliant Greek classicist, embodied poet, radical thinker, and MacArthur Foundation Fellowship recipient. Thanks to her essay "The Gender of Sound" from *Glass, Irony and God*, loaned to me in 1996 by fellow URGE member Linda C. Smith, I read that physicians in ancient Greece believed that the mouth a woman uses for speech reflects her mouth below—for example, you could tell when a woman was menstruating through the sound of her voice. There is truth to this, as the vocal cords,[*] along with the rest of the body, swell when water is retained. In the case of a singer this can affect the quality and range of her voice, rendering high notes unwieldy, or even inaccessible. In some leading opera houses a singer is still contractually permitted to cancel, without penalty, when she is menstruating—a hangover from the nineteenth century—and a previous Russian singing teacher of mine always asked his female students to cancel a lesson, even last minute, on the first day of their period. Vocal cords, when swollen, are fragile. They can also feel rough, like gravel, due to surface dryness. But more than two thousand years ago these medical observations were not applied to the general female population for a woman's benefit; they were used to limit women's voices in public space during a time when male intellectuals were debating whether or not women were actually human, or a different species altogether.

In one of our development workshops, Anne offered me a new way to view and organize the world. As I was struggling to find the right placement for one of her poems within the emerging libretto, she asked me, "Is it *bound* or *unbound*?" This simple question became a clean way to look at energies I had been defining as male or female. *Bound* and *unbound* are less weighed down because they speak to physical feelings found in both male and female bodies, before allying these sensations to our cultural construct of gender. *Bound* and *unbound* reflect the natural expansion and contraction of a singer's vibration—and exist in orgasm as well as a myriad of other bodily functions, from shuddering and shaking to digestive processes. Our bodies thrive on ebb and flow.

The give-and-take of the human body rose to the surface in the next show that Good Hair Day Productions produced. In 2004 singer Kazumi Tsuruoka and I, along with pianist Sageev Oore, created a piece that brought Kazumi's cerebral palsy to the fore while revealing his passion for R & B and his desire for intimacy. We did not shy away from his disability, drawing on his spasms to fuel the show's voice and movement

---

[*] I use vocal cords, vocal folds, cords, and folds interchangeably.

aesthetic. Kazumi's profound understanding of songs by Smokey Robinson, Bob Dylan, and Willie Dixon was used to unite singer and audience through shared musical culture.

Kazumi's hard, handsome looks could typecast him as a samurai, but his emotions sit close to the surface when he sings. His voice is rich and burly—connected. Kazumi does not control the sound, because he can't—he has to fully commit to get the air out of his lungs in one usable stream. Because individuals with a disability often have to rush to keep up with the mainstream we took extra time to allow Kazumi to pay attention to his insides during rehearsals. Based on the timing of those impulses, and the full team's honoring of them, our focus then turned to outward theatrical values.

Because the transparency of Kazumi's performance offered very little by way of an emotional safety net, I designed the show as a salon that would ideally play in the intimacy of a home, starting with mine. This proximity allowed *CP Salon* to reveal Kazumi's disability as integral to his identity, and part of an exchange rather than something to look at. The staging was often participatory: for "The Tracks of My Tears" Kazumi sat on an audience member's lap, and for "Little Red Rooster" he used a stranger's hand for his harmonica ... eventually grazing his way up their arm while gazing into their eyes. Gently insinuating his body, disability and all, into another person's space was risky for Kazumi as well as the audience member. Gratefully, we discovered that audiences were more than willing to receive his strength and vulnerability. Tears and laughter flooded every home we visited. In 2006 we toured the show to Regina and Vancouver, in 2008 to Whitehorse, and in 2009 to three university campuses in Toronto, always asking both a disability organization *and* an arts group to host us—bridging communities. Post-show we facilitated breakout conversations that were revealing and courageous.

After *CP Salon*'s first incarnation, I returned to my own singing and flew to Rome to work with composer Maurizio Squillante; he had a creative process I could not resist, and Italy held a big dose of nostalgia for me given the amount of time I had spent there in my twenties. For Maurizio's electroacoustic opera *The Wings of Daedalus,* he and I painstakingly developed the Daughter of Cocalus's arias over two separate weeklong creation sessions. We refined each and every vocal gesture based on how I improvised David Haughton's texts while under the influence of Maurizio's evocative tape part. We recorded our results, and then Maurizio made subtle pitch and tempo adjustments to the vocal part while deepening the layers of his electroacoustic track. Maurizio's invitation to collaborate was aligned with how I thought the operatic voice could sound, and the vocal part that emerged was sensual and potent ... radical.

For Maurizio's next opera I was cast as Alexander the Great's mother. To embody this high priestess of Dionysus, I used the very top of my voice—quietly and intensely—to shape my son into a man hurt and hungry enough to conquer the known world. Olympias's power emanated from disturbing and haunting scraps of sound that seduced rather than bullied, her own wounds informing her vocal reach. Treading Rome's rounded cobblestones on the daily walk home from the recording studio, I felt buoyed that at forty-six there was even more to discover about my voice.

These arias live on in my body to this day, but despite my personal elation over this approach to birthing vocal creation, each story centered on a man, his historical importance, and his neuroses. In *Wings* I sang partially naked in an aquarium while tethered to my father, the king. In *Alexander* Olympias operates behind the scenes, regardless of her ordained status and personal drive. Despite being more than an equal participant in the creation of my vocal lines, I had to insist that my creative work, as well as that of the other singers, was recognized in both the performance program and the liner notes for the eventual CD.

Returning from our first *Wings* tour in 2003 I sank into the premiere of URGE's final piece, commissioned by Theatre Direct. Artistic director Lynda Hill had felt that body-based, interdisciplinary work would be a fantastic way to get at the issues that most concerned Grades Seven and Eight girls. Joanna McIntyre, in her dramaturgical wisdom, suggested the creation of a young company, and URGE's four core members (Marie-Josée, Katherine, Linda, and I) learned to co-create from the other side of the directorial table by assembling a young company: Lauren Brotman, Andrea Donaldson, Christina Sicoli, Amber Godfrey, and Diana Tso. Over the show's two-year development period we gave workshops at six Toronto schools, spoke to girls from a wide variety of backgrounds, and discovered that friendship was the most important theme, bar none, for this age group. We read about, and identified with, the indirectness that adolescent girls adopt in order to be "good girls" when trying to communicate difficult feelings like anger, or handle their drive and aggression. ·

The premiere of *And by the Way Miss ...* won its commissioner and the ensemble two Dora Awards and was later published by Playwrights Canada Press, thanks to Heather Fitzsimmons Frey's initiative and the one hundred hours that it took me and Victoria Stacey—an intern at Theatre Direct—to convert the opening night video into script form. This final piece allowed us to better understand and pass on our collaborative, interdisciplinary URGE-y ways, and in the ensuing years we have each continued to weave those methods into individual performance and creation contexts. As with other URGE shows, the central theme was so current to us at the time that the friendships within our core group were challenged. Eventually we worked our way back to one another, and years later have strong personal and professional ties.

The second *Wings* tour in 2005 took us from Italy's heel up into the French Alps. Immediately after, I returned to Toronto to finish creating and rehearsing *Yours to Break*. I had collaged together many narrative cabarets in the past but this melding of pop songs—ranging from Hank Williams to Jann Arden—enveloped fictional letters, texts from Helen Humphreys's novel *Wild Dogs*, dialogue, movement, and boxing. My onstage colleague Danny Wild and I spent two years learning to box under the watchful guidance of Canadian silver medalist Tristan Whiston. I wanted the show's elements to help me tease apart instinct, intimacy, and intensity.

I insisted that Danny and I engage in unchoreographed boxing during the performance to keep our exchanges immediate and unpredictable. Could learning how to land and take a punch set a productive template for giving and receiving within difficult conversations? Despite our exhilarating, evenly matched, pre-show sparring, I pulled my punches in front of an audience—always the good girl—and Danny, under the influence of performance adrenaline, hit hard. Tristan had cautioned us about boxing out of our "weight class," but I was not yet ready to take this idea seriously—physically or emotionally.

In 2006 I was tired of interdisciplinary work—both the collective nature of URGE and the collaged quality of the boxing show—but I had no idea how to make things outside of a collaborative process. To return to the wholeness of opera I decided to commission one. I approached writer Tom Walmsley after reading his novel *Kid Stuff.* Tom had captured a horrifying mix of arousal, humiliation, powerlessness, and emotional need in a short scene in which his central male character, Moth, was pressed over the hood of a car during a rough sexual encounter. It begged the question of consent long before that public conversation began. Perhaps because both characters were men I could see what was happening purely in relation to agency.

Tom agreed to meet, and over that first coffee I proposed a story about a brother and sister. It would start with the two of them downstage, their parents' dead bodies bagged somewhere behind. I wanted to kill off inheritances to see if masculine and feminine could come together through a not yet imagined origin myth. Rebalance. Tom informed me that he had already written an "incest play"—which wasn't quite my point. Three short weeks later he returned, on his own terms, with a piece about "love at first sight."

The libretto for *Julie Sits Waiting* is succinct, erotic, and thrilling, and though the plot made the feminist in me uneasy, I could picture Montréal composer Louis Dufort's gritty electroacoustic music doing it justice. I had been in on the creation of Louis's first opera, *L'archange:* first, through improvising to Alexis Nouss's texts; and then by inhabiting Louis's melodic writing using sculpted vocal textures. I knew he would not shy away from Tom's language. After auditioning a number of performers for the male part, we asked Richard Armstrong to join the project—his remarkable vocal instrument was the inspiration Louis needed.

Tanja Jacobs, who directed the early development workshops with generosity and flair, called it a sexual-catastrophe chamber opera. She was right. *Julie Sits Waiting* takes on adultery, violent sex, loss of faith, and core identities. Its love triangle is made up of: Julie, essentially Lulu as stay-at-home mum; her husband, Rick, a cop we never see; and her lover, Mick, an Anglican priest who ends up leaving the church to, as he puts it, "follow Julie to hell." In short, Julie and Mick meet online and have earth-shattering sex in a house she and her husband are renovating. The depth of this connection causes Mick to have a crisis of faith, leave his parish, and murder Julie's husband because he thinks this is a good idea. Julie finds a body under a tarp in the undone house and assumes it is Mick's. When Mick bursts in on the scene, she realizes that it is her husband's. She is horrified—it was not her intention that Mick should kill Rick. In an attempt to foil the cops Mick and Julie stage a home invasion. Both of them decide that Mick should hit her on the head to add to its credibility. Julie suffers brain damage and ends up losing custody of her daughter and living in her sister's basement.

I found myself once again playing a woman whose sexuality and agency were in reaction to the male character's. Despite the broad palette that I had accessed for Louis's first opera, only Richard sang with extended sound in *Julie Sits Waiting;* my part required nothing beyond clean, conservative singing. If Julie's character had been less socially *bound* would Louis have allowed her to use wilder sounds? Less cultivated vocals might have changed the opera's inevitable, tragic outcome. In the final scene Julie is unable to recognize Mick as her "lover" despite his recounting of their torrid past and their plan to foil the cops. Once their fingertips touch she instinctually knows that this man is a threat to her integrity. Undone, Julie avenges her psychic death by stabbing Mick to death. If only her voice had come undone, too.

Moments after the final matinee ended, my eighty-year-old mother and I stood outside Theatre Passe Muraille's grungy back space in the tender spring light. I asked her what she thought. I was more worried about Mum's reaction to Mick's blasphemy than the graphic lyrics of his "I climbed through your cunt" aria. Mum's response was swift and direct: "At the end of the day Julie knew what was most important: her love for her child."

It took me a little more work to make peace with the opera. As a producer it was simplest to think of it as a cautionary tale. Inhabiting its words and music over the six years that it took to evolve from libretto to award-nominated new opera, I came to wonder how many of us have been raised to politely lose our minds when it comes to Western culture's romantic narrative—one that still has a hard time coupling a woman's agency with her desire. It breaks my heart that Julie's pristine singing might still accurately reflect the limitations of my daughters' times, as well as looking back to those of my mother's generation.

———

I can count on one hand, a thumb, and a finger the number of composers I have worked with who have accepted a broad palette of female sound-making as legitimate vocal expression. R. Murray Schafer, Louis Dufort, Maurizio Squillante, Nik Beeson, Jeff Corness, Wende Bartley, and Rainer Wiens were open to furthering their art-making by encouraging and including what I had to offer through my lived understanding of opera's architecture and my need for unhampered vocal expression.

For more than three decades, not only have I experienced layers of resistance within opera to realistic female sounds, roles, and stories, I have witnessed a paucity of female librettists, composers, and directors. If an opera's vantage point is voyeuristic or objectifying, or if the female lead's function is to serve the masculine, she is not being represented fully; she is not a woman telling her whole truth.

The laws that govern grand opera have always guaranteed that its women will suffer while bringing a man's story to light. To choose something other than death or madness, transgression is necessary. Female singers need to stop measuring up, but rather take the measure within. We have to want change, *and we have to offer it.* The next generation of opera composers—male and female—need to reconsider the use of the female voice … allow it to move without hesitation into the twenty-first century.

9

Crying from the Neck Down

We have been taught to apologize for our tears, to suppress our anger and to fear being called hysterical.

—JULIE HOLLAND*

WHAT IS AN ARIA?

Clara settles into the leather armchair across from me, wrapping her lanky frame around her younger sister. She is also cradling a bowl of brownies made by her mother, who, along with several other women, is carrying weekend food supplies into the adjacent kitchen. The two sisters nestle in more deeply as we debate the virtues of brownies versus broccoli. Clara makes it clear that her choice to have the sweet and not the vegetable is a no-brainer. We have hardly met, and already I like her. She looks to be in her late twenties, with an intelligent gaze that outshines the tiny blue crystals glued high on her cheekbones. As these two bright young women talk and laugh, I see how deeply attuned they are to one another. I wonder if my own daughters will have this kind of intimacy when they are grown.

---

* Julie Holland, "Opinion: Medicating Women's Feelings," *New York Times,* February 28, 2015.

We are staying at a log cabin on the shore of a remote lake for a voice retreat tailored to mothers and siblings of individuals with disabilities. We've driven for more than an hour on icy northern roads to get away from the everyday. There are only three beds for the nine of us and as the late afternoon sky darkens I begin to worry that we will feel crammed in as well as remote. Several inflatables materialize: modern-day pioneering. I decide to sleep on the couch, placing my pillow so that I can lie face out on my uninjured left shoulder. For three days we are going to be intimate, sharing food, toothpaste, and stories ... as well as undressing vocally with one another.

I wonder what to serve for our first evening's session: broccoli or brownies? I weigh the desire for emotional catharsis against the sobriety of "technique." I think of catharsis as the brownies, and, like sitting down with a girlfriend to dish over something sweet, it usually brings relief and immediate chemical change. The broccoli—working quietly with the nuts and bolts of breath and resonance, and, through this, changing old habits that no longer serve—is the building and sustaining part of the diet. But then again, brownies are a thing to share at the best and worst of times. I take in the group.

Each of these mothers has shouldered more than her fair share. Denise, the force of nature who organized this weekend, is as adept at wheelchair dance as she is in a kayak. In both public and private roles she lobbies the government on behalf of families dealing with a wide range of disability challenges and access issues. Annemette's young son died some time ago; her capable bones, wild laugh, and ready-to-share case of beer are the tools she uses to support other parents dealing with loss. Maria Gloria, petite, sparky, and of South American origin, has several children, two of whom are on the autism spectrum. Mona, a serene, willowy visual artist, has opened her home time and again to foster children diagnosed with fetal alcohol syndrome, one of whom, now an adult, is with us for the weekend. And finally there is Katherine, whose daughters are still cuddling and bantering with one another in the armchair. She is compact and capacious, with an open, radiant face. Only a few months past a family tragedy, she and her daughters are tenaciously supporting one another through a landscape of tender grief and rugged acceptance.

I am still considering what to offer as we climb the stairs to the second-floor studio. It is after 9 p.m. and everyone is tired … possibly reluctant to engage too soon or too deeply. As I settle behind the electric keyboard I decide on broccoli. We yawn, we sigh, we sing some long tones. I draw each woman into an unthreatening solo moment, grateful for the trust they have built with one another over the years. As we lay vocal ground I ask them why they are here. Sisterhood, healing, curiosity … a few are not sure. I teach a song—one of my favorites. *Tell me more and more and then some.* Its sensuously attuned melody by singer Billie Holiday puts the narrator right in the center of her own needs and feelings while providing a safe container. When we end at around eleven, everyone is happy and a little more alive from all the vibration we've shared. As we head downstairs for a glass of wine, no longer road-weary but ready-for-bed tired, I ask them to notice their dreams.

How will we tell our stories if we can't catch our breath?

The next morning, after a fun and epic walk to the far end of the frozen lake to fetch freshly baked cinnamon buns for breakfast, we head back up to the studio. Again I can feel their reluctance; they are open and closed all at once. I let them know that our work will invite unlatching and that I do not want them to be taken by surprise. I have too much respect for their strength, for what they have put in place to cope with the intensity of their lives. So many things not in their hands.

We start off with a partnered exercise—softening our organs while following one another's breath through touch that travels from crown to toe. Flesh remembers weight as it slips toward earth.

I lie on my back to demonstrate the *dark breath;* invite the women to surround me. They kneel or sit cross-legged, and while I breathe and sound they voice their thoughts:

movement	*fluttering*	*open*
bear	*speaking*	*broken*
alone	*possessed*	*chamber*
vibration	*depth*	*fueling*
belly	*help*	*soft*
swell	*back-and-forth*	*wave*
lost	*slow*	*whisper*
release	*last breath*	*delicate*
rapture	*opposing*	*rise and fall*
oh	*life*	*feminine*
snake	*emptying*	*vulnerable*
grieving	*at ease*	*surrender*
pain	*billowing*	*life*

I explain to the group that they will take on the *dark breath* under my guidance. I let them know that I have been involved with this exercise for longer than I have been with any partner, longer than I have parented, almost as long as I have sung. Some of them will open quite quickly to its release, whereas others may take a while to give into its parameters. I note that two of the women sat silently as we debriefed and did not add to the list. I want to make space for whatever they are feeling and tell them that they are welcome to watch the others if that feels better than joining in.

One woman slips back to sit against the wall while the other lies down on the floor with the rest of the group. In the quiet each woman invites breath into her body, searches for space within. For twenty minutes the in-and-out of the *dark breath* maps feelings and encourages release. I ask the women to coax their animal beings out from hibernation, crawl and growl their way into companionship. For another ten minutes they become rowdy little bears rubbing up against one another, exhaling pleasure, play, and pain. Tears of all sorts fall on the paint splattered floor.

We head to the piano to sing our long tones, rediscovering the depth of last night's work. I lead them semitone by semitone up to middle C and the F just above it. We spend a little time straddling the *lower* female *passaggio,* the terrain of our speaking voices. Lips softly pursed and kissing forward we shape the vowel *oooo*—as in *blue* or *who*. We *oooo* our way up several more semitones, trusting the divine nature of female overtones. I single out a few of the women, including one of the sisters. We get a taste of each woman's voice.

Katherine is next in the circle; I ask her to sing for a bit on her own. She opens her mouth fully and her sinuses—eight pockets of reverberant air—shine. I indicate that she should touch her sternum with one hand. Her sound grounds, becomes a vertical tube of resonance, lustrous with height and depth. I follow her voice into its brilliant top range, ask her to change the *oooo* to a more open *aaah*. Her whole being radiates softness from a core of natural, well-earned steel. It is magnificent and connected. Without warning she bursts into tears and bolts from the circle.

I ask the group to keep breathing while I cross the room. I touch her back. That is all it takes for Katherine to turn and clutch onto me. She sobs and sobs and sobs. I feel the release of her diaphragm against my torso, the violent spasms necessary to exorcise feeling. I stay connected to my own breath as Katherine lashes herself to me. What an honor to hold her within the storm she is raging. Mouth against my sternum, she wails into my flesh, strips bare her pain.

When Katherine is done, she apologizes. I tell her it is not necessary to say sorry; she has done such solid work—a gift to us all. She says that her partner had hoped she would get to cry from the neck down, something that hadn't yet come.

———

An aria.
Emotion flowing on air … transmitted through air.
An aria is air, after all.
A story without words.

I return to the group while Denise, Katherine's close friend, holds her with care and expertise. In the afterglow we speak respectfully about what we have witnessed, contemplating how it touched us, and what it brought up. The women share things they each have gone through, mapping their feelings to the recent vocal vibration that shook this cabin to its rafters. We are fortunate that Katherine owns her past and her present. That she already balances broccoli with brownies allows us to learn from and integrate her experience. Maria Gloria, who has been watching from the side, breathes a sigh of relief and joins the conversation, opening to the rest of the weekend's work. We break for lunch. Undone by breath and washed by sound.

What would it mean for a woman to flow sound on air ...

Free of worry?

Sing her story without any fear of disease, madness, or death?

What would it mean if all women could tell their stories without *any* fear of retribution? Escaping not just death but false perception, judgment, limitation.

My own included.

Oh, for the courage to experience myself head-on.

No sidestepping.

(What do the personal resources for this feel like? How can it be practiced?)

Imagine that your story is interesting enough without any extra "drama" ... and that you recognize this from within.

Picture *sounding* like yourself.

Now ... *erase* the male gaze ...

Your father's and your mother's ... your own.

No need for pillars to hide behind ...

No one else's internal need exacting a tale, night after night, for their own pleasure and amusement.

Imagine that when you tell your own tale you are supported by other women.

Not just opera would be different.

What matters could become whole.

PART II

What I Teach

IO

A Studio of My Own

WITH THE BIRTH of each daughter, teaching became an increasingly family-friendly way for me to earn a living, as well as a reliable support and outlet for my own creativity; I loved it right from the start. I taught privately from my home, and occasionally ran weekend intensives or weekly night classes for groups of twelve to sixteen students, usually in a rented dance studio with a piano. I also taught at two diploma granting institutions: for eighteen years as a faculty member in Humber College's Theatre Arts program, and for more than a decade at The CREATE Institute in the service of expressive arts therapists in training. I was lucky to have a short waiting list of new students as well as the long-term faithful, which included a variety of professionals and a dozen apprentices devoted to regular vocal exploration.

Coincidentally, as the Great Recession of 2008 began, I tried to take my first sabbatical. For almost two decades I had dealt intimately with dozens of nervous systems a week while developing and producing lyric theater projects after dark or before dawn. For eight years the girls' father and I had met the challenges of co-parenting in separate homes. Tired and in need of nourishment I decided to slow down for a few months—take the fall off! But my students resisted.

The compromise I came up with was to teach one day a week: three two-hour prepaid group classes on Wednesdays in my home. No more privates spread out through the week, no drop-in night classes in a rented studio. Students used to one-on-one attention would have to share the space around the piano with six or seven other individuals on a regular basis. I might not have cut down on the number of nervous systems, but the change to my schedule made time for my own replenishment.

Most of my students committed to the proposed weekly groups. Wednesday after Wednesday they filled my home. Week after week they witnessed and supported one another. For three months they learned to listen more deeply and became much less nervous when taking center stage. A living lab emerged founded on unbiased, democratic space and the potent exchange between student and specialist. My understanding of the human voice burgeoned.

The groups were half the size of the intensives I had offered previously and their content included more technique. Weekly groups are not the traditional context for this kind of vocal structuring. As singers we think we have to hear ourselves, but truthfully we can't—at least not accurately. A teacher's job is to listen, reflect, evaluate, and correct, without letting their aesthetic preferences overshadow the free and balanced functioning of their student's voice. Focusing on vocal process, not imitation, in a group—*feeling* the technique—can help a singer connect to their own individuality without becoming distracted by how they think they should sound. Aesthetic sculpting can come later as a vocalist finds their own musical style, whether heavy metal or opera.

Through figuring out how to deliver both cathartic relief and technique, or house-building skills, to a regular group on a weekly basis, I was able to avoid the things I had not liked about teaching voice intensives. Two- to three-day group workshops are often overwhelmingly intense, no matter how hard a teacher tries to pace the experience. I had begun to wonder if they were cruel. Some students love the ecstatic feeling of "razing themselves to the ground" over a weekend, but often these transformations are not sustainable. Other students appear to close down after a weekend of "breakthroughs," unable to make sense of, or incorporate, such rapid change. Integration takes time and rest.

In January, when I returned to full-time teaching, the recession's negative effects had trickled down to the artists I serve, so I kept the classes going. The groups were more affordable, but that wasn't the only reason. I had seen growth within the studio that could only be credited to a healthy ecosystem: commitment to one's own sound in front of others; sensitive, unbiased listening; and responsive, nuanced communication. Egalitarian support among peers.

Kind and truthful reflection between co-equals, based on sensed, shared experience, promotes insightful, moving conversation. "Speak from your body! How did it feel when your colleague sang? What did you enjoy? What did your body learn?" I might demonstrate the way I want a student touched to awaken their senses, but stepping away so that a classmate can do the hands-on work invokes more layers of learning. Together the class enters the unknown, lets go of self-criticism, becomes complicit in each singer's unique unfolding. Opening up my "air space" to other voices—while holding the technique's pedagogy and managing time—lightened my touch. My sense of responsibility was blessed by the buoyancy of "group."

My home studio, ringed with art and lit by a string of brightly colored lanterns, is a far cry from the neutral, and sometimes grubby, rehearsal halls I used to rent, and there is just enough space for a small group to lie on the floor if needed. During the day my family discreetly passes the curtains that separate my workspace from the hallway. Sound crosses easily, but classes don't seem to mind; they understand that we are bringing full human expression out from behind closed doors. A student might wander off to use the bathroom, or into the kitchen for a glass of water, chatting with the girls if they happen to be home. My daughters have rarely complained about my early-morning classes and I can hear that they have benefited from this regular acoustic diet. Their adult speaking voices are free and grounded.

I have experienced an integration of private and public space through my approach to the human voice, as a teacher and as a performer, and even between these two identities. The more I have woven what is outside of my home with what happens in my personal space, the more integrity I have had to ask of myself. I do not feel less professional since breaking down these boundaries; I feel more competent and whole. And, of course, there is more for me to learn.

In 2010 I received a Chalmers Arts Fellowship from the Ontario Arts Council to survey my vocal practice, create a small women's choir, and write about my pedagogy while exploring the newly available neuroscience that might apply to voice. The Chalmers is a coveted mid- to late-career grant and has the potential to set the course for an artist's coming decades. The grant funded research over an eighteen-month period, but to keep contact with my students and support my family, I had to keep on teaching. Limited time begged an even more streamlined format, one geared to establishing and maintaining the basics. Simultaneously my performing students—dancers, actors, and singers alike—were asking for a vocal warm-up so they could become more self-sufficient when rehearsing or touring. What a perfect fit!

Their growing independence and my desire to reflect and refine were met that summer through the introduction of Slipper Camp: a one-hour progression of clearly articulated, distilled skills that could be practiced within a group. As much as I wanted the rigor and regularity of a "boot camp," it was essential that *rest and digest* weave with *fight or flight*. This camp would require the softness of slippers.

I sold the "Slippers" in packs of five classes for fifty dollars to encourage frequency, which I thought would be necessary for this experiment. Each Tuesday and Thursday morning at 8:45, a dozen or so bodies tumbled into my home having braved Toronto traffic and humidity, often by bike or public transportation. For sixty full minutes, or around one thousand breaths, in a way that was not spectacular or dramatic, Slipper Camp warmed us *in* rather than *up*. Starting with breath and yawning for release and integration, we moved on to long tones at the piano in order to engage with phonation, pitch, and resonance—finally tackling "*oooo* slides" over a musical fifth to become even-keeled with melody.

Focusing regularly on inner physiological sensation, we foraged, deepening our relationship to breath and our understanding of exactly how healthy singing grows out of the inhale, which feeds, and the exhale, which expresses. Within an empathic context we practiced specific body-led tasks that, through healthy, conscious repetition, forged a balance of light and dark, of height and depth, of *bound* and *unbound*, of compassion and aggression. An economy of activity from the inside out.

Slipper Camps don't engage with the processing of emotion through exploring the topography of personal temperament and life experience; that essential and transformational work is engaged with during group classes and in private lessons. Instead, I treat emotion as something normal, necessary, and reliable; consider it central and reasonable with regard to survival—weave it right into the technique. The resulting organic skill set functions collaboratively within the body, creates a reliable foundation to support cathartic release in private or group contexts.

This breath and voice routine can be taken home and practiced alone, but, as in group classes, working alongside others creates a spacious arena for under the skin change and exchange. Anyone new to the studio senses that this is a reliable culture to join while remaining true to self, and each week I see my students band together afresh while fostering individual potential. When a student commits to four or more sessions a month, I observe increased ease, freedom, flexibility, authenticity, range, composure, stamina, sustainability, and longevity.

Trying to sing "in our own sweet time" within community sets a template for negotiating complex tensions, and when on tour, or far from Toronto, Skype and Zoom are effective ways to stay connected. During 2020 and 2021's pandemic lockdowns the Slipper format translated online beautifully, though in each singer's home the class would have sounded like a duet between the student and me, despite the chorus of faces on the screen.

I am cautious about teaching remotely as long-distance practice can degrade pedagogy over time. However, when technology provides a solid connection, and a group class is small enough, I can see, hear, and feel what is happening in a faraway singer's body in surprising detail. In combination with online groups of four or five students Slipper Camp has provided a good container during the pandemic. Interestingly, the lessening of social distractions can give some students easier access to intimate space within—inhabitation versus performance.

A healthy singing practice is like a balanced yoga practice. Going to the mat brings relief through regulating multiple systems in the body—breath and chemicals, muscles and fascia, heart and mind. Sitting down at my piano to sing does the same. And like my body, my voice never lies. It provides a universe of realization through telling me what is going on: maybe I am pushing too hard, at odds with myself, or having a rough ride with my emotions. Slipper Camp mends me by rejigging the binary systems I juggle every day: instinct and learned behavior, individual and social drives, self-healing and professional goals. Its vocal nuts and bolts lead to a deeper inhabitation of self. Paying attention through all my senses, body finds heart, heart finds soul, and my mind doesn't mind so much anymore.

I now call what I teach Emotionally Integrated Voice. To make it available for readers of this book I have given each vertebra of the technique a chapter. Every discrete pedagogical piece has "real life" Slipper Camp experiences as illustration. Some of the Slippers were in the summer and some in winter, so time appears to jump, but each study is in order and when strung together flesh out a complete warm-in. I invite you to enter the studio—share precious air while engaging in the ancient, knowable art of breath and voice. Change is possible, and best wrought in community.

II

Slipper Camp One— Loving Gravity

A STREAM OF students pours through my front door, spilling early-morning sun onto the foyer's stone mosaic floor. Slipper Camp is starting in five minutes and everyone is on the verge of being late. Without wasting any time a dozen city dwellers from across Toronto wiggle their feet into the warm cherrywood of this erstwhile Victorian parlor, now my voice studio. Nairobi, Reykjavik, and Regina flash green on my laptop's screen: three long-term singers joining via Skype from cities far and wide. I place a wastebasket in the center of the room and plunk a tissue box beside it. Live and online, we ready ourselves to go into the human engine through breath and sound.

I cast my gaze over this morning's faces. Evalyn, a renegade theater creator and singer/songwriter, uses her well-trained focus to find neutral. Michelangelo's soft eyes juggle desire and excitement; he is a composer, performer, and instrument builder. Natasha's usually limpid brow has her PhD-furrowed look of "I will become expert at this!" Aviva is already dropping her belly, a dutiful yet daring cantor continuing to deepen her ability to lead others in prayer. They raggedly ring the room along with the rest of the class. Knees unlatch reflexively as I start to speak.

"Take a few steps forward and backward. Note the space between your feet as they swing past one another. Try not to plant them when you come to a stop. Most of you will now have a narrower stance than the one you first took. You may feel a little wobbly through your legs. This is what I want! Invite your soles to enjoy the soft wood underfoot while celebrating becoming 'unfixed.' Note how much softer the sides of your ribs feel!"

Most students will take a much wider stance than needed. They are used to feeling "grounded" by working through their thighs to push into the earth. But I don't want this feeling of adeptness ... of arming. We have a lot of habit bound up in standing. I want a wobblier place so that being grounded comes out of having a free, released diaphragm, based on a responsive, at-ease pelvic floor.

I ask my students to place one hand low on the curve of their abdomen, thumb at belly button and baby finger on pubic bone—the back of their other hand can rest gently on their sacrum. I model dropping my belly into the palm of my "front" hand, reminding my students to marvel at the lower abdomen's ability to *kerplunk*. Aided by gravity, guts and organs settle a little deeper into my pelvic basin, prompting—not forcing—the downward pull of my diaphragm ... leading my breath engine to believe I am relaxed!

"Invite your genitals, perineum, and anus to become soft, expanding, and undefended. Cultivate a deep love for gravity. Imagine the flesh on your buttocks, thighs, calves, and shins sloughing toward the earth. Sink down ... but don't bend your knees more deeply! Instead feel earthy and moist throughout your core by imagining your plumb line in relation to gravity.

"Be your own field. Take time to replenish by letting your flesh lie fallow. Take in your whole torso three-dimensionally. Notice the continuing swell of your belly, the complementary swoon of your back. Imagine a melting sensation on either side of your spine right down to your sacrum and tailbone. Slouch your lower lip toward the floor. Risk a little drool—it's the only thing that will get you a gold star in my class!

"Open your mouth tall and wide to let air flow down your throat and into your lungs, *all by itself.* Remember that it wants to. Let it flood in of its own accord, filling lower, middle, and upper lungs, undulating your spine from tailbone to skull. No need to yank up through the shoulder girdle to guarantee air's complicity. Listen carefully. Can your mouth and throat be so completely open that the inhale becomes silent, as well as slow and passive?"

I go over to a recent student, Roula, to see how she is doing, asking if I can place my hand on her belly. She looks a little "set" and I want to encourage a deep and true "swoon" within her core. I want her to allow her diaphragm to do what it does best when we are asleep: inhale involuntarily, without worry or interference from the ego.

Softening the pelvic floor encourages the diaphragm to work involuntarily, promoting *rest and digest* in the autonomic nervous system. The ANS regulates the intestines, heart, and glands: things we normally don't pay attention to but that are essential for life. This nervous system is designed to work homeostatically—in other words, sustainably—without any help from its "owner." Typically, we don't feel or see it unless something is wrong; but as singers we need to access it consciously, even when nothing is amiss, to enhance balance within both calm and excited sound-making.

Dropping the belly and softening the pelvic floor ungirds my loins. Each breath, based on receiving and not on grabbing, asks me to trust that the world would like me to thrive, reinforces that things are okay, reminds me that I already know how to breathe.

"We are such beautifully designed breath machines," I say to my class, "but some days are harder than others."

This makes Roula laugh. She is a gifted singer of Arabic music and one of the juiciest belly dancers I've ever seen, but today she is having a hard time releasing her guts.

I note something practical in Roula's body. Her stance has become dogmatic. Her feet have crept about two inches wider apart than I would like, and her weight is back in her heels.... She looks more warrior than lover. As she brings her feet closer together, a few other students adjust theirs. We like to feel competent, and pushing against the earth, against anything, can give a false impression of sturdiness.

I encourage Roula to let go of any feelings of responsibility that she might still be holding through her upper chest and shoulders by touching her gently in those places. I ask her to become somewhat simian, bringing her upper torso slightly forward by folding minutely at the hip hinge—*not by slouching*. She eases out of the straitjacket of "good" posture without crunching through her front ribs. This minuscule shift of weight toward the front of her body—while maintaining a pleasant, earthy sensation through her buttocks, and equal contact with the floor through the front and back of her feet—changes everything. She looks as if she could move equally easily to crawling on "all fours" or to plopping down onto her bottom like a toddler; her balance is that fine. On the next belly drop she finally *kerplunks*, feels the thrill and terror of abdomen unlatching and organs slipping downward ... an almost pre–toilet trained state. I ask her to open her mouth a little more, to go soft through the lips, and to veer toward a yawn so her incoming breath is completely free of friction ... silent.

As she shifts into fully letting go—receiving air, not demanding or guaranteeing it—even her exhales change, quivering as they release from behind her sternum. A sigh, a shudder, unforced small gushes. Roula looks undone and receptive. She inhabits herself with ease and simplicity, self-love deep in her bones.

Collaborating with the earth by yielding into gravity is transgressive in our culture. There are so many situations in which we feel we need to measure up, impress, or defend. We are supposed to look like we have control over our bellies. We like neither the vulnerability nor the aesthetics of a rounded tummy. When I first started to demonstrate this dropped breath, I used to blush. My face burned. I did not know what to do with the fertile curve of my womb in a culture that does not value untrammeled female sexuality.

I share my own struggles so as to underline that it takes time to shift habits, especially when a new paradigm is at odds with what we see around us, with what we have absorbed into our flesh in relation to safety and values. It was after I had birthed and breastfed two babies in my thirties, and felt more *mother* than *singer*—impressed by my body's innate abilities and humbled enough by life to have stopped caring about certain external things—that I was finally able to yield into this breath. Once I had identified thoroughly with the dropped belly inhale, I used it for all my professional singing gigs and began to teach it. I experienced immediate improvements in digestion and a new ease for my neck and shoulders from not holding the world together, but rather letting it hold me. Through consistent, repeated demonstration of this low abdominal release, I escaped my unconscious mistrust of—and my very early learned shame over—the female body. The blushing stopped.

"Each of you has good reasons for why the passivity required to receive air feels wrong. And yet it is profoundly right, and important to find and integrate into the everyday. It was through allowing this drop, over and over again, through thick and thin, that a compassion grew within me for my worthiness as a human being … as a woman.

"Use these moments to learn how to indulge in the inhale," I tell my students. "There is no need to suck at air! I promise that the drop of the belly—as long as your mouth and throat are open—will bring air in without any conscious or added effort."

We are making a new weave of *rest and digest* with *fight or flight* by discovering how profoundly gravity can influence our insides. We are realizing how little work or volition breathing takes by releasing unnecessary grips on both of our lower diaphragms—the pelvic leading the thoracic. This rest within the breath cycle provides the basis for sustainability and longevity within the singer's instrument, as well as within a human's body/mind ecology.

The room is full of sincere connection to self, to quiet, to rest. Time has started to shift as flesh and spirit become one. I plant a new thought in these ready and receptive beings: "Why does air come into the body?"

The answer? Because it wants to. It is there for the asking. No, as long as I am open, *I don't even need to ask*. Once my diaphragm pulls down and out, opening my lungs from bottom to top, air floods into each lobe's expansive, stretchy recesses with ease.

Air is all around me, and free. Even at night when I am asleep and busy with dreams, air comes into my body over and over again. Such beautiful design.

"As your insides dance subtly with this room's air, find pleasure in your body's sophisticated sensations," I tell them. "Don't be shy about noticing that you are sharing space and air with other people. For those of you on Skype, remember what it was like to breathe with your fellow students the last time you were here. People you have shared calm breath with can accompany you over time and across distance through memory's constructs. Consciously imagine your senses to life."

Diaphragm pulling down without impediment, expanding and dropping a little farther, shaping into a gentle bowl. Ribs floating sideways and outward as if we could take flight, gradually tugging the lungs fully open so that the alveoli can exchange oxygen for CO_2. Loving gravity leads to the kind of deep nourishment found in sleep. The start of this vocal practice is so relaxing that some new students think it is called "sleeper" camp. Not so! We are waking up.

"There is one last thing I want us to include in the dropped belly breath cycle ... something to weave a small dose of *fight or flight* into the *rest and digest* you're already accessing. Trace a line between your pubic bone and your belly button. In tandem with each unimportant, fluffy exhale, mimic a small zipper-like action upward along this line corralling your lower abdominals ever so gently. Please don't pull these muscles back toward your spine or yank them up toward your chest; instead, gather them slightly, just like a zipper's teeth coming together on a pair of low-rise jeans. When you do this smoothly and easily you won't create tension farther up in your throat. Your exhale—deep, small, audible, and fluffy—will flow without impediment from behind your sternum, sounding like the somewhat self-possessed older sister of a fully relaxed sigh."

A few students question what happens with my pelvic floor—do I pull it up along with the zipper action?

I tell them that I let my pelvic floor glide forward in gentle response to the zipper-like action. It reminds me of a toboggan on snow. I say, "No, I don't pull up, but my perineum does feel a little more tonic on the exhale. And in case you are wondering, I don't feel my anal sphincter tighten."

They seem satisfied and include this first piece of *bound* energy without sacrificing *unbound*. A roomful of humans thrumming harmoniously, enjoying their "in common" engine.

This is the easy part of my job. Our urban, Western bodies are in need of these reminders in order to reconstitute healthful breath patterns. In between classes I am prone to pulling up through my whole body. I may rush, drive, defend, or collapse. I display the effects of walking on concrete and the overwhelm of tall buildings, thick air. My face mirrors the stressed faces that pass me in the grocery store aisles, the city's squeeze making us insensitive to how tense we've all become.

In Slipper Camp we take ten minutes to enter fully into receiving air. I call it the "spa" in the breath cycle, and know it can lead to ease, an exquisite inertia, or deep sleep. As much as it is seriously missing from most people's breath diets, on its own it would not guarantee survival. However, it is the crucial building block upon which all our creative efforts will be based.

I suggest practicing the dropped belly in the everyday: while waiting in line at the grocery store or for the streetcar, while talking to a trusted friend or cutting vegetables at a counter, eventually taking it into riskier situations like asking for a raise or arguing with a loved one. Based on receiving and not on grabbing, each inhale reinforces well-being and the right to listen to the deeper self, as well as the ability to hear others. In not too long this breath will become a welcome and reliable daytime resident in any new student's body.

While teaching this first Slipper Camp segment, I map my students' bodies onto mine, using breath to become aware of what we share and how we differ. My body opens to fundamental, contrasting human need—the one to bind and make order, the other to spill and dissipate. This approach makes my students' bodies easy to read and a pleasure to offer pleasure to.

After decades of teaching, I remain in awe of breath: the beauty of it, the intimacy of it, the health of it. It is no accident that in many languages *breath* and *spirit* share the same word.

12

Slipper Camp Two—
Mouth Orgasm

A CRUSH OF activity fills the tiny entranceway next to my studio; boots, coats, mittens, scarves, and hats pile high. This colder-than-usual winter has demanded endless bundling and unbundling. The swish of fabric and whispered *excuse me*'s are accompaniment to my words as I start the lesson without waiting for my students to settle.

"I know you think you're late—but please don't rush. While slipping off your coat and bending over to take off your boots, begin the gentle work of softening your belly to receive breath; you likely girded your loins to traverse slippery sidewalks. So, even if the snow slowed you down, take a few extra moments to enter this room by giving in to the mundane task of arriving—coax your mind out of its tendency to push. Use this as an opportunity to rebalance tension by weaving soft, deep breath into the everyday stress of feeling late."

Each student slows down to enter the studio by following the inner rhythm of dropped belly breath as it softens down past the pubic bone and across the pelvic floor. I remind them to give their anal sphincter time to blossom, and then to take their mind's eye up toward their sacrum. Our two sacroiliac joints connect this triangular-shaped bony plate—also a foundational part of the spine—to the left and right hip bones, and along with the iliac crest and navel form what feels like a top rim for the pelvic basin. There is so much space available in and around each sacroiliac joint when a soft pelvic floor initiates the breath cycle, leading to a subtle broadening and narrowing of the pelvic rim with each in-and-out of air.

I want my students to keep their attention focused on the back of their body. "You have two anal sphincters—one you can control and one that has a mind of its own. Your external anal sphincter is connected by the anococcygeal ligament to your tailbone; that is why softening your anus can set up a wave of release through the spine. Given time this undulation encourages your diaphragm to find itself anew through integrating the easy release of *rest and digest* with *fight or flight*'s desire for more airspace.

"The ribcage, which protects heart and lungs, is extremely malleable. In German it is called the rib basket. I like this change of focus from guarding the organs to holding them. And it is true that the muscles between the ribs—the intrinsic and extrinsic intercostals—are similar to the weave of a basket.

"The bony frame of this basket is kept together through connective tissue—multidirectional joints where the ribs meet the spine, and costal cartilage where they connect to the sternum. More than eighty points of articulation! In addition your ribs are unique bones within your skeleton, as their material is flexible, even elastic.

"Return to the release of your anus. Imagine the quietest pull of ligament on coccyx. Then take time for the expansion of your sacroiliac joints. Several inches above this, where ribs meet spine meets diaphragm's wing-like efforts, are your 'floating ribs.' Our eleventh and twelfth ribs are attached to the spine but not to the sternum. Grant them an outward 'float' so the lower lobes of your lungs can fill with air in a way that feels *effortless* as well as *expansive*. No enforcement necessary!"

I walk around the room, sweeping my hand gently across each person's lower back—first the sacrum and then the bottom few ribs on either side of their spine—waking up sensory awareness through touch.

"Take your focus a little farther up the back of your body to the space between your shoulder blades. Let air spill into your upper lungs after filling the lower lobes. Permit ten more pairs of ribs to feel as if they are moving more freely around your spine from the inside out. You might even notice the front of your chest expanding in response to the unlocking of space between your shoulders. Posture is aided by breath's movement. No need to ape an idealized shape."

Again I circle the room, gently touching the space between my students' shoulders, often gripped from too many hours spent at a computer, or in a car, or holding the universe together.

Each breath follows this sequence of soft expansion, beginning with the dropped belly down toward the pelvic floor. The spreading sensation continues past genitals, perineum, and anal sphincter, then scoops up to include the sacrum, the lumbar vertebrae, the lowest back ribs, finally inhabiting the space between the shoulder blades. The expansion of the torso from *bottom to top* will feel as if it mirrors a ballooning of the lungs, also from *bottom to top*. A small, natural shrug of the shoulders will likely occur as inhale turns to exhale. A gentle affirmation of the breath cycle rather than a "doing." How perfect that an exhale provides the opportunity to notice give-and-take, engage with ebb and flow. *We are designed to let go of burdens ... as well as shoulder them.*

Now that my students are more at home in their bodies I want to see if neck and head can have a new relationship to torso. I invite them to picture a little coyote opening up through mouth and throat. I want the air hovering around their lips to play in the space we call the pharynx as well as the upper chest ... without sucking in willfully. *Make space and receive.*

I go to each student one last time, tracing the curve of their neck bones right up to the occipital joint, where skull floats on vertebrae. This cue encourages our ten minutes of dropped belly breath to transition seamlessly into yawning.

"Our studio has become a safe harbor today, especially given the temperamental weather outside. Yes, the geography of piano, books, and art is well-known terrain for your body, but the coziness you are feeling comes primarily from your own breath cycle's increased receptivity. The climate of trust now hovering between you and your classmates' bodies further invites the releasing height of a yawn. When dropped belly partners with yawning's upward suspension an important relationship is fostered within each of you, that of levity with gravity."

I yawn into my next thoughts, priming my students' nervous systems through "impolitely" smearing my own words.

"Fully inhabit yawning by flying in the face of physically encoded taboos. Unfortunately, social repression can be even stronger than a yawn's deeply wired contagion. If you are resistant today to the pull of another person's yawn, or even to your own … well then, lustily fake a few. Let your mouth gape wide. Haul in a little ragged air. Shrug your shoulders for no good reason in case they are holding your yawns in check. In no time your yawning will become real, sincere, authentic, and yours."

As my students follow their yawns, their torsos twist and their hands reach wide. The wave of each delicious pandiculation spreads through the entire body, stretching open more than just ribcage. We aren't making our physiology *do* anything; we are becoming devotees of what it *wants* to do.

The word *pandiculate* comes from the Latin *pandere*—to spread out. A pandiculation spreads out the human body under the purview of the autonomic nervous system through what appear to be stretch-like motions. Not only are muscles implicated but also fascia, the tissue that bundles and connects us from head to toe. This interconnection is why tightness in one part of the body is reflected throughout the whole musculoskeletal system—can show as restriction or pain elsewhere.

"Note how a pandiculation gathers your muscles before releasing and lengthening them. This gathering provides feedback to your cerebral cortex about how your body is doing 'in the moment.' An *haute couture* stretch—designed for my 'in the moment' body thanks to a pandiculation's rapid-fire reconnaissance team. In contrast, a will-based stretch can override my spine's healthy, protective 'stretch reflex.' Good thing, because I can be bossy about what I think my muscles should be able to do …

"The yawn is a particular type of pandiculation—comprehensive and holistic through working from the inside out with the breath equipment, the pharynx, larynx, vocal cords, lungs, and trachea. These are moments of ecstasy designed to take us out of daily limitations. Notice how tension and release climb on top of and through each other as you yawn.... Let this remind you of lovers wordlessly following desire. Both yawn and orgasm model an intelligent relationship between *fight or flight* and *rest and digest*, and, in bringing together contradictory energies, reset tension levels. Things the mind has a hard time governing alone.

"The design of all living organisms is to seek balance, or homeostasis. We humans can promote allostasis—the process by which we recover from stress and return to homeostasis—through embracing pandiculating. With or without the yawn a pandiculation is expert at coordinating strength and release; it has a precise understanding of energy and effort. In my experience it is hard to injure yourself yawning ... so go further! The magic happens when we don't think.

"Let your palms broaden—or ball up into fists—both of these actions are in the yawn's tool kit. Let yourself compress as often as your body requests; yawns and pandiculations know that both *bound* and *unbound* feelings are effective, necessary. You know, sometimes the back of my neck feels like it is being squeezed out like a little sponge! I love that feeling ..."

I share my current yawning stories, explaining that I now yawn whenever I go for a walk. This body and brain love affair began in Vancouver during the 2010 Paralympics. I was coaching vocalist Mark Brose in Peggy Baker and Ahmed Hassan's dance/music performance *Geometry of the Circle* and on our day off went for a long walk in Stanley Park. Its old-growth forest inspired massive release throughout my breath body—hundreds and hundreds of personal yawns unleashed by centuries-old trees.

"A variety of hormones, peptides, and chemicals are released when you yawn, ones that are chronically low in Alzheimer's and Parkinson's patients as well as in individuals living with diabetes or ADHD.

Oxytocin, the bonding molecule, flows more freely. Neurotransmitters too, processing sensation, clarifying thought. Yawning helps us sleep and lifts our blues. It also lowers pain levels through the release of natural analgesics. Yes, free drugs! I can't think of a single good reason not to yawn to your heart's content."

I describe my nightly ritual of reading and yawning. "One of the benefits of intentionally linking yawning to this pre-sleep transition is that I have lowered my nighttime jaw tension significantly. Post-yawning, I have a hard time remembering the things that bug me—things best left untackled late at night. Sharing that yawns soften away the day's emotional barnacles can start me on a fresh yawning jag, even while writing. I picture the warm lighting of my bedroom, feel myself sink into the pillow-top mattress; I am as good as there."

How can anyone not trust the body/mind connection?

I invite my students to yawn outside of our studio, make space for it daily—a time and a location: over morning tea in the kitchen, as a late afternoon pick-me-up in front of the computer, or a bedtime ritual between the sheets. I tell them, "Your body will learn that certain spots in your home or at work are safe for yawning and releasing. My hunch is that we could all yawn for around twenty minutes throughout the day for optimal health. Start each day by yawning and pandiculating your way from night's modest, relaxed breath into your daily agenda of activities. I just heard that laughing for fifteen minutes a day is necessary for emotional well-being, so why not have a prescription for yawns too!"

Mouths widen and necks arch backward, leading several bodies into finely sculpted upper backbends. Hands clench or spread, ribcages twist, torsos elongate, bottoms drop, and hips grind. The movements of this disinhibited gang of yawners are ever surprising as well as ample and connected.

"Be extravagant, extroverted, exuberant yawners. Lose your sense of good taste, and for goodness' sake, never cover your mouth. Feel the gorgeous—*and free*—massage of sinuses and eyes as you grimace your social face away."

I witness a display of untamed facial expressions that are not usual within our civilized repertoire—an episode of *Mutual of Omaha's Wild Kingdom* without the TV. One after another, today's students reach for the tissue box next to the wastebasket in the middle of the room. There is a symphony of phlegm as noses blow and throats clear. Pandiculating has opened space in the head and chest by encouraging the natural functioning of sinuses, trachea, and lungs. The free flow of phlegm comes as a result of mechanical actions through the yawn's massage. It also indicates that hormonal and chemical levels are changing for the better throughout each person's body.

"Remember that yawns understand and love asymmetry. A pandiculation knows the needs of your spine, neck, and occipital joint, and can expertly chart the remarkable length of your body from toe to fingertip and up through the crown. Even wrists and ankles want to twist their way out of our mental and physical shackles ... especially the ones we adopt in front of a computer, typing up a report or essay, relentlessly surfing the web—or writing a book like I am.

"I think of language as the biggest and best birthday gift imaginable. And, now that it has been opened, hard to put down. I feel possessive of this gift for many good reasons: it tracks my narrative, constructs my identity, defends a position, and reframes bad experiences. It helps transmit inherited beliefs within the family, as well as cultural beliefs within a group ... beliefs we may no longer believe. A subtle grip in my speaking voice can point out tension or tiredness, and it can also underline that I've been sidestepping my truth, toeing someone else's line, or have a really, really, really important point to make! The nerves, muscles, and cartilage of my voice box map the sound of mind winning out over body and soul; its tension patterns make willpower audible. Yawning is one of the few ways to release the larynx and give ourselves a break from all the blah, blah, blah. Free ourselves from what we've made of ourselves.

"Stay away from 'good ideas'—resist the neck circle or side bend you think will fix things. The yawn knows best how to undo before assembling once again. *It seeks balance.* Your voice box, or larynx, is almost entirely connective tissue; enjoy how reclaiming balance throughout your body massages tension away from your habitual use of your vocal folds."

Occasionally a student will dissolve to the floor as the connection between diaphragm and psoas* becomes more liquid. Sometimes little shakes quiver through the neck; I imagine all the *nos* a person might have censored seeping out of their nervous system in a moment like this. A recent immigrant from Palestine—who had grown up in a predominantly Arab town in Israel (not the occupied territories)—discovered an intensely militant looking yawn one day during Slipper Camp. It was not his usual sensual pandiculation, which seemed to fit so well with his generous, friendly personality. His body's new yawn action was undeniably tonic, definite, selfish, and productive. He told the class that, all at once, he felt that he had found a missing part of himself, one that revealed his full range of experience.

I encourage my students: "Let the yawns surprise you. Let them teach you something new about yourself, your body, your feelings. Let them misbehave and be creative. I am starting to think that yawning is akin to art-making. Both come from the unconscious—feel improvisational.

"In between yawns, touch base with your dropped belly breath. Celebrate how malleable and responsive your entire torso has become. Notice that the yawn and the dropped belly breath are melding into one!"

Ribcages widen and sternums rise while remaining flexible—open-hearted, expansive, and capacious. Together we are supporting a healthier relationship to the autonomic nervous system. Some students start yawning outside the front door of my studio, others during the walk from streetcar stop to class.

---

* The psoas major originates at the spine around the bottom of the ribcage and runs down to the thigh bone (the femur). The psoas major acts to flex the hip. The psoas minor also originates at the spine around the bottom of the ribcage, but it runs down to the bony pelvis. It acts to flex the lower (lumbar) spine. The psoas is connected to the diaphragm through connective tissue or fascia, which affects both our breath and fear reflex. (Liz Koch, CoreAwareness, https://coreawareness.com, an educational website.)

Our ten minutes of dropped belly breath has melded into a ten-minute full-bodied "yawnga" festival. A day care of adults releasing habitual grips. Twist after twist, their increasingly unsocialized bodies have stopped shouldering the world. Crotches practically explode, ribs take down barricades, ramparts crumble. Maybe our soft bits—lungs, heart, liver, trachea—have no real need for armed protection. This rebellious therapy for conditioned minds and busy hearts knows how to celebrate the body's intelligence. We are not pretending anything.

Yawning is a completely integrative, nonhierarchical activity in which the body leads the mind. Along with its benefits of physical expansion, yawning, I believe, offers an opening of spirit. Could the empathy promoted through its physiology consistently lead to doing good *with* others: using yawns to reset tension levels within a group, not just an individual body? Maybe yawning could teach us to live within community rather than as a part of society—coming together instead of telling each other how to behave.

Enough of sense-less, repressive taboos.

13

Of Yawns

IF A STUDENT asks for homework, I suggest that they investigate yawning, sighing, belly laughing, sobbing, and orgasm. I remember blurting this list for the first time in the late 1990s as an off-the-top-of-my-head answer to a student's query. Over time, it has become increasingly clear that each of these ecstatic diaphragm-, sinus-, and voice box–releasing activities is not only good for the body, but food for the soul. These five intrinsic human activities have so much to reveal about breath, emotion, vocalization, and the body's ability to restore itself.

When I first became obsessed with yawns there was very little research available to the general public. Most online articles—written by doctors or medical researchers—ended with some version of "and we don't really know what they are for." I would often rail aloud: "Isn't the fact that they make you feel better information enough?" To encourage my students to take the yawning plunge, I had to rely on what I witnessed in my studio or gleaned from alternative health practitioners as well as the occasional scientific tidbit.

1. Tight jaw hinges and gripped voice boxes find relief through regular yawning.
2. Once a yawn has completed, increased mouth space encourages greater vocal resonance.

3. Our eyes, nose, and mouth moisten, which is good for a singer's mucous membranes.

4. Yawns bathe the cells of the body in chemicals that are deeply relaxing.

5. Most yawns occur as we transition from one activity to another.[*]

6. In primate studies, when the big baboon yawns all the other baboons get to yawn as well.[†]

In 2009 my student angela rawlings—a fantastically intelligent, sloe-eyed poet—sent me a two-page article by Andrew Newberg. Reading it brought one excited nod after another. Dr. Newberg's research illuminated the breadth, complexity, and value of yawning's chemistry. His research showed that a yawn's cornucopia of natural drugs leads to self-reflection, empathy, and consciousness, as well as improved memory retrieval and neurotransmission. "Yawning may be one of the most important mechanisms for regulating the survival-related behaviors in mammals."[‡] He explains that yawning may promote self-awareness through evoking unique neural activity in the precuneus region of the brain—the part that lights up in mature meditators. He also notes that the contagiousness of yawning is not as mysterious as we think. It syncs us up with one another socially, which speaks to the yawn's valuable role in meeting the human animal's specific survival needs.

It is easy to feel how beneficial a yawn's neurochemistry is when a yawning session is not curtailed. First I become aware of all the places

---

* Maria Konnikova, "The Surprising Science of Yawning," *New Yorker*, April 14, 2014, www.newyorker.com/science/maria-konnikova/the-surprising -science-of-yawning.

† Alessandra Zannella, Roscoe Stanyon, and Elisabetta Palagi, "Yawning and Social Styles: Different Functions in Tolerant and Despotic Macaques (*Macaca tonkeana* and *Macaca fuscata*)," *Journal of Comparative Psychology* 131, no. 3: 179–188, https://doi.org/10.1037/com0000062.

‡ Andrew Newberg, "Yawn," *Pennsylvania Gazette*, November–December 2009, www.upenn.edu/gazette/1109/expert.html.

I am holding, of the tiredness I feel. Full-bodied stretching follows so that aches vanish and vigor renews. As my nose drips and eyes water, mental space opens, making transitions easier, transformation imaginable. Together body and mind dissolve power structures, embrace cooperation. Yawning can be used not only to warm up for rehearsal or to imagine a new character, but as preparation right before stepping onstage. Performing difficult roles in the theater requires well-honed, in-the-moment survival tools as well as emotional transparency. By freshly combining relaxation and alertness, yawns lead to a more flexible interpretive instrument.

As you learned in the preceding chapter, the stretch and twist of arms, torso, and legs that accompanies a yawn is called a pandiculation. This beautiful and rarely used word came to me from a Wikipedia entry found during one of my late-night online yawn safaris. A few clicks in, I found myself staring at the back of Joseph Ducreux's mouth. Caught mid-yawn, his gob gapes, its open, fleshy aperture matching the red of his jacket. Ducreux's belly slackens into his fawn-colored waistcoat, relaxed flesh gently straining at the buttons. Both arms are spread wide into the dark negative space surrounding his head: one leading from the elbow, the other reaching a clenched-fist conclusion. I can feel the lift of air under his armpits. As work and release combine, Ducreux's brow furrows facial features away from their usual socialized set and his facade crumbles. An unguarded, intimate self-portrait.

It is 1783, six years before the French Revolution. I don't know about the late 1700s, but I do know that today we might allow ourselves a fulsome, wholesome, some-kinda-big-ass stretch only around those with whom we feel extremely safe, or maybe only when we are on our own, or maybe not at all. We have lost faith in yawning. Life in a big city's push and shove leaves little room for an open mouth. Too much adrenaline too often and elevated cortisol at barely disguised levels are things that cause a soft palate to pull down. Locked into chronic *fight or flight*, we "keep a lid on it" as a way to feel safe.

Ducreux's interest in physiognomy—the belief that the study and judgment of a person's outer appearance, primarily the face, could

93

reflect their character or personality—led him to break from the constraints of traditional portraiture. His ability to capture the individuality of his subjects through warm, insightful works resulted in a free trip to Vienna in 1769. Louis XVI had commissioned a miniature of Marie Antoinette so he could see his bride-to-be. I am more grateful for the right to comfy-ness that Ducreux's self-portrait proclaims than his portrait of the future queen of France, and I wonder if his appreciation for yawning could have led an ass-backward charge against the class system through tender care for the expressivity of each individual human body. I also wonder, *When and why did yawning become so repressed?* We think it indicates rudeness, tiredness, or repressed anger, but when we keep it caged up we keep ourselves caged up too. When we yawn with others we are on even footing. My yawn is just as good as the next person's. My yawn is just as real, as inviolable, as Marie Antoinette's. (Ducreux also drew the last portrait of Louis shortly before the king was executed in 1793.)

When my second daughter, Oksana, was very little, she had a hard time waking up. I would set a small wooden plate of mini-croissants and Nutella on her bedside table at 7:30 a.m. to start the process, giving my early-morning princess time to luxuriate. She was a grounded little creature right from the start—earthy and playful. Both girls went to primary school on the Toronto Islands and caught an 8:30 a.m. ferry five days a week. The drive to the docks, which had begun when her older sister was two, was a reliable source of stress for me, eventually resulting in the girls' gleeful suggestion of "Fuzzy bunny!" as a fantastic replacement for the F-word. Regardless, explaining to Oksana that we had a ferry to catch in under an hour only ever elicited a puzzled, indignant—and achingly sensual—"I stretching!" And that is exactly what she had to do—stretch and stretch and stretch until she was ready to get out of bed. Oksana couldn't fall asleep either until she had done her requisite thirty yawns. Little did I know that she was spreading herself out, making room internally for day or night to come. I can't say I was always patient as she transitioned into or out of this world, but watching her listen to her body educated me.

Entering yawning's liminal space class after class, I am struck by how much this bodily function feels like musical improvisation. Despite its being spontaneous and surprising, there are laws that govern its actions. It has flow, flexibility, and purpose, without too many hang-ups. As with improv, it is worth exhausting the yawn's process to get to the heart of the matter. When I am leading a rehearsal and give yawning its full due as part of the warm-up, censorship falls away, making room for a flood of creative impulses and ideas.

Yawning has taught me and my students that integration happens from the inside out and is not something the mind can do alone. Through lowering the larynx and completely adducting the vocal folds, over time yawning can stretch a singer past self-imposed limitations as well as keep her healthy through the stress and strain of rehearsal. Over the years I have learned that not only does yawning illuminate how I am doing in the present moment, but giving time to a flood of yawns offers a perfectly tailored physiological solution for tension, pain, and inattention. The yawn's ability to regulate affirms and promotes resilience while excavating shared body truths.

It is Monday morning and my women's choir is singing Antônio Carlos Jobim's "The Girl from Ipanema." Playing between sensual satisfaction and the longing for "more," our hips sway cool and gentle, lips articulating the text with enough ambiguity to render our English translation Portuguese-sounding once again. We are singing the song as part of a fundraising performance for Ernestine's Women's Shelter, and I will place the twelve of us along the length of hallway that takes the evening's guests from registration table to silent auction.

For our next pass through the song, I ask the women in the choir to yawn randomly, whenever they want to, each woman interrupting her connection to the song's melody and lyrics to indulge in her own body. Maybe open-mouthed duets will occur, or a series of solos—maybe we will overlap, or yawn all at once. I want to get inside the sensual, self-sufficient protagonist of this song through each singer's nervous system.

The yawns are serious magic; they are sultry, intensely private, and authentically exposing. From time to time a delicious sigh slips out of the yawn, flirting with the *aah* of the song's lyrics. How easily we've tumbled into autonomic nervous system storytelling. As the song installs itself in our bodies, I am reminded of "installation art," though our distillation of the female body may function more like "instillation art." I hope "The Girl from Ipanema"'s nonchalant nervous system will slide playfully under this audience's skin, trigger a yawn or two to help shed their workday bodies.

On the day of the fundraiser, everyone in the choir is a little nervous, including me. Fortunately Jobim's music puts us at ease as we sink into ourselves and sync up with one another. Some guests laugh and linger as they move down the hall, and some speed up, wondering if something unexpected will be asked of them. The yawn's aural/oral profile might be a little too intimate for those unaccustomed to its wisdom … might seem too close to female orgasm in its sensual ebb and flow.

We sing fourteen times through the song. The yawns prompt spontaneity, refresh our focus, teach us about sustainable performance. Most importantly they provide inhabited entry to an evening designed to treasure the bodies and souls of women who have suffered domestic violence.

14

Slipper Camp Three—
The Little "Huh"

MY HOME STUDIO is about ten feet by twenty-four. Its walls are lined with a smorgasbord of art: an ink-brush Chinese landscape, a large saturated oil painting of a bodhisattva, the portrait of a heavy-lidded woman, blank book open on her lap, in creative anticipation. A string of lights crisscrosses the space: bouncing, colorful, homemade shades of irregularly perforated Japanese paper … a bit of circus. Another lampshade, covered in silk flowers glued on by my daughters, counterbalances an actual silver-birch tree trunk wedged between ceiling and floor … the relic of a past theater production. The effect is organic, creative, and homey. The piano is at the opposite end from where I drop the tissue box to playfully invite bellies to soften and *kerplunk*. About fifteen minutes into a class, once the group yawning ripens, I head to the piano's bench and sit down.

I ask my students to give full-blown permission to any vocal sound that comes unbidden out of their yawns—especially when accompanied by a pandiculation's full fascial stretch of mouth, face, neck, chest, ribs, diaphragm, psoas, hips, and thighs. "Notice where all these wildly varied, nonverbal utterances are coming from within your torso, your throat, your head. Witness how they twist, squeeze, and gush to emerge from your body. These organic sounds, birthed from flesh, reveal your uncensored voice."

I am used to hearing my voice sound a certain way. It is easy to become accustomed to neck muscles working a bit too hard when speaking. Long hours typing at my computer, lecturing in front of a university class, unresolved home or work stress, justifying what I have to say—all these things can cause me to jut out my chin, throwing voice box and vocal cords out of relaxed alignment. This physical mapping of "taking it on the chin" abuses the neck's many fine muscles, especially when it is chronic. I compensate for this misalignment—maybe even an out-of-whack life—with more pushing or contorting. Becoming oblivious to excess emotional work happens because bad habits creep in over time. But these lingering short-term coping responses can be acknowledged and changed. A pandiculation gathers information before setting chains of muscle and connective tissue into motion—knows how to be fully engaged without working too hard.

I encourage my students: "Risk being unfamiliar to yourself by growing fascinated with your inner wilderness. Allow for any and all of the sounds your yawn wants to make, especially as breath and muscle come through the greatest part of the inhale's stretch into the exhale. Embrace less-than-pretty—maybe even gently gripped—sound."

Coaching humans to make the sounds that a yawn prompts may seem a little ridiculous, but, more "yawn charmer" than instructor, I am teasing out what's already there. If you have been covering your mouth since childhood, you can bet that making sound mid-yawn will require more than one invitation.

"That's right, a little high-pitched squeak might scrape out from somewhere behind your nose, or a wide-necked, inarticulate moan from your throat. Let yourself be surprised. Maybe these unbidden vocalizations are at a higher pitch than you expect, maybe lower, maybe rougher, maybe sweeter.... I am starting to sound like Dr. Seuss!"

Everyone laughs; our diaphragms' easy bounce further loosens body and mind.

"Observe these intimate, precise sounds without manipulating your yawns one tiny bit. Are they *real*? Are they *genuine*? Are they *authentic*? Are they *yours*?"

As the yawns progress, shyness around unintentional vocal "noise*-making" eases up. The sounds *are* high and low, rough and soothing, curved and angular, anything they need to be, anything the body is letting out through pandiculating. In these initially elusive, intensely private sounds, the truth of a student's voice emerges—sounds forgotten or locked away, sounds never before uttered. Befriended by the yawn, the voice box conveys sound that simply is ...

I want us to observe this specific sound-making moment with care, but also a bit obliquely. Glance at it. Hear it, but don't judge. Learn to recognize it and trust its veracity. Yawns reset and rebalance the voice. A yawn's vocal texture reminds us how to retrieve free *and* connected sound through resetting and rebalancing the cords and larynx. Its action invites a collaboration between work and pleasure, between expansion and contraction. To sing we need to value fulsome, uninhibited communication that is not word-based. Mid-song it is helpful to remember the yawn's disinhibited, natural use of voice—slip a little of its attitude into what feels like a more "organized" or "important" musical activity.

"Rushing from repression to refinement won't work, so don't try to *employ* this sound. Imagine that we are sourcing a palette of noncapitalistic human expression. We so often use our voices professionally, as singers, as actors, as teachers, as lawyers, as baristas, as children, as parents ... to fulfill a role. Please do not try to get this right—don't even try to get the job! I don't want you to pimp out this intimate part of your voice, your *self*. I don't want you to risk making it too tidy for deeper truths. *You might even need to pretend that you are not in a voice class.*"

---

* The word *noise* comes from the Latin word *nausea* to indicate disgust or literal seasickness. English and French etymological meanings include quarreling, damage, scandal—even praise, or a pleasant sound, depending on the century. I use the word rarely and am always interested when a student says they are making "noise" while following the body's sound-making desires.

Given the audacious sounds in the studio, tidiness and employability appear unlikely. These moans and groans and peeps are thriving far away from language and song. Nothing is "put on." The freedom of these sensations is how singing feels, how actors engage with text genuinely, how anyone speaks from the heart—whether out of joy, sorrow, or anger. I want my students to take *such* good care of our species' sound-making gifts.

"The human voice *means* to communicate," I continue, "but for this to happen we need *permission* for true expression. This has not been a given in human history: speaking out can be dangerous. It is hard to simply say what we want and need, given that reasonable things have been illegal, and unreasonable things, legal. In 1928 the Canadian Supreme Court ruled unanimously that women were not persons and could not be appointed to the Senate. From 1876 to 1996, as mandated by the Indian Act, First Nations children were taken from their homes, placed in residential schools, subjected to unbelievable horrors and death. Throughout the last century, the Albertan government oversaw the sterilization of nearly three thousand individuals deemed 'unfit.' The Holocaust's extermination of six million Jews was legal. Until 1968 Jim Crow legislation segregated and marginalized African Americans, furthering the catastrophic myth of supremacy while ensuring a legacy of trauma. As late as the 1970s, in many Western countries, a marriage bar required a woman to resign from her job once wed—limited her employability even when widowed. At the time of this writing, gay men and women are not allowed to express their love in seventy-one countries, threatened with death in eleven. We have more often than not learned that it is unsafe to express. The legacy of a silenced voice is tangible and continues many, many generations past the overt silencing."

The harsh truths I am voicing have paused some of my students mid-yawn.

"Can you stay with your pandiculating voice while listening to mine? Can you stay in touch with your insides while taking in what another person is saying?" Once their yawning resumes, I resume.

"We can be so seduced by the words of another that it is possible to be taken right out of ourselves and lose the ability to speak our own truth. I can end up saying something I think someone else wants to hear. I might find it easier to advocate for another person's needs than for my own. How often do any of us take our most intimate thoughts and feelings to heart? It is increasingly clear to me that not expressing myself simply and honestly has been bad for my health."

It takes a supple nervous system to take in someone else's words while staying flexibly engaged with one's own breath and sound-making body. We can practice listening from a direct, nonreactive place by valuing our own voice's nonjudgmental, yawn-based sounds. I suggest that my students let what an incorrigible yawn knows from the inside out get tangled up with the yawns of their peers, and with my words.

"Don't modify yourself because your teacher is speaking to you. Love your yawns utterly!"

It is time for the class to leave their cluster around the wastebasket and tissue box to move toward my piano at the other end of the studio. Only a hop, skip, and a jump away, those ten feet can be daunting.

"Start to locomote toward the piano via your yawn.... See how it moves your body. Its effect on your diaphragm will affect the way your legs move. A friend told me that Roman soldiers thought that their lungs were in their thighs. Whether this is true or not, it makes sense to me! Anyone walking from Rome to England would need a pretty unified sense of breath, muscle, and movement. Luckily, thighs, hips, psoas, diaphragm, and lungs are all connected. A full-bodied yawn reminds the body of this."

I am giving my students a destination while yawning so they can see what it is like to have a goal while maintaining the yawn's interiority. I don't care if it takes them five minutes to cross the floor.

The scene unfolding in my studio has been touched by *Night of the Living Dead* filmmaker George A. Romero as twelve undone zombies shuffle, stumble, and slide from wastebasket to piano. Shifting allegiance away from learned physical patterns is taking us into the creative twilight of not knowing.

"Please don't rush. Pretend you are more beast than human—imagine that you don't even know what a piano is for. Once you arrive, lean on it casually, let it support you. We are so used to this big, black piece of furniture taking up center stage—so behave a little inappropriately with my piano. Lounge. We are about to take a big leap, and I want you to do it from a brand-new place, without overworking, without thinking that you are working at all. For this you will need to distinguish between *making* and *allowing*, so that *allowing* revolutionizes *how* you make a sound."

I don't want my singers to control airflow by using their neck muscles. I want the throat to provide an open, equanimous environment for their voice box to respond intuitively to pitch. The larynx houses the vocal folds and is situated in the throat at the mouth of the trachea, whereas airflow originates at the base of the trachea. I want this flow to emerge as a nonverbal vocal gesture from behind the sternum ... a satisfying sigh of relief.

I invite my students to prop their elbows on the piano, to lean their forehead against hand or fist. Anything in order to take the last remnants of work out of the neck. Each person adjusts their body, sloughing off the responsibility to get this right. The feeling around the piano is languid, casual, unimpressed, relaxed ... almost *louche*.

"As you exhale, ask your vocal cords to gently engage *on their own terms*. Remember the independence of your yawn while choosing the timing of your sigh. Trust-based acceptance of air on the inhale will provide the context for the voiced exhale to express a small 'huh' of relief. This little puff of sound is the body speaking for itself ... subtle, transparent, and fresh. I know where I am 'at' when I make this sound and so does the person next to me."

A most wonderful range of intimate sound is escaping each and every mouth. Vocal cords are phonating without excessive throat-muscle engagement—without the mind dictating what the sound should *be* or *be like*.

"Your *huh* is not loud … but it is clear. Feel how emotional clarity is birthed behind your sternum."

One of my Humber students offered a word for this feeling. Checking in after the summer holidays, she said that the way she was able to maintain the little *huh* over the break was to think of it as "vomitrocious."* Good for her! The feeling *is* as easy as a baby or kitten vomiting. Her word also reveals how disturbing she found it to not control her airflow, or the sounds from her body.

At the end of the previous school year, this student's voice reminded me of a defenseless young girl caught trying to please everyone in order to stay safe. A whine slid through every sentence. We know that the throat tightens for many reasons: when we are stressed, or holding back a feeling, or having to censor a thought or push forward an opinion. The throat also compresses for good things like squealing with pleasure—or even laughing—restoring once we relax. It is not about trying to stop the throat from narrowing; it is about allowing the little *huh* to feel raw and natural. This is how this young woman began a shift away from disenfranchised voice toward self-discovery and agency. In doing so she became clearer to herself as well as others.

Don't underestimate what the yawning sounds do for the voice box, how they make its physiological functioning less cultivated, simpler, more direct. The yawn teaches the little *huh* that it can be smaller, less biased, less busy. Its intimate, integrated nature allows each of us to become our own relaxed point of departure.

It is true that singing requires heightened states of emotion: because of the story we are telling, and the way a melody is shaped. But sometimes the extra effort we put in is entirely unconscious and from the wrong place. This extra work might arise from wanting to do well, making us sing a little louder than necessary in order to be "seen." Identify your own chronic, habitual tightening through neck and throat. If it is unnecessary to the moment, slough it off.

---

* "Vomitrocious" is the title of an episode of the children's animated television series *Arthur*.

103

A singer is not only learning how to use their instrument; they are in the process of making it each time they breathe. Just as various parts of the body need to feel undone for breath to come in by itself, something similar needs to happen for breath to release from the body in a way that is unforced and yet connected. The pool of feeling that helps with the *out-hale* includes blue, sad, sloppy, comforted, comforting, relieved, trusting, and pleasurable. We might worry for our safety when making these sounds publicly, but a small, fully present *huh* is capable of simultaneously offering a reassuring *there, there* to the nervous system that birthed it. When *there, there* resonates at the base of our windpipe, and marries with vocal cord vibration as it slides out, it provides a reliably connected basis for elongating tone. The horizontal sigh.

I remind my students that last week's "lazy" homework was yawning. "This week I want you to become obsessed with its close relative, the sigh. Why not have a crush on both! Remember that humans are part of the natural world—don't be afraid to observe the other 'sapiens' around you honestly. Investigate how you feel about their sighs, how they react to yours, and what you learn from this. An osteopath once told me that sighing is the most effective way to relax the diaphragm. Between now and next Tuesday, see how your whole being benefits from frequent sighing, as well as regular yawning."

If I could change the word *sing* to *sigh* I would.

15

Of Shudders, Sighs, and the ANS

LIKE YAWNING, SIGHS are natural to humans. However, finding and maintaining unprejudiced access to this subtle vocal gesture requires a little work. At the turn of the millennium I was trying to teach a group of eighteen bright-faced Humber students how to consistently access the little puffed sigh. A young man with thick dark hair and a ready playfulness was the first to come up with a perfect, repeatable, seated-in-the-chair-of-the-dirty-corset *huh*. He was also the student who had been having the most difficulty matching pitch at the piano.

I asked him how he managed this integration: his pitch (vocal cord phonation), his airflow (originating from behind the sternum), and his resonance (body vibration) felt completely integrated. He said it was simple! One morning his girlfriend had dashed naked from his bedroom to the bathroom. At that exact moment his father opened his own bedroom door and, seeing his son's unclothed girlfriend, responded with a small, discreet *huh*. That was it. A truthful little puff of attuned air.

This story might make the listener uncomfortable; however, identifying with his father's natural, unapologetic, and un-acted-upon nonverbal sound helped my student trust his own vocal expression of impulse. It is a challenge to integrate instinctual rawness within nuanced, evolving social mores—whether the distance needing to be covered is geographic from Old World to New, or temporal from generation to generation. The beauty of this father's honest "slip" is that from that day forth his son's pitch improved at root.

In a romantic novel a sigh's expressivity is typically linked to passion; however, this unguarded release of breath is just as likely to convey frustration, sadness, or anxiety. Being subjected to such intimate emotional leakage can cause the listener to want to get away from what they've felt in the sigher. They might even judge the sigher's right to feel their own raw truth. *What have you got to complain about?* Because sighs are so revealing, many of us censor these nonlinguistic vocal impulses to the point that *no* self-betraying sound ever escapes our lips ... *even when we are alone.*

Into the Woods with the
Autonomic Nervous System

The ANS is the network of nerves that governs bodily functions like digestion and heart rate. Gut feelings—excitement's little butterflies or a churning, anxious belly—originate in the ANS. Like yawning, a sigh can slip out without forewarning as it, too, is under the purview of the autonomic nervous system.

Scientists have divided the activities of the ANS into "sympathetic" and "parasympathetic" processes to better understand and describe how it works. The sympathetic, *fight or flight,* mode kicks into action when we are under threat, need to get something done, are excited by an intense thought—or a cup of coffee. It activates. The parasympathetic, *rest and digest,* function calms the body back down, readies us for sleep, makes us feel safe. Humming is a musical activity that promotes *rest and digest* for most hummers and almost as many listeners.

Even though we don't need to monitor the ANS consciously, making friends with it allows us to engage with somatic, of-the-body intelligence. I want us to consider "feeling" as a thing in and of itself, rather than something that needs to be immediately labeled (possibly incorrectly) as an "emotion" and therefore turned into a "story line" with a supporting "worldview" or "value system." *Take the time to absorb the raw information that feelings offer before jumping to conclusions.*

Early each term I pass out a colorful diagram of the ANS to my students. Everyone *oooos* and *aaahs;* the image is cheerful and clear, easy to take in. We chat through the differences between the two "sides," noting when organic functions slow down and when they activate. I tell them that I was surprised by the opening of the bronchi in *fight or flight* mode. Of course, it makes sense that we need more air when in danger—to run or holler—and when we are at rest the body doesn't necessarily want, or need, to make loud sound. I point out that orgasm is on both the *fight or flight* and *rest and digest* sides. Its flesh-and-blood action doesn't ask for either/or but fulfills active engagement and passive receptivity equally. Recalling the orgasm's integration of *rest and digest* and *fight or flight* when singing can help balance vocal effort. And it's a fun piece of homework.

I tell my students that we will make a new weave of the sympathetic and the parasympathetic—not just for singing but for everyday health. I don't want them to choose between excitement and calm. Family and culture have separated us from our dynamic urges by labeling them good or bad, rendering us antagonistic within. Perhaps consciously holding contradiction can foster a somatic understanding of deep-seated collaboration—balance the essence of various worlds. Instead of eyeing duality suspiciously, let's embrace the poles, chart and value each degree along our feeling continuum. Let's use our deepest fibers to yield whole cloth.

Exploring the ANS reminds me of entering the forest in a Brothers Grimm fairy tale. I cannot see or feel my ANS's activities like I do the sensations and activities regulated by my peripheral nervous system, the nervous system that allows me to play the piano or pick up a cup of tea. It takes a lot of awareness to hear what the ANS has to say, let alone interpret its subtle jumble. Instinct is rooted in its functions. Through investigating how intuition flows from instinct, I can tune my mind more finely. These connections already fuel my subconscious, mold my dreams. As an artist this affects what I choose to make and how I make it. In practice, if I can tease apart and look honestly at both ends of the ANS's spectrum—the highly stimulated and reactive as well as the deeply fallow and occasionally depressed—I may feel less buffeted about or duped by life. The story of "Little Red Riding Hood" remains a valuable cautionary tale because despite her immediate suspicions she struggles to see and name the wolf inside the grandmother. We are only beginning to listen to a woman's body-based knowing. Her hunches. Each person's "but grandmother ...?" voice.

An Introduction to the Vagus Nerve

To understand and engage with the ANS, we need to meet the longest of the cranial nerves, the vagus nerve. Its name is derived from the Latin word for "wandering," and it does just that, from the brain stem through the organs in the neck, thorax, and abdomen. In the thorax, branches go to the trachea, bronchi, lungs, esophagus, and heart. In the abdomen, it wends its way to the stomach, pancreas, liver, small intestine, large intestine, and colon. The vagus is both viscerosensory and parasympathetic; in other words, it feels what is going on deep within the organs and responds accordingly, counterbalancing the action of the sympathetic nerves to create a calm and regulating experiential loop.

When it comes to the head and neck, the vagus nerve supplies the pharynx, the soft palate, the cricothyroid muscle, and the muscles of the larynx. It also conducts sensation from the epiglottis, the base of the tongue, the aryepiglottic folds, the upper larynx, below the vocal folds of the larynx, and the pharynx. All of these body parts become intrinsically linked to how we express emotion as well as being employed for language. The vagus nerve also manages our hearing, having under its purview the external ear and external auditory canal, as well as the external surface of the tympanic membrane. To travel to the voice box, one branch of the vagus nerve wraps around the aorta to the heart and ascends.

"Speaking from the heart" or "getting something off the chest" existed as body-wise turns of phrase long before we could prove a functional link between heartbeat and vocal cords, or between the vagus nerve and sighing. How we are wired allows the voice—cords and airflow—to intentionally betray the deepest part of our survival self. Perfect for singing. This is why we feel that a singer's voice spills secrets, can turn us inside out, strip us of defense. The stakes are so high that many people say that their worst nightmare is to sing in front of others.

In an interview Hugh Jackman equated singing live in front of a film crew for the movie version of the musical *Les Misérables* with shooting nude scenes.* It is sensible to feel naked when singing. A professional singer uses the part of the body that knows how to digest and how to sleep and how to make love in order to make vocal art. Instinct and logos connect through the simultaneously delicate and robust activity we call music. In order to meet its demands, whether generating or interpreting, I need to be a master of many potential dualities: soft and hard, expansive and contained, brilliant and contented, happy and sad, furious and self-possessed. My mind and body need to collaborate in this balancing act. I need to understand, and then dance with, all the potential tensions inherent in how *fight or flight* (I like to add *fuck* and *fun*) and *rest and digest* come together. The practice of singing—as I teach it—demands that I find equanimity, grace under pressure ... healthy vagal tone.

Breath Is Inspiration Is Creativity Is Story Is Song Is Breath ...

I say to students that singing is being on the verge of both crying and laughing—and still being capable of murder. Why murder? Because setting a boundary on one's own behalf can feel as extreme as committing murder.

---

* The producers of *Les Miz* took extraordinary risk by having their performers sing live to camera rather than following the usual practice of lip-synching to vocal takes recorded in the relative privacy of a recording studio.

This way of looking at emotion, or energy, or survival responses helps me shape each line I sing out of a malleable balance of mad, sad, and glad. When I let the mix stay raw and chaotic it might sound like I am growling or screeching. It only takes a little aesthetic organization for a scream to become operatic, something we accept as beautiful and legitimate, but first, unsocialized sound must be embraced and understood.

I have been using this understanding of vocal process as the stuff and muscle of my art practice as well as my teaching. In both situations the yawn is my inhale, the sigh my exhale.

When I compose with less normalized vocal sound, to shape feeling and contain expression within a larger frame, meaningful communication emerges, as in "real" life. In both the mundane and the artistic I use vocal dramaturgy to bring sense to light.

Choreographer Peggy Baker calls what I do "vocalography." For her first full-length piece, *locus plot*, based on mathematically defined conditions related to space, she has invited me to create vocal material on her dancers. Now, as well as moving, the five performers will vocalize throughout the show, their sounds partnering with John Farah's muscular composition. I am profoundly touched by the willingness of these dancers to integrate voice into previously silent artistic identities.

I have asked the two men and two of the women to breathe out a warm, generous tone each time their hand passes the body of their dance partner—either an *oh* or an *ah*, depending on whether their movement phrase is "x" or "y." They are to listen to each other, and to the piano, but they do not have to match anything, just commit to whatever pitch is freely chosen by their vagus nerve as it acts upon their vocal cords. The result is an improvised quartet of beautifully and accidentally layered clash and consonance directly from the ANS, especially fragile and volatile when encountering the piano's thoughtfully chosen, shifting harmonies. Several duets, or "collaborations," are on the go ... woman dances with man, *oh* contrasts to *ah*, high voices ring with low, and voice and piano relate to one another through gently agreeing and disagreeing. The literal algebra of the choreography is $x=y^2$, but the way movement and sound come together creates new equations. Emotional math emerges from all of the near hits and misses. The whole is conscious and also happenstance, an ambiguity of overlapping feelings.

The dancers' sung notes increase in frequency, intertwining more densely as their movement quickens, bodies circling one another before leaping upward or plunging to the floor. This thickening vocal embrace wanes by the time each woman comes to a stop beside her partner, bowing her forehead to rest on her partner's back. A delicate sound creeps in under the shimmer of John's music, cresting slightly above it in pitch and volume. A plaintive glow tinged with that ache birthed only behind the human breastbone.

The women are keening, vibrating a delicate, trembling arc of emotion in the tissues we use to cry, our sinuses: frontals, ethmoids, even a hint of sphenoidal* resonance. A serendipitous trellis of interwoven minor modes. Each man slips an arm around his partner's supplicant body to better contain the spill of grief. Four bodies wrapped into a quietly intense sonic tableau.

In canon the men drop their supportive arm from their partner's waist into a weighted pendulum swing, launching the women into a cascade of shudders … breath releasing more breath. The men then take on the keening, floating whimper-high and gentle into this residue of their boy-bodies … nongendered, prepubescent vulnerability … fear and sadness bound together with nothing to prove.

In that shimmering afterglow I feel my heart squeeze … and just behind my eyes a pinch of salt. A vocal filigree of emotion bearing witness to the human "stuff" beyond logic. But before I can settle into sorrow our fifth dancer cuts her way through the tableau, a growl furrowing her chest.

---

* The frontal, ethmoidal, and sphenoidal sinuses are three of our four sets of sinuses. All four will be discussed further in Slipper Camp Five.

16

Slipper Camp Four—
Pitch Is Something We Are Made Of

TODAY'S SLIPPER CAMPERS—an assemblage of actors, dancers, singers, a rabbi, and a few other healers, teachers, and clowns, ranging in age from twenty-two to sixty—are expressing an array of nonverbal sound. In twenty short minutes each person's face has become more off guard, more authentic. Eyes are being wiped, noses blown, mucus cleared. Some of my students look a little embarrassed by this.

Easing my way through the dozen melting bodies toward my baby grand piano, I speak gently, as I might to a skittish animal. "Don't let the phlegm bother you. Yawning has exercised your sinuses and given your lungs a good massage—mucus and phlegm are natural by-products. Your vocal cords are designed to clear gunk out of your lungs and trachea first thing in the day through an undulating upward action, just under the line where they meet to phonate."

Everyone likes this explanation; singers and actors think something is wrong if they have phlegm. Much as it can indicate overuse of the voice or general tiredness, a little phlegm is absolutely normal first thing in the morning and does not need to be cleared forcefully. It helps to start the day with a large glass of warm water to render phlegm more fluid and therefore easier to move along.

I listen to their small *huhs* while settling myself quietly on the piano bench. Not wanting to put a single body into *fight or flight or freeze* I encourage even more time and space for intimate sound. "You've pan-diculated your way out of guardedness, some of you moaning pleasure and ache, some groaning disgust and frustration … normal, uncolo-nized sounds given our 9 a.m. class time! Take note of how your throat feels when you are not trying to identify with external measures such as pitch or politeness—cords phonating easily, sound carried by the air flowing from behind your sternum. In touch with *connected sound … sound* connected to *feeling.*"

I especially don't want anyone to feel obligation toward perfec-tion or good behavior when I play the ivory keys of this sweet-toned, matte-black 1926 Hardman, Peck & Co. These relaxed beings should not become achievers in any way as we head into the low, easy, relaxed range I call "What the fluff!"

Speaking from the solid ground of ass on piano bench, I announce, "If I were to write a chapter for my book today, I would call it 'The Unimportance of Pitch.'" I am hoping to provoke a little. I ask them about how we understand and use the word *pitch* in speech. The answers come quickly.

pitch a tent
baseball pitch
nail the pitch
hit a pitch
get a pitch
fever pitch
pitch an idea … a ball …
pitch-perfect
pitchy

I tell them that I believe our ability to identify with pitch is based on our ability to connect to how we feel … without inhibition. I cite a study that claims that the human animal is born with perfect pitch.[*] This makes sense to me, as an infant's voice is in tune with her inner state: she sounds how she feels. She also uses the mechanism of perfect pitch to recognize her mother's voice, maybe even decipher her tone of voice.[†] We all begin life as uninhibited criers sensitive to human vocalization because we don't know any better. By eight months we lose the specificity of perfect (or absolute) pitch and begin to adapt our emotional states to external prompts. Part of becoming socialized is that we no longer express freely.

I value the human ability to bind emotion and sound through self-control and words, but I am also aware that most of us have not learned how to do this with equanimity or finesse—in part because human life is often not true or fair. As we approach "What the fluff!" I want my students to allow their vagus nerve to do its job of meeting pitch through nonjudgmental identification with the inside of the body, not through strong-arming the vocal cords. Our culture has tied us into a fine knot around being "in tune" while stripping us of the tools that would help us connect with ourselves and with others—to be better "attuned." To substitute *sigh* for *sing*, we need to start by undoing the piano.

"When I was four my parents bought this very piano for two hundred dollars from an estate sale posted on the bulletin board at the local grocery store—it was my mother's money, a gift from her godmother."

My lessons started at the age of eight when we moved, piano in tow, from Québec to Burlington, Ontario. The group classes were held in the parlor of a large Victorian house and our teacher—who had Joni Mitchell's flaxen hair plus a Finnish accent—made us play on foldable cardboard keyboards. We never heard the music we were playing! Just before Grade Six my family moved to Northern Ontario—for me, the end of civilization and several close friendships—but at least our piano

---

[*] University of Wisconsin–Madison, "Born with the Perfect Pitch?" *Science Daily*, February 27, 2001.

[†] Quoting Dr. Jenny Saffran, a psychologist at the Infant Learning Laboratory at the University of Wisconsin–Madison, in the *Science Daily* article.

came with us. When I left home for college after Grade Eleven, I continued to study. Practicing with tension led to tennis elbow and after a summer of left-hand repertoire in Seattle, I turned my back on the piano and started to sing.

"I assume that most of you have some history with the piano—good or bad," I tell the class. "Maybe you did *not* get to play, or see it as a foreign culture. Maybe you wanted to take guitar lessons instead of piano. Maybe you haven't been able to match its pitch since the day your Grade Two music teacher pointed out your 'struggle' to the whole class."

I want them to rethink this big beastly emperor of the classical world … feel how it shakes and shudders anew. I'd like the piano's vibrations to encourage them to sink into it—as they might a good friend—eventually dropping into their own resonance.

I ask them to rub up against the body of my piano, to crawl under it, to behave in ways they wouldn't normally, to let the piano become something to explore through touch and movement while breathing and sounding. At the end of five minutes they are draped on it, oozing out from under it, pawing at the wood. I ask two questions: "How old is the piano?" and, indicating all of our bodies, "How old is the *Homo sapiens* edition of the human body?"

Curiosity shines from their eyes, but no one risks an answer. I ask them to link the piano to a composer, which helps narrow down one guess, but their attempts to date *Homo sapiens* range from ten thousand to five million years!

The modern piano morphed into existence in the period between 1790 and 1860 … Mozart's time, and then Beethoven's. It is just over two hundred years old. Even if we go all the way back to its obscure inventor, Bartolomeo Cristofori, the man who had the idea that a harpsichord's strings could be struck and not plucked, it is still only over three hundred years old. Anatomically, modern humans originated in Africa about two hundred thousand years ago, reaching full behavioral modernity around seventy thousand years ago. We are much older than the piano, but like many of our devices, it can rule us with an unpleasant grip.

"Stand in a relaxed, wobbly fashion, the way we undid ourselves in order to receive air … orifices soft and welcoming, mouths open. Close your eyes if you'd like. Now, listen with your whole being."

I play the lowest A-flat the piano can manage, and then the one above it, and the one above that one and so on, till the piano runs out of A-flats. Seven in total. Despite being an octave apart, these notes all agree with one another with regard to *pitch,* but they *resonate* in different parts of the human body. I do the same with the G a semitone below, and then the F-sharp one more semitone down. I want the men and women in this room to feel their way into pitch … into the sensation of dwelling within themselves.

"What did you experience?"

They show me, hands charting pubic area, low belly, chest, throat, cheekbones, third eye—some map space above the head and below the pelvic floor.

"Yes! A tube of resonating potential runs through the human body. Now, why is this happening?"

There are many creative, sensitive, and accurate answers—but the one I long for is the one I want them to start believing in, the one that will require a paradigm shift.

"These sounds already exist within us." Although I may never sing the piano's lowest or highest notes due to the length and thickness of my vocal cords, we are *all* able to vibrate with the resonance of the pitches we hear coming from the piano because that is what it is to be human. And, when we make a tone, we do not need to match an external source. We need to be like archaeologists and expose the tone or note within ourselves. *"Pitch comes from us … it is not just an idea, an extension of our imaginations … it is something we are made of."*

There is a look of delight on some of the faces before me, on some an impish *aha*—as well as the wistful twist of a mouth or two.

One of the ways Beethoven coped with his hearing loss was by chopping the legs off his pianoforte so that its belly—the sounding board—rested on the floor. I picture him sitting on the ground in front of it, imagine his playing resonating from the room's floorboards up

117

through his pelvic floor (genitals, perineum, and anus), flooding his whole being with vibration. How amazing that he had the necessary irreverence and drive to come up with this solution. Fully deaf when he composed his adamant "Ode to Joy," this champion of sound does not engage with despair, but marches hope straight home. It is wondrous that he continued to experience melody, texture, and harmony, shaping the density and breadth of his longing, joy, and fervor, note by note. As a teen and Beethoven fanatic—we share the same birthday—I thought his hearing loss the worst thing imaginable. Now I think his continued ability to compose underlines the fact that pitch lives inside us, much deeper than the rudiments of "hearing." It *is* home.

"Let's start again with the A-flat below middle C. Lean into yourself, and allow the sound to vibrate up and down your whole being even as some of it streams out of your mouth."

Mouths wide, bodies soft, ease setting the standard, they all *aaaaaaah-hhhhh* in unison. The sound makes me think of how we wrap a blanket around those we love when they need comfort.

"Beautiful. Enjoy the fact that you are doing this in a group of bodies that your body feels safe with … but do not for a second try to blend. Instead, acknowledge that your vibration is winding in and out of the vibrations of the other humans in the room. Delight in nonpartisan sharing."

We proceed down by semitones: the G, the G-flat.

"Excavating foundation takes time. I just heard that we are made up of quickly moving molecules—we are, in fact, mostly space. If the movement of these molecules is vibration, then this space must be where pitch and resonance live. Adopt this thought as we descend a second time."

We repeat the G and the G-flat, then continue down another pitch or two.

"Remember to inhale fully without grabbing. Align yourself to your own sweet time. Trust your own delicate beauty while being determinedly carnal and recklessly spiritual."

Entertaining unusual partnerships helps my students stay open and flexible. We sing down past the F, E, and E-flat.

"It is not accidental that I call this lowest range 'What the fluff!' I used to call it 'What the fuck!' but that seems a bit violent now. My desire is to encourage a gentle lawlessness when it comes to engaging with pitch. Relaxed, connected sound in our lowest range gives us time to recognize ease when 'matching' pitch. Why? Because lower, slower vibrations are simply not as intense as the vibrations of the mid and high ranges."

We finally settle on low D.

"If this was not called singing, what would you call it? What is this low end all about?"

Puzzled faces shrug back at me.

"Remember what you just did—remember it through your body. When you made these sounds, what were you actually doing?"

I give them a few odd and exaggerated physical cues, trying to replicate the simplicity of comic-strip emotions as I make sound. They finally get the gist of what I am asking for and come up with words like *moan*, *grunt*, and *groan* to name the basement of the human voice.

I feel the burr of an F below middle C as a *groan*. I appreciate where an F comes from in my body and understand what that means for me today. It is of expressive and communicative value to make and hear a *groan*. The feeling that goes with a *groan* and what it communicates, in partnership with a melodic line of pleasure, frustration, or determination, is why a particular pitch belongs in a song's phrase. It is why a good composer might set a word low in the voice. Songs we come to call standards—the pieces that last—understand this emotional geography.

I would rename the whole span of a singer's voice in an onomatopoeic way, from the lowest *huh* of intimate connection to self through to the top screams of danger and excitement. I would not use letters for pitch but rather the physiology of human feeling as it resonates through the body. The entire span of my voice from bottom to top: grunt, groan, moan, sigh, laugh, coo, sob, holler, whine, shriek, scream, snarl, squeal, peep …

I trace the terrain of each of these nonverbal sounds on the keyboard. Three to five notes for each fleshy feeling—often overlapping a semitone or so—starting from the low D below middle C and moving to the top C to F Queen-of-the-Night notes, covering close to three and a half octaves.

I want to establish direct lines between how we sound by nature and what I believe singing is. Natural sound has been socialized out of us, and not only do these sounds have a lot to say, but if a singer gets comfortable with them she can learn a lot about who she is.

We "What the fluff!" our way back down through the G, the G-flat, then F, E, E-flat, and finally the D.

I love witnessing a group relinquish their mind's will to match pitch by giving over to the autonomic nervous system's accessing of authentic frequency. When I taught myself to trust pitch-making through my vagus nerve—after twenty years of professionally guaranteeing "being in tune"—I had to repeatedly tell myself to "walk out of the room." Yielding into long tone after long tone replaced the muscular management of a note with the human animal's innate capacity to engage with pitch.

I say to my students, "Being in touch with your own truthful, nonreactive emotions helps you to identify with external tone—the feelings of others. It can also keep you from agreeing or matching at any cost. Staying true to inner geography can lead to spacious self-identification. Allow your notes some wiggle room. Trust the beauty of wandering. See what this fresh abandon offers."

We return to fluff the A-flat down to D. The sounds emanating from these students' bodies have become lush, spacious, extravagant, inclusive—beautifully attuned to self, and to one another. Letting go has led to deeply caring, resonant connection. Pitch, breath, and voice *are* empathy.

17

Sex with Schoenberg

I HAD ONE of those dreams that doesn't shake off in the morning. In it I was having sex with Arnold Schoenberg, the late-Romantic Viennese composer who broke with tradition to formulate his acerbic "twelve-tone row" pitch proposition as a means to construct music. In any picture I've seen, he does not look like a sexy guy: receding hairline, worried frown bordering on a scowl, some-kind-of-tidy cravat.

Schoenberg could no longer tolerate the gilded impasse that Western music had arrived at after centuries of tail-eating iterations. Its twelve more or less evenly spaced pitches, when followed horizontally, make melody; when stacked vertically, create harmony. This thousand-year-old harmonic system came to rely upon intervals such as thirds, fourths, fifths, and octaves, all of which are found in nature. Depending on which note is the root these intervals add up to keys. This resulting "tonal" music surrounds us, entrenched in pop songs, symphonies, and movie scores. The lullabies we teach our children are made up of its building blocks, grooving predictability into collective musical thought processes. As late-Romantic composition became more and more over-wrought, Schoenberg devised a melodic and harmonic sorbet to scrape clean the early twentieth century's classical sound palette.

Schoenberg was compelled first to deconstruct the use of Western music's twelve pitches through free tonality, and then to restructure it through a rigid serialization of those same twelve pitches. In his new system, each composition required a fresh pitch sequence. This unprejudiced ordering, and an accompanying egalitarian use of the notes, became new scaffolding that he and other members of the Second Viennese School played with creatively. His proposition was boldly reactive and left many musicians unsettled. Its cerebral aesthetic remains difficult for audiences today, but his pioneering acoustic vision influenced and enriched musical composition on both sides of the Atlantic throughout the last century.

Schoenberg's monodrama *Pierrot lunaire* (1912) became part of my standard repertoire when I was twenty-six. I embodied its angular, anxious beauty on several continents during the late '80s, using *sprechstimme* to speak-sing the text. To learn the score I had to cut myself loose from agreed-upon tonality; I had to reinvent my understanding of melody—learn it as a function of rational, revolutionary ideology rather than one of my culture's hand-me-downs. My equal love for both *Pierrot*'s rebelliousness and precision pulled apart previously reliable musical beliefs, setting the tone for later vocal experimentation. His music appealed to something "cool" in my psyche: "cool" to hold romantic rot in check by intoning Belgian poet Albert Giraud's blasphemous texts; "cool" to perform something so musically difficult, staged and from memory; "cool" to take on the challenge of making Schoenberg's system accessible to an audience through embodying the music's unpredictable intervals with my whole being. My nervous system trusted being elbowed by Schoenberg more than it did being pumped up by Wagner or plumped up by Strauss.

So, back to sex with Schoenberg. I am lying on a red velvet divan and Arnold is spooning me from behind. For the life of me I can't make out what he is actually doing, but I am erotically satisfied to the core of my being. Waking in a happy, aroused state, I laugh out loud! Has this dream come to me now because I have finally released myself from thinking about pitch in the way I *learned* to think about pitch: something to get right, something to conform to, something outside of me? I wonder if Schoenberg's need to free himself from using culturally sanctioned pitch rules was his way of becoming more attuned rather than less "in tune." Not atonal—a term he deplored—but iTonal. I am grateful to Schoenberg for steering me away from mass musical inheritances. His modern, prickly approach to pitch was in sync with how out of step I felt with the stories fed to me about how women should align.

Struggling to match pitch or track melody can cause any individual to feel inadequate regardless of how easy or difficult the song. Richard Armstrong's teaching, based on Roy Hart's pedagogy, suggested that pitch problems indicated underlying neuroses. When I was a young singer, this was at odds with my belief that talent and determination led to the successful handling of pitch—a good way to prove one's worth. Singing the difficult repertoire that I loved, and that very few knew or could manage, made me special. Richard invited me to reconsider why a person might have difficulty getting a pitch, by thinking of it less as a skill and more as a symptom, not a question of accomplishment but more an indication of inner states of being, linked to a life story.

I might not have liked this philosophy as a performer, but it was helpful when teaching. One of my students in Regina, Saskatchewan—a warm, intelligent middle-aged woman—could not match the piano's pitches. This confused me because her interest in the well-being of those around her, coupled with her obvious sensitivity and caring spirit, struck me as qualities that would help her voice mesh with a note that was hanging in the air. One day she told me that as a child she had had rheumatic fever and needed to spend months in a hospital on an adult ward. If she cried she would not get to see her parents when they made their weekly visit from another town. How she felt wasn't valid; expressing it was hopeless. At a very young age, she became overly attentive to everyone else's emotional needs in order to manage her situation.

If there hasn't been space for how a child feels, how does she calibrate experience, make sense of how inside and outside match up, stand up for herself ... sing in tune?

Pitch in the Studio

I am leading a smaller than usual Friday afternoon Group Class—only four students. The end of the week, combined with warm and languid late spring temperatures, has made us all a little less city-bound. Time and space are ours.

Each of these mature students has a unique relationship to voice and music. Niloo grew up in Iran, participated as a teenager in the revolution, and moved to Canada in the '80s. Once here, she studied engineering and then taught math in post-secondary institutions, all the while writing poetry and, currently, a novel. She is a high-contrast individual—dark, fiery, and esoteric, with a large hamper of logic. Her singing voice gleams when she lets it go a little wild. Despite a history of pitch challenges, Niloo has persevered with her relationship to voice and sings in my choir.*

Ronit is a newer student. She has a tantalizingly raspy voice and teaches mindfulness meditation through courses designed for schools and businesses. She was a dancer in a previous creative incarnation and is always sporting an ornament or two—recycled fur around her neck, the surprise of jewels in her hair—that speak to her refined taste and wit. Born in Mexico and partially educated in Israel, she is an interesting hybrid. Like most of the Israeli women I have worked with, the "little girl" glisten is missing from the top of her voice.

---

* Of the dozen Iranians I have taught, only one has had an easy time with pitch, though her tendency was to force herself into agreement with the piano. Traditional Persian music is complex and refined; this doesn't help me understand why matching a piano's pitch would be difficult for my Iranian students. However, the extreme turnarounds in Iranian politics this last century, and the danger of imprisonment, torture, and even death if caught speaking out against any of these regimes, might provide a clue. Perhaps chronic self-censorship—in order to stay alive—has meant these students' vocal cords no longer know how to make the match between inside and outside realities? Pitch will suffer when it is not okay to be true to yourself in public.

Doug is the youngest of three singing brothers; all are unusually talented and abundantly sensitive performers and songwriters. His over-six-foot frame and lanky limbs shadow the two much shorter women, but his empathy and delicacy balance any potential threat. Recently, Doug has taken on learning several of Debussy's art songs, and I am in awe of his commitment, intelligence, curiosity, and expansive musicality.

The class is rounded out by Judith. She is mid-fifties and statuesque, and despite her really wild bomb of blonde curls, she has subdued herself vocally. She insists that she has no aptitude for singing. Despite misgivings she comes faithfully to work on this aspect of herself with humor, grace, and wisdom. I am always happy when Judith is coming to class; the comments she shares with each of us teach me so much about the humanity in art-making.

It is obvious that I really like these four students; they are persistent, progressive seekers, as well as highly conscious. They don't fancy being stuck in a rut or deluding themselves just for the sake of feeling better. These individuals *get* process, and magic happens when we work— transformations slowly pervading the body and persuading the mind.

Today I want to deal with pitch and tell them so point-blank. No pussyfooting, even though simply mentioning the word *pitch* could cause a rash or riot in some nervous systems. I want to see if these students might let themselves forget to control the action of their vocal cords and leave it up to their intrinsically "musical" selves instead— through the vagus nerve.

My belief that *the unimportance of pitch* can lead to *permission to attune,* with self and with others, is familiar to these four despite each one's idiosyncratic relationship to pitch. Nonetheless, it takes time to practice a paradigm shift, let it take hold in the soil of our bodies ... in our empathic wetlands. Trusting that these four will be particularly available to one another on this luxurious day, I plunge us into the deep end.

We breathe and yawn, beginning the physical process of getting out of our heads. As they settle I share the details of my sex with Schoenberg dream. Doug and Niloo seem mildly amused but I don't worry about whether anyone understands the meaning of my fantasy anecdote. A new tale can start the unraveling of old belief systems. Because this subtle, unpredictable, oblique work can take time, for now, I simply ask them to "blow" air through their vocal instrument. No drama and not much personal story—more like a small gust moving through wind chimes, unintentionally and under no one's purview.

Once we are less "in the way," I sound the piano notes that lie near the bottom of the speaking range—beginning with the A-flat below middle C for the women, Doug an octave lower. We sing long tones, semitone by semitone, down to low D. There is no rush, just trust. Over and over again I encourage them *"not to care"* in the split second before vocal cord vibrates against vocal cord. I suggest they imagine *"walking out of the room"* at the beginning of each exhale. "Let the part of yourself trying to make pitch 'good' go on vacation."

Not bad! Despite our nonchalant attitude we are "in tune," and I hear a scintilla of warm feeling arise effortlessly from what appears to be an impersonal—perhaps ego-free?—process.

Even though this second pass through the Lower Fluffs sounds more genuine, somewhere behind their Neanderthal stances they still look as if they are near a piano. I remind them that the word *pitch* is, in and of itself, a potentially misleading and even violent word with a history of *hitting* and *nailing*!

"If the vagus nerve—which controls pitch—wraps around the upper aorta to the heart and ascends to the vocal cords, we are meant to sing in tune with how we feel, not through measuring up."

I turn to Niloo.

"Niloo, why don't you put the backs of your fingers on either side of your neck. Jawbone resting on pointer finger, pinky resting on collarbone."

This softens the sides of her neck, and the sound of her next note is much easier, but I can feel that she is still not fully "seated" in herself. Who can blame her! She is singing alone and under a magnifying glass.

"How about letting the corners of your mouth droop slightly? You don't need to reassure me that you are my friend by faking a diplomatic smile—even if part of your expression, likely unconscious, is there just to reassure your own guts that you are not under pressure!"

She laughs.

Releasing from the grimace of a tense smile does settle the next few pitches. I sense that she is ready to make these sounds truly hers without resorting to drama.

"Could you take your hands from your neck and wrap your arms around your torso as if you were hugging yourself?"

This third instruction brings time to a standstill, stops the world from interfering with Niloo's selfhood. The intimacy of the gesture releases excess arming through chest, neck, and face and now, instead of bracing, she embraces her insides. Niloo's sound is warm and round—centered within the tone the piano is offering, centered within her whole being.

It's Judith's turn. She jumps in with each pitch as if on a dare, making the best of an uncomfortable situation. I see the hesitation in her eyes in the split second before she sings. I ask her, "What flits through your mind just before you make a sound?"

"That I can't sing. That it will sound dreadful." I love her for her honesty.

Despite having made astonishing progress over the years, Judith still holds this negative thought pattern, like many others who struggle with pitch. I ask her to start the sound before she thinks she is ready, before "preparing," before her mind can sabotage her vocal mechanism. She takes on this direct instruction wholeheartedly; top and bottom open up. Her sound is beautiful. We all hear it even if Judith is not quite ready to take it in. I explain that it may take some time for her ears to catch up with her growth but that we are here to mirror back the beauty of what we hear until she changes her mind and realizes that she *is* a singer. All she needs to do right now is to practice flow—especially at the moment when the inhale "reverses" or "turns into" the exhale—to silence the negative thoughts that want to slip into that transitional moment.

I make eye contact with Ronit. For her it is not a question of being able to match pitch; rather, it is the connection between what her vocal cords are doing and what her resonance thinks is appropriate to the task. She "gets" the pitch but works too hard physically, pushing upward through her neck muscles to reinforce it. She feels that she has to because she is at odds with the ringing tone of her upper resonance and does not yet value what it can do naturally, even unconsciously. Recently we have been working to reclaim height in her voice. Ronit can now regularly move up into higher scream and squeal zones with much less fear or repulsion. This will help with today's class.

To deal with both the "push-up" and the "guarantee," I would like Ronit to back away from drama and discover that those upper vibrations can be as easy as cooing. I want her to believe that this upper resonance belongs to the middle of her voice as well as the high notes. I call on her inner "airhead" to help me out. I ask her to not care about how well she is doing, ask her to stop evaluating her own sound. To be a little mindless rather than mindful. Play freely. When she stops trying—and no longer defends—her sound glistens and the raspiness fills in, becomes complete. The young feminine, the least useful member of a military nation and the most endangered in a sexist culture, has brought Ronit's voice just what it needs.

I move on to Doug for the last solo work of the session. Doug plays many instruments and writes sensitive, surprising songs; his singing voice has an otherworldly sheen. With these multiple talents, one would assume that pitch would be a "no-brainer." Doug always sings in tune, but I want his sense of pitch to settle in his body, feel less "carried" and more that it carries him.

Playing an instrument asks a musician's peripheral nervous system to move a finger here or there to strike, strum, vibrate, or slide. We take on these learned patterns often enough that they become second nature. I used to think that instrumentalists—including me—were "uptight" about pitch and that this was why we would match it at the cost of connected, communicative vocal sound when learning to sing. I now think of it as a communication challenge between two very different nervous systems: my autonomic nervous system *feels* pitch; my peripheral nervous system *does* pitch. I want a singer to trust that pitch is about revealing their state of being as they move through a melodic curve. Conscious muscular control is necessary to ensure the quality and timing of breath flow as well as the open architecture of resonance, but in order to let the vocal cords match pitch through being attuned, we are better off trusting our ANS over our PNS.

Today I want Doug to *do* in new places, for new purposes. I want him to step into a virile, aggressive, self-possessed resonance behind his sternum without stepping into expectation—the need to conquer a note's vibration. I'd like him to feel more capable and more demanding through the surface of his entire torso, and at the same time less adept, less attached to specific acoustic outcomes. It takes a leap of faith to let go of monitoring or managing pitch, but any concerns about pitch that might have been tended by his neck muscles will be assuaged through the bearings he now feels in his chest. As note after note unchains, Doug becomes beautifully tethered to all that he is; his multiple octaves sound endless and seamless. Pitch is now a by-product of feeling, and less a virtue to obtain. It is okay for the human animal to believe in itself.

I am extremely pleased with how each of these students has stepped out of the way so that pitch can take its rightful place. It is as difficult for the musician who has been measuring up as it is for the individual labeled "tone deaf" to change their relationship to being in tune, to shift their values from something set externally to something that begins with inner accord.

After twenty-five years of professionally guaranteeing pitch, I chose to let go of my need to be competent. It took six years to fully inhabit the idea that pitch can manage itself, that the vagus nerve wrapping around an aorta to the heart means singing is about being attuned to survival states—to feelings. Having the courage to "walk away from the pitch" while singing has taught me that being in tune is something humans have by nature. *We are all special in this way.* This new way of being with pitch—feeling my way through it by feeling my way into myself—makes sense of everything I believe about singing, about emotion, about work, about communication and even relationship. When I connect emotional instinct to internal vocal geography, this not only gauges external musical reference points, it spills into my interactions with others.

Musical forms that stay the course grow out of shared human development. Familiar intervals hold clear chemical and hormonal significance within a culture, and, because many intervals are present in nature, beyond a culture's aesthetic walls. Well-mapped vibratory distances between pitches are how we understand what a song is trying to get across even when we can't make out the words. Each musical tradition's "standards"—whether classical or popular—have recognizable emotional bones. Working on songs with my students is a chance to illuminate the physiological *hows* and *whys* of musical inheritance.

Surprisingly, in my late forties and fifties, I have returned to more easily digestible melodies than what I took on through loving Schoenberg. Listening to recordings of recent live and studio performances, I hear that my pitch has never been truer. I can sit round and fluid within a measurement that in the past could have made me feel restricted, corralled, or even inadequate—needing to push or prove. I now love pitch … my own pitchy-ness.

18

Slipper Camp Five—
Double Fluff

THE EASE SHARED by this morning's Slipper Campers is unqualified. Their lowest long tones ring intimate and true—more late-night confessional than technical building block.

"You've all 'What the fluffed!' beautifully. As you know, this lowest part of the human voice, when unforced, results in sounds that are unapologetic ... free of coping mechanisms ... truly of the body."

If this were a small Group Class, I might look for previously untapped sounds within each of the students. We'd plow new furrows in rich, loamy emotion, weed out old root systems, stumble upon long-lost treasure—exploratory, cathartic work. However, Slipper Camp is for technique building. A reliable practice that cultivates balance through harvesting the essence of human expressivity. For an unprejudiced and sustainable garden, many dualities must come into open relationship, beginning with light and dark.

"Lower Fluff" connects us to sounds and sensations that feel dark, compassionate, down—maybe even "sad." To balance this, we need the opposite—light—and for that we need a little genuine "glad." Light and dark counter and complement each other, which helps manage emotional topography.

I ask the class to sing long tones from the A-flat down to low D one last time … and then I pop us up an octave, my thumb striking middle D on the piano.

"Here we are at middle D. Listen to the piano's pitch as you inhale silently through an easy open mouth. Imagine how the D will resonate in your body and head before you engage with it. Men, please sing the octave lower, as this will resonate similarly for you."

The group responds with a long sung tone, and despite my suggestion that they listen to how the pitch lives in them, the sound emerges with a low ceiling. I play the pitch just below the D—a C-sharp—and ask them to shape the mouth, neck, and face that could sing this note—*without singing it*. They do. We repeat this "unvoiced singing" back at middle D. This time, as they explore the inside of the head that could sing D, they feel the difference. C-sharp lives a little further down, while D asks for fairly equal space in head and body.

"I have chosen middle D as our starting point for holding both gravity and levity because it is a note that understands this balance on a corporeal level.

"Today I want us to revel in levity's ability to accompany gravity in order to become more conscious about balance. I want us to find a second fluff behind the eyes without losing the lower one. While singing this next note, let's pretend that we are friendly people and make a little eye contact!"

Everyone loves to imagine being friendly. As soon as we risk "friendly" the soft palate lifts naturally and resonant space within the sinuses becomes available. My sound lightens up because I've lightened up; this seems to be how we are designed. If there is a new student in the group, inviting them to share the fun and frivolity of eye contact is daring, delightful, and attainable. We sing another tone.

"Those are your sinuses ringing!" I tell them. And then I get specific.

We have four pairs of paranasal sinuses in the upper part of our head. The vibrations that ricochet through these eight resonant pockets are what get called "head voice." The friendliest ring is in the ethmoids—the sinuses right behind the bridge of the nose, between the eyes. Our ethmoids have numerous thin-walled air cells and are one of the most complex structures in the body.

I confide in my students, "I adore the word *ethmoid*; it sounds like a best friend you could tell all your secrets to—an Ethel, or Myrtle."

We all laugh. There is nothing like becoming an instant BFF with a body part you didn't know you had.

I pull out a diagram of the sinuses pilfered from the box of an excellent herbal/homeopathic nasal spray I use to keep my allergies at bay. One student blurts out, "You mean sinuses are empty space?"

"Yes, space within the facial bones that are in the vicinity of the nose and eyes. The size of these cavities varies enormously from one person to the next; anywhere from 5 to 67 percent of each bone can be occupied by space. The uniqueness of a person's physique affects a singer's tone and volume." The anatomy lesson continues.

Each of these air pockets is lined with cilia, tiny hairs that wave mucus forward toward our nostrils so we can clear out irritants or infections. For those unfortunate enough to have chronic sinusitis, the cilia have been damaged and are incapable of this action, though I suspect that my pleasant-smelling spray, and other forms of healthy irrigation, including yawning, can help regenerate the cilia over time.

All four sets of sinuses are connected to one another and the nasal cavity by small passageways in the bone called ostia. The *frontal sinuses* are in our forehead; they can be painful and less accessible when clogged by a head cold, or squeezed shut through frowning. They vibrate where we picture our "third eye," long associated with enlightenment. The *ethmoidal sinuses* are located within the labyrinths of the unpaired, fragile bone between your two eye sockets, known as the ethmoid. You can't cheat, lie, or engineer your way into these sinuses; they need happiness, delight, and pleasure to ring true. The air within your *sphenoidal sinuses*—held within the sphenoid bone, right behind your ethmoid—seems easier to access through levitating the soft palate. These sinuses help create the lofty sound that marks the operatic voice. This domed, regal tone can be present in an individual's speaking voice as well. If it doesn't partner with warm airflow from behind the sternum, that person can sound "out of touch" with mere mortals.

Finally there are the *maxillary*. These sinuses are found in our cheek-bones. A brash and brassy Broadway sound seems to rely on feeling the sound at the front of the face. When a singer tries to push her sound forward into the cheekbones, she narrows in the throat, becomes overly "nasal," and actually misses out on the gorgeous bronze shimmer a belter seeks. Jamming or squeezing resonance forward, a common mis-interpretation of "placing" or "projecting" the voice, is an unreliable shortcut to the big maxillaries at the front of the face, with a resulting sound that is usually driven or inflexible. I avoid terms like *placement* and *projection*. "While flowing air from behind the sternum to keep your throat flexible and generous, access the maxillary sinuses by lifting your cheekbones as if a family of tiny Polly Pockets* lived in those cavities. Try not to crush them!"

We are born with only two of our four sets of sinuses: the maxillary and the ethmoids. The sphenoids and the frontals don't begin to form until around the age of twelve and continue to make space in the bone throughout our teenage years. I wonder if this is why the habits of those who have sung in musicals through high school are so etched, and can be difficult to change; the young musical theater singer's technique is built before all their equipment has developed.

The purpose of human sinuses is still up for grabs. One theory posits that this empty bone space is meant to make our weighty heads a little lighter—easier on the neck when standing. Perhaps. Regardless, like the vocal cords, which were not designed for speech, we have come to rely on our sinuses to amplify our thoughts.

"Maximum resonance grows over time through all four sets of sinuses working together," I tell my students. "Playfulness is a great

---

* Polly Pockets are centimeter-high dolls that my daughters played with when they were young—perfect for car trips. I keep a small Polly Pocket globe with its one remaining inhabitant on the piano as an example for those who didn't have them as children.

way to get them open and communicative. Let's flirt with each other over this next long tone. Don't just make eye contact—actually flirt."

The air around the piano heats up as giddiness takes hold; it does not matter whether a student is twenty-one or seventy-one.

"Have any of you experienced European flirting? Years ago at a market in Ascoli Piceno—a small mountain village north of Rome—I was buying apples from a wonderfully toothless old man. Next to him sat his equally wonderful and toothless wife. In response to my request for an apple he held up two, gently cupping them in his palms, just in front of his chest. His wife cackled in lusty agreement when he asked, in Italian, 'What about two?' Their eyes played with mine as we shared a juiciness beyond the flesh of the fruit.

"Flirting doesn't have to lead to a one-night stand—it is not simply conquest. Be the old Italian couple celebrating abundance."

The next tone is so much better. I hear a bubble of sound behind the chest *and* a bubble of sound behind the eyes. Light and dark. In Italian, *chiaroscuro*. "Double Fluff." I ask them what it is like to flirt in this way. One of the older students confesses it had never dawned on him that another person was a part of flirting, despite his love of sparky engagement.

"You are right that flirting is about giving *and* receiving. To help us with this, let's make sure our anal sphincters stay soft through the next flirted tone."

What a pleasure to enjoy the kind of flirting that doesn't have to end up in an affair, marriage, or feeling harassed. We sing a few more long tones, balancing light and dark, giving and receiving, self and other.

"This sound is generous, attractive, and full … mindful even. Doer, receiver, and listener each maintain space in a way that results in what I think of as 'contemplative' flirting—with third and fourth* eyes remaining soft."

---

* The fourth eye is my pet name for the anal sphincter. I believe that understanding and accepting this orifice is part of becoming fully realized with regard to who we are as human animals.

The class's laugh bonds with optimism to build a tangible and repeatable image of levity. Its genuine ring brings our resonators closer to the space necessary for "Upper Fluff," though we will have to let go of laughter's hearty spasm before singing the next note. We sing note after note with fluff above and fluff below from middle D down to low D, back up to middle D, continuing a few more pitches to end on the F-sharp at the top of the *lower passaggio*.

"I am going to add one more idea."

A barely audible groan seeps out of the group. They know they are doing well, but it has taken a lot of work to stay released into gravity while identifying with height. Adding yet another concept seems like too much, but a new ceiling is presenting itself as we reach the F-sharp, and this will hamper our ability to go higher with ease.

"If you feel you are juggling several things at once, you are on your way to good singing," I say.

This is especially true in the early days of practice. Eventually, accessing duality feels normal—full of leeway and possibility—and less like work. Vocal economy comes from understanding and managing all the resonant rooms in our voice's "house"—their individual dimensions, functions, and needs—as well as how they interact.

"The top of your mouth, the back wall of your mouth, and the circumference of your upper throat are all flexible. Unfold those spaces toward a yawn with each inhale. For a little extra height, take in four quick, light breaths, one right after the other, as if you were mildly shocked. Feel how this quickly repeated action lifts the soft palate. It might even make you yawn for real! Now maintain that space as you sing; in fact, keep unfolding it upward over the course of your exhale."

We sing the F-sharp once again. The ceiling in each student's voice has lifted—become vaulted. We are now ready to move up to the G above middle C.

"Conjure the image of an airhead. How about the main character in the film *House Bunny*—played by the magnificent Anna Faris. There are many female ditzes in pop culture, but who plays a good male example of this archetype?"

Brad Pitt is suggested. A few students cringe, but everyone agrees.

"Both male and female airheads are characters we tend to deride. Reese Witherspoon played one with finesse in *Legally Blonde*—and without sending her character up. Like Reese, we need to love our innocent, naive, hopeful, and unprotected aspects; they are tender.

"Because of this, the top of the voice can be terrifying. By 'top' I don't mean high notes exclusively, but the height within each and every sound. Our culture does not respect sweetness and sensitivity and has divorced these things from power, intelligence, and importance. Access your inner airhead as a 'homeopathic' cure, dosing yourself with the feelings you separated from in order to survive. If there is too little pink in your life, a blast of levity is very good medicine and will not undermine your dark, your gravitas, your drive. In fact, a small Barbie pill will help your depth become sustainable.

"Try out this little sound. *Hahahahahahahahahahahahaha.*"

I laugh a tiny laugh: the sound trips lightly on an easy flow of air. It peals untethered brilliance. I am a dainty damsel, a fop floating in his falsetto, a child responding gaily to a joke whose meaning eludes her. The actual pitch is not terribly high, though it is definitely above my *lower passaggio* and fully in my head voice. Everyone joins in, and once they find their shimmer they can't stop … it is so endearingly silly. The whole group "*Hahahahahahahahahahahahahas*" repeatedly until I bring them to silence. I can always tell what has been in short supply in an acoustic diet. A few are still giggling.

"Did any of you feel you might cry when you found this place?"

Big, wobbly smiles under glistening eyes as heads nod yes.

This part of the voice is the same whether we are laughing or crying, as long as both of these emotions have our full permission. The vulnerability of this part of us is almost unbearable, as well as incredibly responsive; it is too precious to mock.

"Did any of you worry that the next scene in your film might be a really bad one?"

More nodding heads.

A beautiful scene in a film can make us suspicious, nervous, or worried about what the next one will hold. We are wired to look for danger in order to keep ourselves safe, to spot the tiger when we emerge from the cave. This very young, undefended sound—whether a laugh or a cry—is so exposed. We learn to protect it when we're out in the world. Ideally when we were children, adults looked after us, but many of us have had to watch out for ourselves for longer than is fair. The practice of light, hope, optimism, and fragility does not come easily. It takes time to rediscover and value these things—render them useful habits.

"Remember how much you enjoyed 'flaffing' *Hahahahahahahahaha* ..."

The whole group jumps in, a flock of spontaneous, flap-happy birds.

I'd love to use this raw sound in a piece. It is such a beautiful mix of sad and glad. It reminds me of how emotionally flexible my kids were when they were little. Shakespeare described his character Feste in *Twelfth Night* as "wise enough to play the fool." The brilliance of Upper Fluff's resonance is that it allows us to access emotion without forcing catharsis, and through this, we gradually build stamina for our own vulnerability.

"Let's bring this openness into the G, G-sharp, and A above middle C. Remember the feeling of sparkle in this little laugh, and bring this physiological space into your next long tones. Consciousness around light and dark in this malleable and manageable range will set a template for height and depth through all of your registers—including the lowest 'What the fluff!' range."

This airy sound is not a final destination with regard to a complete technique. We've not yet explored the gathering of energy through the midline that will allow our fluffs to fully blossom and fill in. But it does ensure that we know how to release upward and downward at the same time, vibrate the full length of our tube. Air flowing from behind the sternum, up through the mouth cavity, and into all the sinuses—without forcing it into any one place. A "double bubble" of resonance—chest supporting head—gently balancing gravity and levity, compassion and delight. No prejudice one way or the other in this healthy manifestation of *unbound*.

19

Naked Men Crying

STEVEN TYLER IS my boyfriend. Every time I listen to him I fall head over heels. The undisguised pain his voice lays bare pulls me in, heart, head, and pussy. He sounds as if he could use a whole lifetime of me.

I've been listening to Steven obsessively while hunkered down within the moldy walls of Artscape Gibraltar Point's old schoolhouse on Toronto's Centre Island. It is winter, and Lake Ontario's choppy chill—spitting distance from my studio—holds nothing over the goose-bump thrill I get from Steven's voice.

For weeks I have been online tracking down performances by older rock and rollers, searching out the singers who have survived that life's ride: performances in sports arenas with monstrous acoustics; needy crowds absorbing, screaming, demanding; the ridiculous pressure of having everyone think they are your girlfriend. I want to find the ones who have lasted into their sixties with an expressive, flexible voice—and a generosity of spirit. Most of the surviving senior singers are male, in part because there were so many more of them in the first place.

I discover 2010's Kennedy Center Honors tribute to Paul McCartney. Just shy of the thirteen-minute mark, Steven Tyler strides out from the wings, hair and coat billowing behind. Steven's bony hands grip the mic, its stand festooned with his signature scarf. The audience, studded with the likes of the then president Barack Obama, Justin Timberlake,

Alec Baldwin, and Yo-Yo Ma, waits expectantly. Paul is sandwiched between Michelle Obama and Oprah in the front row of the balcony. Nancy Shevell, Paul's soon-to-be wife, is seated just behind him. She places her hands on his shoulders from time to time and Paul returns her touch, but his attention never leaves the stage. Steven performs "Medley" from *Abbey Road*'s B side, singing each song as if he has no choice. His musical prowess reveals the urgency of primal want, transforms weakness into something noble. Wanting this for myself, I run after his joyous abandon from the first ...

"Oh, look out!"

Steven's voice hovers on the thrilling sill of debauch. He jumps off a cliff of his own making, pulling me with him. I follow his *unbound* energy, spill into my own wantonness.

"Once, there was a way to get back homeward ..."

I am amazed by the looseness of this man's articulation. His enormous, malleable mouth opens beyond imagination, sucks air as if sentenced to death. The sounds it shapes resonate through muscle, cartilage, and bone ... nestle into a pocket near my heart. Naked, hollow, bereft, Steven treads my sorrow.

"... And I will sing a lullaby."

Can one adult sing another to sleep?

(How I want to be soothed by this virile, wailing man.)

Today I hate my father ... really hate him. He is sick, decrepit—imprisoned—hardly communicates with any of us anymore. I wonder if he has "locked-in syndrome." For the last few months I have been trying to foster a benign compassion that would allow me to be with him regularly without too much emotional fallout—or pity. Today it's not working.

I take a deep breath and walk back into the bedroom he and my mother share. Everything is as it should be: family pictures on the wall, king-sized bed nicely made. His half has a railing now—to prevent him from wandering at night—and the room's wall-to-wall carpet has been replaced with solid hardwood to better handle any "accidents." I look down at the floor, force myself to imagine my father lying in a puddle of urine.

My father has started to fall recently and Mum can no longer get him back up. More than once she has waited for hours at his side, keeping him warm with a blanket, afraid to dial 911, finally calling my brother at dawn to come and lift him back into bed. I can hear Dad's small groan of pain as Chris settles him onto the sheets; my father never betrayed much. But today Dad is lying on top of the covers, dressed well in pressed pants and a button-up shirt. The dark, rich colors Mum has picked out look good on him.

I gaze down at my father, ask how he is. His eyes are closed, but he is tense with listening. I try over and over again, simplifying each statement. What he would like, what might make him feel better. I sit on the edge of the bed, draw closer. He shrugs the smallest shrug I have ever seen. *He does not know how he is.* I hang on to each precious, verging-on-invisible nod or shake of his head, the very occasional word or two. Everything must seem like weakness, like need. I join him, lying down on my mother's half of the bed. He is part of me. I want to know how that part is doing, but I am exhausted from trying to figure out what I should do—how I should be. I do not know how to help.

When I was growing up, my father was angry much of the time. Aggression and drive fed his successful business life. Though my energy went into making art and not croissants, borrowing his relentless pace was useful when juggling family with career. Overworking became a seemingly safe way to avoid the things neither of us had the time, patience, or skill to sort out—a productive way to escape sorrow and disappointment. I am certain that my father, like me, did not have permission to feel or show his vulnerability from a very young age.

At twenty I discovered that I could sing my anger and despair. The tragic scale and bona fide drama of opera met me. Dad talked to his colleagues about his daughter, the "singer." I thought he was simply proud, but maybe he was envious too? With distance it is clear that my affinity for singing dark material expressed not only my own repressed feelings, but my father's backlog as well. My inheritance includes the things he could not escape by leaving Switzerland as a young man, the things he could not change in his adult life in Canada.

Steven Tyler is in church. He is singing "Amazing Grace" with gospel singer Juliette Hamilton. Steven looks rough and sounds rough, but he is joyous as hell. Wireless mic in hand, he loses himself in front of the choir. Juliette sways ever so slightly from side to side, anchoring his wandering. Her burnished, grainy voice makes visible a stable core while Steven's sobs split light. Mutual trust allows these artists to follow the song's emotional thread in tandem. Two sides of faith—one pulled out from under a park bench, the other cultivated in the crucible of the Gospels—meet through pitch-perfect, effortless phrasing. Delight cracks open shared growls; amazed grins follow. Grace reveals.

I am worried.

My father is in the hospital for the third time in only a few months. My mother has the flu, so my brothers and I visit him daily. At the end of the week I am supposed to go to the Yukon to create and premiere a variety show with a group of young adults who have intellectual disabilities. Before leaving I spend two evenings alone with Dad. Too tired to drive through rush hour, I take the GO Bus from Toronto to Hamilton.

Our first night together is sweetness. He points out a horse suspended above the hospital curtain. This ghost leads him into the early-dawn backstreets of his childhood, and he tells me that when he was little—just six years old—he delivered bread for his father's bakery by horse and cart. The second night is intimate in other ways. We share the most basic things, including a few squares of Swiss chocolate. When he becomes restless, I take him to the toilet. Afterward I stroke his head till he falls asleep.

My mother and brothers, the doctors and nurses—everyone, as far as I can tell—think Dad will come out of the hospital soon. Anticipating a little more loss with regard to his faculties, we shrug a little in reassurance. I get on the plane.

On Saturday Magda visits him and I use this as an opportunity to call; two iPhones and my daughter's sensitive interactions connect me to Dad. I listen to his voice's phlegm and scratch—still a Swiss accent after sixty years in Canada. I imagine his dark, sensitive eyes peering intently from behind his glasses. *Vunderful, vunderful!* crackles through my cell phone's fragile little speaker. Dad thinks that what I am up to with my northern troupe is *vunderful!*

During this final conversation, as well as the last two nights we spent together, I swear that my father lightened up and let go. Revealed himself. His grip on life had always been irrevocably strong. I feel it in my body every day: in actions that could use less effort; in feelings that could flow with more ease; need I could express; weakness I could show. The light I witnessed as Dad neared death is the same light I hear at the top of Tyler's voice; it comes from around the eyes, from the same resonant cracks that allow a person to laugh or cry. Dad would have been horrified by a man as *unbound* as Steven Tyler, but I see essential similarities between these two sensitive, intense, charismatic souls. But Steven Tyler does not need me as his girlfriend; his wailing charts sadness expertly. He radiates joy doing this work, lets me lean into his fractured voice so as to release my own cares and sorrows. I have never had to cry on his behalf.

In the weeks following my father's funeral, I lessen my teaching load, and in that double void accept several invitations to sing. I step out publicly with my voice, over and over again celebrating how *vunderful* it is to express. I sing for myself, I sing for the sake of beauty, for my own ears and heart ... without expectation. I feel and fulfill my own need: I don't question its rightness. I trust my ability to give and take, share space with the audience. Working from pleasure, I begin to taste happy. The universe I inhabited as my father's daughter cracks.

It is 2016 and I have just returned from visiting his homeland, where I met with his two remaining sisters, now eighty-seven and eighty-three. Dad would have been eighty-four. I ask these women—who look so much like him—many questions; their answers flow easily. Yes, he had always been silent. Yes, he had a temper like their father did—a family trait that even my aunt, the nun, battled her whole life. Yes, he loved to sing Swiss songs; in fact, he would cry when singing them during visits back home. This information stops me, tightens the muscles of my throat.

Remembering that the word *nostalgia* has Swiss origins, I look up its etymology. In the darkening light I learn that it was coined in 1688 by medical student Johannes Hofer. He united the Greek *nóstos*—homecoming—with *álgos*, pain or ache, in order to label a condition known as the "Swiss illness." Swiss mercenaries, fighting on the French lowlands, pined for their native mountains to the point of sickness. Military physicians hypothesized that the constant clanging of cowbells in Alpine pastures had probably damaged their eardrums, or brain cells. To prevent further illness, desertion, or death, Swiss "soldiers of fortune" were forbidden from singing *kuhreihen*, or *ranz des vaches*—cow songs! These mournful melodies, based on the intervals of the alphorn and the slow lag of mountain echo, were just too sad.

Nostalgia became a medical diagnosis for a form of melancholy in the twentieth century. Today we use the word to refer to a general interest in the past—a dwelling on the "good old days." A song heard at one time in a person's life and then not again for a while remains undiluted in its association with a "better," "easier" time. It can stir emotion, bring back memories. Smell and touch also evoke nostalgia due to how we process these stimuli. The ethmoid bone's multiple chambers provide passage for the olfactory nerve's many fine fibers as well as vibrating laughter and crying.

Tucked under the eiderdown at my uncle's home in Basel, I risk my own malaise listening to a whole whack of cow songs well into the wee hours. I remember these tunes from the cassettes my dad popped into the car stereo as he drove our family deep into the mountains to ski, gliding over the icy back roads of Québec, Northern Ontario, British Columbia, and Washington State, my brothers and I groaning aesthetic protest from the backseat of the van.

Holding the acoustic scraps of my father's melancholy in my palm makes it tangible—and simpler than I had thought. Acknowledging his feelings and then noting how my own inner landscape differs makes it easier to slip out of my excessive response-ability for his emotional limitations. By staying unapologetically connected to myself—to the light that is *my* sad and *my* glad—I begin to shape a homeland of my own.

20

The Full-Blown Beauty of Anger

I LOVED MY early voice study with Richard Armstrong, loved the permission he gave me to let loose big, rage-filled sound. Thick multiphonics rumbled around within my chest and splayed their way up through my sinuses, many pitches all at once in areas used to being much tidier. I reveled in the tussle of aggressive, complex, layered sound, relied on my "false vocal cords"* for extra heft.

At first I accessed this fire only under Richard's purview; the sounds seemed dangerous, and finding them, mysterious. Sometimes they threatened to knock me off my feet. But my body's physiological productivity was undeniable—and the dare, potency, and release met a need for which I had no language. Growling, shredding, and shrieking became the soundtrack for personal renovation. Soon I was offering these colors as part of my core artistic identity.

---

* "False vocal cords" refer to the vestibular folds that are above our regular vocal folds. Each vestibular, or superior, fold is made up of one thick fold of mucous membrane that encloses a narrow band of fibrous tissue. Tuvan and Arctic throat singing, Tibetan chant, and various forms of metal, as well as voice actors wanting to add a little growl to an evil character, ask for these folds to come together in a vibratory pattern to achieve depth of sound. These "cords" are not normally used for speech; they aid in the life-preserving acts of breathing and swallowing.

Rehearsing for an Autumn Leaf Performance fundraiser in artist Vivian Reiss's exquisitely idiosyncratic mansion, I launched into chorded sounds within an URGE group improvisation. When the scene ended I felt surprisingly depleted and hollow. After eight years of vocal catharsis, had I come to the end of my anger? Had there been a backlog? Was I "done"? Though I dredged up the feelings needed for that night's performance, the experience left me unsettled.

When I displayed my temper as a child, my mum called me Fifi rather than Fides. I was not "me" when I wasn't a "good girl." I can appreciate my mother's wariness in relation to anger. Her father was known as Red for more than just his hair color, and she married a man who used anger to mask his sadness. Both Dad and Grandpa had ample drive, which helped them become successful, and although neither was physically violent I regularly witnessed my mother counterbalancing Dad's quickness to rage. She typically defused my feelings of anger before I could acknowledge what was pent up inside. I didn't learn how to work with anger, honor its strengths, or curtail its excesses. Its useful drive remained emotionally unintegrated, and I ended up using it as fuel for overworking, or as a way to sidestep sadness, just like my father before me.

When my oldest daughter was moving into puberty—all breasts, hips, and hormones—I found myself avoiding her when she brought friends to the house. I couldn't handle the sound of their voices, which had risen in pitch over the course of Grades Seven and Eight. This alarming ascent was not caused by any biological changes; if anything, their voices should have deepened as they matured. I believe that their high, grating, skittish vocal timbre was in response to losing the more equal footing that girls have with boys in primary school. Learning to balance estrogen's nurturing feelings with innate human aggression is difficult when female anger is taboo, when its healthy manifestation is rarely modeled. These young women sounded as if they were trying to please everyone, all the time, to stay safe ... even within their own circle.

I recall Magda's younger sister, Oksana, waltzing down the stairs late one morning, her eleven-year-old abandon expertly shredding,

"Rrraaaarhh ... Rrraaaarhh ... Why did your students have such a hard time with this today? Rrraaaarhh!" That morning's 9:30 a.m. choir practice had brought up some potent stuff, and the group's sense of politeness was challenged as they groped internally for more vocal space, more sensate permission. It takes time for a woman to free herself from socially sanctioned constraints in a culture that doesn't acknowledge, value, or deal responsibly with either male or female anger and drive.

Both Oksana and Magda had permission to express anger at home through direct vocal aggression. I let them say *no* to me—listened when they yelled and hollered in response to the culture at large. I wanted them to understand and own their drives, flex their vocal muscles without fear. They had heard all sorts of sounds emerge from my studio and seen me work artistically with those sounds onstage. Both girls kept alive what was elemental in their presexualized voices as they moved into the first stage of womanhood: firmly rooted chest resonance partnering with the playful ping of head voice.

Like many women of my generation, I have spent time talking to a therapist. Depression might take us to our first appointment, but it is often anger that arises next, pulls our suffering out of despair. Sometimes it seems as if we are trying to change or fix ourselves, but I think we are trying to make sense of how out of sorts we feel within the dominant culture ... how out of touch we are with our right to be mad.

Freud's theory of "hysteria" is named after the Greek word for womb, and equates a woman's neurotic behavior with having a wonky one. Two millennia before his psychoanalytic theories, ancient Greeks blamed female "craziness" on wandering wombs. In the early 1900s the vibrator was second only to the vacuum cleaner in catalog sales—doctors were tired of inducing "therapeutic orgasm" at the office to treat mental health symptoms. Thanks to Sears, women could finally take care of their "madness" by themselves in a dust-free home. These attempts to "fix" a woman miss the obvious point: It is crazy-making not to own your own pelvis. It is enraging to grow up in a culture that doesn't respect a woman's body right down to the bottom of its grounded floor. If I were my own womb, I'd want to fucking flee more than wander.

149

Many cultures have tried to figure out how to deal with women who break (down) from cultural norms. Up until the 1950s in Puglia, southern Italy, a ritual known as the *tarantella* was used to treat a woman at her wits' end. The Pugliese believed that a woman no longer "herself"—at odds with the world—had been possessed by spiders. As cure, a small ensemble of male musicians would arrive at the troubled woman's home armed with guitar, violin, accordion, and voice. In response to their frenzied tunes the woman let herself roll around erratically on her kitchen floor, flinging herself against the walls, jerking spasmodically, following whatever her flailing body compelled her to do. This exorcising went on for several days until the woman was fully wrung out, and ready to return to her social and familial roles. Looking at black-and-white Italian footage from the early '60s,* I am struck by the contrast between the woman's "out of bounds" movements and her painfully mundane setting: her children bear witness perched on the kitchen table; neighbors peer in through an undressed window.

We need more than the fervor of the *tarantella* to resolve the gender inequalities still gripping my generation. I'd love to listen to a woman's voice figure itself out given permission to be on the planet without reserve. And although singing has long been my personal life raft, I am only now hearing the breadth of my unadorned, godforsaken voice. How much freer would women be within our sounding bodies—head and chest resonance as well as vocal cord function—if we had not been denied academic inclusion until the mid-1800s, the vote until the early part of the 1900s, or a bank account until the 1960s.†

How much corset is still in our breath?

Where are the female singers who have explored their emotional geography through transgressive, progressive sound? Human songbirds with the temerity to dilute the domestic with the instinctual, using 100 percent of their air. No second-guessing. A bird's superb

---

* *La Taranta*, directed by Gianfranco Mingozzi, 1962.

† These dates correspond predominantly to gains for white women in Canada and the United States.

syrinx, the siren's call, a feminist's unapologetic spit and spill. A self-possessed muse.

Richard Armstrong introduced me to the African American singers who had shaped him as he came of age in 1950s England. African American female voices have been inspiration and balm over this last century for countless men and women wanting to embrace and express a wide range of forbidden feeling: unimaginable sorrow, bristling rage, joyous abandon. Ma Rainey, Bessie Smith, Marian Anderson, Mahalia Jackson, Billie Holiday, Sarah Vaughan, Ella Fitzgerald, Nina Simone and her daughter Lisa, Etta James, Lorraine Ellison, Aretha Franklin, Mavis Staples, Patti LaBelle, Dianne Reeves, Tina Turner, Tracy Chapman, Lauryn Hill, Queen Latifah, Mary J. Blige, Lizz Wright, and Beyoncé. This list brings me to my knees, though it hardly scratches the surface. These women have more than earned the vocal command that comes from integrating textures birthed in pain as well as joy. Resiliency pours through every crack of every nerve-jangling multiphonic, as well as through the creamy flow of pitch-perfect phrasing.

Blues and gospel descend from call-and-response "field hollers" distilled from the melodies and rhythms of multiple West African savannah and rainforest cultures. The pitch bending, the ornamentation and polyphony true to this music—once an integral part of everyday African tribal life—became allied to resistance, rallying, and protest in the New World. Survival. This music came from community and was further developed within community over hundreds of years through the shared trauma and legacy of enslavement and anti-Black racism. It is real.

I have frequently returned to African American female singers for their clarity, power, and emotional vitality. Their voices galvanize and nurture me. But I am descended from ancient Greece, fully shaped by the strictures placed on women born into a western European patriarchal culture. I was molded by the *bel canto* tradition—a technique that took shape around the same time that human beings were first abducted from the African continent. My female forebears, familial and cultural, were charged with maintaining Western religious and economic structures. Grandma and Mum, who slept next to the wounded beast, taught me to bury "mother tongue." Distrust of the female voice lies under my skin as a normalized practice.

I appraise Joni Mitchell's ethereal soprano prophesying obliquely, her voice never settling, never challenging directly. I take in Joan Baez's sweet soprano centering slightly high in pitch as she politely and earnestly sounds protest for others. Remembering Australian Helen Reddy's cheerful rendition of her 1972 megahit, with the famous opening line "I am woman, hear me roar," I come across an equally bouncy a cappella version at the Los Angeles Women's March in 2017. Janis Joplin is dead, despite her flight from middle-class Texan suburbia and her thrilling musical cries for help. And then I stumble upon Ann Wilson.

I was not a fan of the Seattle rock band Heart in the 1970s, but as a grown woman I can't get enough of Ann's voice. It is monstrous. It is enormous. It has fur, purchase, blade, poise, precision, and opulence. Its wild terrain maps the unruly articulation of emotion. I drink in the Kennedy Center Honors 2012 Led Zeppelin tribute. A brilliant piece of musical casting puts the "lady" central to "Stairway to Heaven" right into Ann's mouth, *the mouth of a woman*! I indulge over and again in her gritty, mature Women Rock! 2000 concert performance of Heart's 1976 debut hit "Crazy on You," created with guitarist sister, Nancy.

Ann must be about fifty: hair piled high on her head, blue tinted glasses masking her beautiful face. She has raised two children, gained some weight, battled drugs and alcohol. Fans and detractors duke it out in the comments below the video. Men and women are changed when Ann connects to herself, and they don't always like this. In the verbal melee the hunger and passion of both female mouths are "moshed" together using bad spelling and indelicate punches.

Ann is misstepping. She is loud, strident, and breathtakingly sublime. She takes her own sweet time, slowing the song down to match the soul speed of her body: she follows her voice, tells the truth, and gives us time to absorb. She stays loose and undefended through her body, vibrates with the intelligence of feeling. The unfettered expansiveness of Ann's chest vibration, allied to a sweetness of head tone, makes it clear that she is not taking anything out on herself. She is juicy, like her need to *go crazy on* her lover despite—or maybe because of—the divides that make partnering difficult. None of her drives are disguised. Ann is not matching pitch, she is making *her* pitch the marker; her intonation is exemplary.

I want to devour Ann's delicious vocal umami. I envy her wise, fecund timbre, her unplowed wilderness. She sounds fresh and vital despite working a lifetime toward this performance. In 2006 Ann was listed as one of "Heavy Metal's All-Time Top 100 Vocalists" by *Hit Parader* magazine, joining the high priests of aggression. She is that and more: Cassandra warning us of things to come; Aphrodite, the goddess of love, beauty, pleasure, and procreation; and Calliope, the muse who presides over eloquence and epic poetry. Calliope was also the lover of Ares, god of war. Is Ann's embrace of aggression, her translation of this energy into song, a way to bring anger back home?

Many classical Greek plays begin with a woman waiting for her man to come home from war. She has usually been faithful for decades, often while running the country. This begs so many questions: Are men always off fighting? Is warfare on foreign soil the only way to handle aggression? Do we hope that violence will stay out of domestic and civic spheres if acted out on someone else's land? What would happen if we learned to handle aggression without going off to war? What have I done with my own aggression? Do I have the courage to bring *my* anger back home and integrate it with the rest of my feelings? Set new bearings for the wonderful resources and energy it can provide? Can a self-possessed core take the place of armor within a singer's musculature and a woman's emotional architecture?

"Barracuda" was written by Nancy and Ann to express their fury with how the record business was treating them. The driven, repeatedly climbing vocal line that Ann launches into at the top of the tune shows a lack of fear in relation to the swagger in her chest, and the zing behind her nose. Her flute playing seems imprinted in her brilliant upper register, which partners consistently with earthy chest resonance. This balance makes Ann's singing renewable and sustainable, helps her avoid tightening internally when engaging with anger. Her in-the-body sense of vocal light and dark plus her attitude prevent Ann from backfiring emotionally. She is having fun while letting loose.

I decide to bring "Barracuda" to my women's choir. At the next rehearsal I sing the first line's robust, ascending sweep of five notes to the assembled group. Actually, I hurl it at them, leaving my voice ringing in the air. The look of shock on their Monday morning faces makes me laugh! I ask them to sing the line back at me from a place of uncensored, unworried, abandoned pissed-offness. I sing it again. Something a little disoriented and halfhearted comes back. I explain that eventually we will access self-possession within aggression, but first we need to holler with pride.

One of the choristers, Lee, tells us that something I shared with the group the previous week had affected her in a paradigm-shifting way and she thought it might be useful for the work at hand. She reminds me that the previous Wednesday I had said to my partner, while making and bagging lunch for tired kids, "I won't let the fuckers get me!" Listening to the 6:30 a.m. news, mouth half full of breakfast, I realized I no longer wanted low-grade, chronic stress to get under my skin when there was no immediate life-threatening situation in our predawn kitchen. I had relayed this story to the women while reminding them to love their pelvic floors. I suggested that softening their anuses could promote calm as the underlay for any storm. Lee remembers me saying, "Nothing will get between me and my anus!" It is a revolutionary act of intimacy to check in with our anal sphincter, see whether or not it has tightened, register how rectum and colon are doing, especially when feeling inflamed or under threat.

A fierce, petite bleached blonde, Lee has a dozen gorgeous tattoos covering her arms and chest. In contrast, her speech is quiet and careful. Lee's opening comment encourages me to ask her to "haul ass" vocally. We start by singing a long *noooo* on middle D; Lee digs out the basement of her sound using this first raucous note. I ask her to protect her turf over the next four ascending semitones, and then explore her rights as she continues up another five, all the while singing *no*. By the time we reach the octave above, Lee has discovered a proprietary relationship to her own voice. I ask her to switch the word *no* to *mine* and she sings *Mine! Mine! Mine!* soaring well above the song's demands, embodying the most glorious, full-blooded screams, pitch by pitch to the absolute top of her range.

The air in the room quivers with permission as I continue to tune up everyone's anger through call-and-response—my teaching style borrowing from African American music as does Ann's rock and roll tradition. I barrel the opening pitches of "Barracuda" at Chris; she barrels them back. I ask her for a little more fun behind the eyes and she replies with fire in her sound. The upward feeling in her resonators drops her further into her legs—lightness partnering with resilience—and her sound rounds out. I fury the line at Deanna. What returns is balanced but errs on the side of caution. I want abandon! I use my whole body to three-dimensionally illustrate the impolite incarnation needed to support this much productivity. She adopts my Incredible Hulk posture and sings back five dynamite notes. A shiver of excitement runs through the group. We are feeling the chemical zing of *fight or flight* but we are not fleeing, hitting, hiding, freezing, tending, or befriending; we are hollering while remaining receptive and flexible "breath beings." Staying the course. Occasionally a cough is triggered when a woman's cords balk at the amount of subglottal pressure they are experiencing, but that will pass with a bit of practice, and I am careful not to push things.

Unexpressed anger can turn inward, leading not only to depression but to physical illnesses. Visiting a friend on the gastroenterology wing at Toronto's Mount Sinai Hospital, I learn that the ward's population is over 80 percent female. Diseases like Crohn's or irritable bowel syndrome are related to chronic stress, a result of *fight or flight* constantly simmering rather than safely and creatively discharging when necessary.

Singing "Barracuda" asks a woman to express the feelings we weren't raised to share. Inhabiting its melody teaches us how to locate aggression in our bodies, set it ringing in the surrounding air. Anger is confusing because it is often repressed, twisted, apologized for, or disregarded. But its potent, coalescing drive is a fundamental part of survival. Singing an angry song, written by a woman, can help us learn how to see, accept, and most importantly hold this kind of energy without doing damage to ourselves. If I can express anger cleanly and clearly, I can let it go.

Lee is right: "Nothing will get between me and my anus!" is fully related to "I won't let the fuckers get me!" It is a woman's birthright to stay healthy through staying in touch with all her primary drives. This demands a full-bodied commitment to anger's truth, in balance with sorrow and joy. Easier to access when supported by a community of women.

21

The Dilemma of Pelvises and Chests

LYNN AND I are holed up at the Manitou Springs Resort and Mineral Spa near Watrous, Saskatchewan. Outside a blizzard rages, obscuring the lake that lies only fifty feet from our window. We are going to soak in this town's warm and muddy mineral water to regenerate after a weeklong singing workshop that Lynn organized for me to teach a dozen variously abled adults in Regina.*

I grab a yogurt from the mini-fridge and go online to jump-start my early-morning writing. Up pops a picture of Sean Penn and his recent, much younger girlfriend. They are walking down a Malibu beach, he in trunks and she, a bikini. His chest looks puffed up—held well past what fifty years carry naturally. Under Sean's girded gut the caption says he is "buff," but I am afraid he will explode.

Just behind me Lynn sets a mat on her hotel bed and lies down on her back. She floats her legs up into the air, spreading them into a wide "V." After a few minutes they begin to jostle in fine, erratic patterns. Her psoas muscle—pent up from hours of holding right foot to pedal

---

* Lynn has developed training programs for a variety of individuals and has created a body of disability-based performance for close to two decades.

over icy roads—is in need of release. Lynn is also letting go of other grips put in place to censor or protect a woman's pelvis. The voice accompanying her physicality reflects pain as well as relief.

Trapped in the outdated motel decor, I can't avoid eavesdropping on Lynn's unmediated, body-based vocalizations. What is it that we humans release into when we let go? My work is to midwife the unchaining of preverbal sound—the body's complaint—but today's rawness makes me ask how much moaning and groaning is healthy. Bathed in the sound of Lynn's release while looking at Sean's puffed-up chest, I try to imagine a balance of energies that could voice what lies beneath the surface of being human without risking exhaustion or the reigniting of trauma.

Prairie wind howls past our window. I rummage for my swimsuit and head to the water, slide my tired bones under its muddy skin.

The Cost of Armoring

The work and place of pelvises and chests has been culturally problematic as long as I can remember. As a cis-gendered, heterosexual woman born in 1960 I'd like to bring some of my complicated inheritances out of the closet, starting with Joan of Arc.

Electric Flesh was the last opera I worked on with Thom Sokoloski, just before our marriage ended. Thom's intense, disturbing libretto was based on the relationship between Joan of Arc and her obsessive, depraved right-hand man, Gilles de Rais. Wende Bartley was hired to compose the score, Richard Armstrong was to play Joan's companion-in-arms, and I the maid-warrior.

When Joan of Arc was thirteen she heard divine voices, donned a tunic and breeches in black and gray, and set off to convince Charles VII of France that she could lead his armies during what we now call the Hundred Years' War. She was a remarkable leader, capable of inspiring King Charles's followers as they attempted to wrestle France back from England's Henry V. Joan was eighteen when she was taken prisoner by Henry's supporters, the Burgundians. She was charged with heresy. During her trial Joan astonished church clerics with her intuitive avoidance of theological pitfalls, remarkable for an illiterate peasant. But neither her astute defense nor the signing of a document renouncing her divine mandate mattered. Joan had returned to masculine costuming in prison because she believed she had been granted permission to cross-dress when necessary by the clerics at Poitiers.* As on the battlefield, she knew that looking like a man would keep her safe from molestation or rape. But it was the wearing of men's clothing—part of the heresy charges—that ultimately led to her execution by burning on May 30, 1431.

Thom loved Leonard Cohen's song "Joan of Arc" almost as much as its central figure. The lyrics begin with Joan confessing that she is "tired of the war" and that she'd better get married to disguise her "swollen appetite." In verse two fire declares his love for her solitude and pride. Joan asks him to "make his body cold" so that she can find refuge. Too late she realizes that she will be consumed. In response to Joan's anguish Cohen questions why "love and light" must be so cruel and so brave. I am left asking why her appetite—sexual or professional—was problematic in the first place. And yes, Leonard, why did Joan have to be so brave?

I have never had a thing for Joan of Arc. When Thom and I separated in 1999 I was relieved to have another singer take over her twisted emotional duties. However, walking away from the opera and our marriage invited me to look at my own maid-warrior tendencies, to how often I played the heroine offstage. Women are more likely to be volunteers at work, as well as shouldering more than their fair share at home. Overwork makes for stress. Being continually stressed clouds judgment, interferes with decision-making, and makes remembering how to "step away" difficult, no matter how tired we are of the

---

* Even though cross-dressing was considered a heretical act, medieval Catholic doctrine evaluated individual charges based on context thanks to St. Thomas Aquinas's writing, which stated that if it was a necessity—for example, as protection against rape—cross-dressing was permitted.

war. Burnout is a natural result of not valuing and balancing giving with receiving.

I have used the practice and lens of my vocal technique to probe the complex struggle between working too much and the need to replenish inner resources. I have spent decades looking at how differences between male and female physiology affect singing. I have questioned the commonplace performance of gender and how this can limit health and expression. I am tired of how opera has been framed by the male body. I am sick of Western culture's "take" on a woman's pelvis and her chest.

Beast of Burden

A strong-featured woman with honey-blonde hair and smiling eyes introduces herself from the soft bristle of my front door's welcome mat. Ciara flows from foyer into studio, all the while telling me about her excellent training at a British drama school and her ability to sing in many styles, including opera. Her easy laugh betrays Irish roots. She finishes by handing me one of her CDs.

Ciara has also brought a picture of her vocal cords. On one cord there is what the ear, nose, and throat specialist has called a gelatinous mass. It looks like a small, flat blister. It is preventing Ciara's vocal cords from meeting easily, and so, with each note she sings she applies a little extra force—just under her radar—to guarantee tone and pitch. It is now habit to work a little "louder" or "harder." Employing fine neck muscles to make this happen places further pressure on the mass, and could eventually lead to a polyp or nodes. This incorrect application of effort through the neck and throat is also undermining the balance of her upper and lower resonance. The ENT would like to correct the mass through surgery; I'd like to get to the root of her body's vicious work cycle.

Like many women who come to me in their mid- to late thirties, Ciara suffers from long-term shoulder tension. Over the weeks I

learn just how hard a worker she is. As a core member of an exper-
imental theater collective successfully charting new artistic territory,
Ciara contributes to writing grants, scheduling rehearsals, and orga-
nizing tours. Responsibilities that demand many hours in front of a
computer. A fairly recent neck injury resulting from the demands of
another theater company's aesthetic has also contributed to her vocal
struggles. I think of her chronic upper torso tension patterns as post–
second wave feminist fallout. The chest and shoulders of most of the
women I teach—much like mine, or Madonna's—remind me of Sean
Penn aping a younger man. Armed and rigid. Not enough testosterone to puff up easily ... muscled past sense. Maybe, like Joan of Arc,
we are going to battle for someone else, or wearing men's clothing to
keep ourselves safe in public space. What a lot of work! Work that's
not actually ours.

Oh, to Be a Shrugging Feminist

When I started singing professionally, shoulder pads ran rampant.
Some days I wore as many as three sets—T-shirt layered with sweater,
then coat. To me that looked normal: shoulders dwarfing breasts and
hips. Like other women in the '80s, I was taking on big and public
challenges. The terrain was unfamiliar, frequently perilous, and certainly unfair—and women hadn't yet learned how to support one
another in newly useful ways. Arming the upper torso and girding
the loins felt necessary within a culture not grounded in the feminine,
a culture that still insists on undermining and ignoring the value of a
secure and expressive pelvis ... a pelvis owned by the woman living
in it.

Over one long winter that bled into spring my daughters and I
drove past a billboard featuring a high-heeled, miniskirted female
Santa straddling a massive vodka bottle. It looked like the model would
be "fucked" by its neck if she fell off her stilettos. Each afternoon on
the way home from school the image etched its way more deeply into

me. I began to pull up through my own pelvis to protect myself before rounding that bend in the road. Disrespecting a woman's pelvis does not only stunt the emotional growth of an individual or couple; it warps the sexual development of a whole culture. Maybe it is holding back the evolution of our species.

For all humans a healthy relationship with the pelvic bowl is essential for a healthy breath cycle. Releasing into the pelvis to inspire the receiving of air allows the pelvic basin to become a cushioned foundation for a flexible spine. A spine that is not gripped is a spine that trusts its environment. The sacrum is part of both the pelvis's bony structure and the spinal column; no wonder it's sacred! Together a free pelvis and flexible spine encourage the lungs to inflate *without fear* from bottom to top. The ribcage's magnificent mobility encourages the lungs to feel as if they are floating within the chest. A malleable ribcage supports a soft heart. Courage takes the place of bravery as we learn to "hold our own" without holding on for dear life. No single woman's physiology should have to shoulder the world. No one should have to be Joan of Arc ... or Lady Gaga ... for too long.

When a woman—feminist or not—doesn't remember how to shrug off heroic archetypes, the thoracic and cervical spines lock. This holding prevents the subtle, intrinsic neck muscles from intuitively expressing a wide range of feeling through the vocal cords. A held voice box compromises the quality and variety of sounds available for communication, especially the upper range. Pitch—meant to reflect emotion, not hide it—becomes limited or forced. An impoverished, tightly managed vocal range denies full human expression: we lose the upper sparkle of a silly laugh; the vulnerable sound of sobbing just behind the eyes; excitement or anger's fractured shards. Over time a restricted emotional regime tires us out, puts our cords in harm's way—as well as the muscles and connective tissue of the larynx that regulate their movement. A singer might sound as if she is constantly yelling to get any sound out.

Vocal cords, or folds, are made up of three things: ligament, muscle layered over the ligament, and mucous membrane coating the muscle.

For breath to become sound, vocal cords vibrate against one another. The air that flows through this quickly tremoring action travels up to the sinuses where it gains amplitude through the thrumming of these modest air pockets. Short, thick, and relaxed vocal cords vibrate slowly, sounding low, breathy tones. When pulled long and lean, their vibrations quicken, less air escapes, and when a fine stream moves into the uppermost crevices of the sinuses we get crystalline tone. Head voice—high pitch and resonance—also relies on the vibration of our cords' mucous membrane. Jamming vocal fold against vocal fold forces the underlying muscle to do all the work without the help of this delicate membrane, depriving a singer of renewable acoustic sheen. When this glimmer is gone, it tells me that I haven't managed my resources, that force has trumped balance.

Not My Chest

In opera, the stream of air necessary for balancing light and dark is based on what revered *bel canto* pedagogue Lamperti[*] described as a military chest. This bracing of the ribs provides subglottal pressure, which can lead to a fine, even tone. The origin of this style of singing is based on the physicality of men's voices. Soon after opera was freshly minted in the sixteenth century, female roles were taken over by *castrati:* male singers who were castrated before their voices could break, in order to retain the beauty of their boy soprano range. This practice originated in the Roman Catholic Church as a papal response to St. Paul's edict that women should be silent in matters of worship. Soon after, it was determined obscene for a female to appear onstage, which made *castrati* valuable in both sacred and secular space. Between 1720 and 1730, it is believed that four thousand boys were castrated annually throughout Europe.

---

[*] Giovanni Battista Lamperti (1839–1910) set the golden standard for *bel canto* pedagogy. He was taught by his father, whose method descended from the great *castrato,* composer, and teacher Antonio Bernacchi (1685–1756).

During puberty a boy's vocal cords increase in size to become about two-thirds larger than adult female cords. Hormonal restrictions resulting from castration meant that a *castrato*'s vocal cords remained lean and limber like those of a prepubescent child—allowing for lots of high notes as well as flexibility. His chest became massive as ribs, as well as the long bones of arms and legs and collar, continued to elongate well into adulthood—another hormonal by-product. A *castrato*'s ribcage remained unusually flexible, which meant that his capacity for air, and its management, were extraordinary. The daily training a *castrato* received in church schools was supervised by men and, of course, men wrote the music for religious services as well as operas.

Male lungs are 30 percent larger than female lungs, and due to a male's generally greater upper-chest musculature, engagement with subglottal pressure comes naturally. Subglottal pressure is a feeling of compression within the chest: imagine lifting a heavy object or getting ready to land a punch. By nature the female voice has a little more airiness in its weave than the male voice. Female bodies do not access subglottal pressure—air held between the vocal folds and the base of the trachea—to the same degree as males because females do not have as much natural upper-body muscle mass. Women are also not habituated to saying *no* as directly and unreservedly as men do.

An abundance of air in the female voice—Catherine Deneuve's sultry Chanel No. 5 commercials, Marilyn Monroe's quivering *happy birthday, Mr. President*—signals that a woman is relaxed and receptive ... maybe a soothing or seductive presence ... possibly "ready to please or be pleased." Men unconsciously dose their sound with a little extra air when they want to gain a woman's confidence. By mirroring a woman's breath texture, they mirror women's history of inhabiting nonthreatening vocal patterns—an acoustic tool many of us have used when trying to stay safe in compromised situations. The vocal equivalent of "playing dead."

Subglottal pressure is the opposite of this. Typically a classical singer achieves the sensation of subglottal pressure by judiciously bracing within the upper torso, using the *appoggio di petto*—a lean in the chest—to firm up intercostal muscles: something the ribcage does instinctively when a person yells, hollers, or screams. Press the heels of your hands together just in front of your sternum. That classic female singer pose should make your upper torso feel mighty and competent. The *appoggio* asks for a productive relationship to aggression and drive. It is the physiological antithesis of getting something off the chest, or singing the blues; the opposite of what giving in to fear feels like. The military chest arms us for battle.

As well as playing women, *castrati* performed powerful roles such as generals and kings. Celebrated for vocal prowess onstage, reputed to be tireless lovers offstage, they were the glam rockers of the baroque and rococo eras. But despite the extreme fame of many *castrati*, by the end of the 1700s they were out of fashion. Why? Over the years thousands of young boys died during castration, not from the surgery but from makeshift anesthetic practices; a thumb to the neck was enough to cut off blood flow to the brain by blocking the carotid artery. The surgery had to be incredibly swift …

The threat of death has never stopped us from sacrificing young men to higher causes such as war, but the kind of voice that appeals to a public does change over time. Today, *castrato* roles are sung by mezzo-sopranos or countertenors—baritones who sing virtuosically in an extended upper range we call the *falsetto*. What a tragedy to label the male body's vulnerable crying range "false." Ironic that today women take on men's roles and physiology unconsciously in the public sphere; we are such an excellent point of departure onstage or off.

Justin Time

Justin is a third-year acting student in Humber's theater program. He is tall, intelligent, handsome, and conscientious. His genuine interest in the well-being of his classmates and his ability to laugh at himself soften his privilege. Justin always picks interesting songs; for today's class he has brought in "Guess I'll Hang My Tears Out to Dry" written by Sammy Cahn and Jule Styne in 1944, and made popular by Frank Sinatra.

It's not an easy song. In the introduction its unpredictable melodic line climbs upward at the end of each phrase, just when a singer is running out of air. Two full verses follow in rapid succession, each one beginning with sustained high notes. The bridge takes us unabashedly into the sensitive pocket of a man's boyish sob zone. So even though the words tell us that the protagonist is ready to stop crying over lost love, first he has to weep his way through this song.

I remind Justin that softening to his pelvic floor with each receptive inhale supports any song's challenges. I ask him not to reach for the intervals but to be open simultaneously to resonance above and below—soft behind the eyes as well as through his sternum—available to sob. Suspended between those unarmed tender spots, the song's sophisticated intervals come easily; Justin looks pleasantly surprised to find that they are already part of him. Then the unexpected happens and, wide-eyed, he blurts between the lines of the song, "My pelvis is moving!" *Dry little teardrops.* "My pelvis is moving!" *My little teardrops.* "In small circles!" *Hanging on a stream of dreams.*

It's true—Justin's pelvis has freed. Small ripples are moving up his spine thanks to the easy, released depth of his breath cycle. This physicality is supporting his emotional journey through the song. Feelings are being held and rocked by his pelvis; its freedom is connecting him to his entire being. One of Justin's fellow students tells him that the hair on her arms stood up as he sang. He replies that he didn't know it would be so easy to be on the verge of crying without spilling over.

Hope Chest

Sometimes I feel a wicked pain on the right side of my neck. It starts somewhere under my shoulder blade, pulls around to the front of my collarbone and up under the jawline. I attribute it to several things: working too hard and pushing too fast; taking on responsibility for things I can't change; not expressing what I am ready, or almost ready, to voice. And not crying when I need to.

I have more often than not taken on the work of "guarding relationship" by trying to make everything go well for everyone. I have avoided conflict by staying quiet about my own needs and truth. These traditional ways of being a woman seeped under my skin through shared stories: song lyrics, TV commercials, film plots, novelistic twists carved deep into flesh ... flesh that so easily turns to stone. Learning to be indirect undermined my ability to relate to another woman's aggression, limited my maturation within difficult situations, and stunted my imagination regarding equitable relationships between men and women. Admitting that I wear a flesh-and-bone costume began the rewiring of internal beliefs and external practices, started the process of casting off the heroine's, or maid-warrior's, chest and shoulders.

The well-being of any singer's neck is dependent on the flexibility and freedom of their shoulders as well as their ability to engage with their sternum, the bony plate that runs down the torso's midline, knitting together the front of the ribcage. The neck appears to be separated from the torso by the collarbone or clavicle, the only long bone to lie horizontally in the human body. This important structural bone integrates the shoulder girdle by serving as a strut connecting sternum to scapulae, or shoulder blades. The clavicle is the first bone in the embryo to begin ossifying—at five to six weeks' gestation. And it is the last bone in the body to finish ossification, usually between twenty-one and twenty-five years of age. The layer of fascia covering the clavicle stimulates the ossification of adjacent tissue; how much we shoulder affects the formation of this bone's compact shell.

Muscle, fascia, and connective tissue are all influenced by thought. They, in turn, affect the alignment of the skeleton, and in the case of the clavicle, the actual growth of that bone. Our childhood and teenage responses to life can shape the clavicle, just as they form our personality. Bearing the weight of the world or taking on too much responsibility too soon can change us structurally.

The shape of this bone tells who I am and what I have experienced. The responsibility of running my father's business from the age of nineteen years to twenty-one, shouldering huge sacks of flour to prove to my employees that I could carry my own weight (almost exactly), transformed my skeletal structure. These patterns underpinned my approach to singing and partnering. My tendency to carry the world on my shoulders was noted by my close friend Eve as I walked to the podium to deliver my father's eulogy.

It does not surprise me that the clavicle varies more than most other long bones in the human body. In a skeleton, clavicular form is used as a criterion for sex determination. In males it is thick and curved; the sites where muscle attaches are pronounced. In females it is thinner, smoother, and lighter. In a bird it is the wishbone.

Transitional Shoulders and Chests

I have worked with gender diverse students, including transgender men and women, some of whom come to me because their voices are changing and they want assistance or accompaniment while moving into uncharted vocal terrain.

When someone assigned male at birth takes the necessary hormones to transition to an estrogen dominant physiology, their chest and shoulder muscles soften, and their airflow becomes breathier. When someone assigned female at birth becomes testosterone dominant, two major things happen that affect the voice: their chest and shoulders become more muscled, which intensifies airflow; and their vocal cords go through puberty, become larger, and deepen in pitch. But the cartilage in the larynx does not enlarge correspondingly, which can cause vocal cords to sound "boxed in." These things are neither good nor bad; they are simply what can happen.

Observing the effects of hormonal change on structure has helped me support vocal freedom and connectedness during a student's transformations. Spending time with transitioning students has made me less worried about noting differences between male and female physiology while affirming gender diversity as part of the human appetite for integrity and fluidity.

No More Armor

Traditional operatic values promote a performance aesthetic that is not drawn from unmediated female physiological experience. Until recently, there have been few female librettists or composers. Those currently venturing into opera tend toward the traditional classical voice, a voice that is not rooted in the authorial female body. The foundation of a woman's *bel canto* technique is biased toward a biological reality that is more male than female with regard to muscular structure, hormonal makeup, and emotional expression. Inhabiting its rules affects how a woman feels when she opens her mouth to sing in rehearsal or onstage.

The integration of chest and pelvis is tangible in the sounds a female's body makes when climaxing during orgasm or while giving birth—deeply creative acts that require both *give* and *take*. Still, it is far too easy to misuse my chest as an unconscious response to being a woman in this day and age. It breaks my heart that women don't start from a place where our *no* is believed and understood. That we have had to work so hard to be heard in the first place. But constant puffing up and bracing do not lead to honest, flexible expression from a woman's—or a man's—or any human body. I wish our culture respected transparency, fragility, the sorrow spot, humor, and ductility in everyone.

We all deserve to inhabit a pelvis that is not constantly simmering in *fight or flight*. Finding airflow that is founded in the pelvis's patience, freedom, and strength helps me let go of what is reactive or locked down in my upper body, releases my coping patterns of strong-arming through chest and throat. We need to find an authentic *no* that does not overwork the vocal cords or shoulder girdle but comes from an honored, earthy pelvis. For the chest to soften and the pelvis to come to life, the rigidity of the military chest needs to yield and swagger, not simply work and defend.

In singing, as well as in life, there are other ways to find narrow, predictable, firm airflow from behind the sternum to access full range. Trusting my body's own sweet time sings me out of neck tension and into what I have to say … recovers my full-gender self.

22

Slipper Camp Six—
Core in Place of Armor

FORTY MINUTES INTO Slipper Camp I remind my students that today I led into our lowest range—"What the fluff!"—by asking how many years each of them had been "performing." One said six, another seventeen, and a third twenty-five, charting their onstage careers. Others offered thirty-six or forty-three, measuring their time on the planet. In all, there are more than two hundred performance years in this room! I then asked them to pretend that this was "day one" with regard to "performance" and that there was no agenda, no need to succeed. I want everyone to be clear about how we accessed *release* before introducing *productivity* and *core.*

"Not 'performing' affected the quality of your airflow, which made a big difference in your emotional tone and acoustic presence. Next we brought more light into the Lower Fluffs. How?"

No one seems to remember. Bringing light into the lowest pitches is new for some of them. I demonstrate singing a low note with ample resonant space throughout my sinuses by opening my eyes, lifting my eyebrows, and floating everything inside my head above the jaw hinge higher and higher until I resemble a zany. They remember the feeling in their own face and head, look ready to expose a shameless capacity for fun and joy—*not through the artifice of a smile but the inner unfolding of "awe."* This upper shine might appear unnecessary for low notes, but over time the light accompanying dark will become normal and sustainable, lead to less physical effort and easier projection, even in the basement of the voice.

"What about Double Fluff? How did we manage to hold a love of gravity—the sigh of relief—while maintaining our newfound love of levity, over and over and over again?"

I shrug my shoulders ever so slightly to remind them of what they already know. "You invited a natural, minuscule shrug into the tricky balancing of Upper and Lower Fluff in the midrange. This shrug helps us to not 'care too much' by softening the back of the neck, which in turn means that the muscles and cartilage that control pitch can do their own thing. When we don't arm the chest we allow the ebb and flow of the upper lungs to become the wave upon which our shoulders crest. Just like the sigh of relief. A less performative body learns to trust its desire for, and ability to, balance. The cords act in accordance with themselves."

The little shrug helps soften the divide between head voice and chest voice—between mind and body. We have been shouldering this culturally constructed separation physically, and spiritually, for generations. Bringing light into the voice is not only about the mechanics of opening the sinuses and lifting, or better yet, unfolding, the soft palate's ten muscles. It is the practice of delight within real life. Plumbing the depths of a voice is not a pushing down into lower resonance but a "dropping in" to inhabit the darker, more shadowy aspects of ourselves. As a singer I thrive when I embrace the subtle, tangible paradox of light and dark resonance cohabitating.

I laugh while saying, "This is less of a stretch when I remember that my head is actually part of my body!"

One of the dancers smiles at this. She understands exactly what I mean and how much work it takes to reintroduce the head to the body as a practiced aesthetic.

I sum up for my students: "The theme of today's refinements has been to follow the body rather than trying too hard. Not performing has helped balance 'inside and outside' as well as 'light and dark.' Let's look at balancing another perceived dichotomy. Without losing any of our recently practiced *rest and digest*, I want to introduce a dose of *fight or flight* to make our sound productive, and the top of the voice more brilliant. As a by-product, this will also encourage a natural elongation of your tone.

"When we access direction and movement from behind the sternum, it feels like vitality, virility, oomph, drive—life force! To find this touch of *fight or flight* within our sound, without losing the openness of 'sad' or 'glad,' I propose a bit of 'mad.' Let's corral vocal sound through singing the word *no*."

Just hearing that word causes everyone to widen their stances and square their shoulders.

"No! Not like that! That *no* is old-fashioned, heroic, and adversarial. It undoes all the fluff we have just become so good at. To maintain openness, I would like to replace that 'arming' action with the physical practice of 'core.'"

I ask my students to narrow their stance back to walking width. We shrug our shoulders and yawn a few times. Wobble.

"Now think of something that you would like to say *no* to. Not the most difficult thing you can imagine standing up to … maybe number five on your list! Use this thought to access healthy aggression."

A few balk at the word *aggression*. "*Nothing ever makes me mad!*"

"Aggression does not have to lead to violence. Think of its energetic imprint as productive—necessary for survival.

"Some of you saw *The Girl with No Door on Her Mouth*. During its development I worked with Anne Carson to find the right dramaturgical order for her texts. When I became stuck as to what should come next, she asked me, 'Is this moment *bound* or *unbound*?' Her use of these two nonjudgmental words offered an intellectually unprejudiced way for me to name and understand counterbalancing energies. Using them now can help us physiologically with our singing practice.

"*Unbound* in the voice comes from fully investigating the released movement of breath into and out of the lungs, and through the trachea, mouth, and sinuses. Soft feelings like delight behind the eyes or compassion in the chest help us do this naturally. To find *bound* we need to access the tougher, energetic feeling of aggression ... without prejudice or dogma."

We rarely see anger used in proportion, as an effective, even force. We so often deny our own until utterly provoked or at the end of our rope. I change my tack: "Have you ever felt angry on someone else's behalf?"

A murmur of appreciation swarms through the group.

"Okay! Take that energy and, without losing the fluff above and below, bring the ability to say *no* right behind your sternum. To help us locate it, let's place our fingertips down that bony plate's centerline while singing."

Their next long tone's volume triples.

"Did you hear how much sound spilled into this room? You are all louder and yet none of you is trying to be louder."

The class's sound became clear without harshness or shrillness creeping in. Staying open in the head while not pushing or "placing" sound into the mask allowed each singer's upper resonators to become optimal natural amplifiers. Our human ability to stand ground, to resist, to draw a line narrowed the airflow below the vocal cords, making it less wasteful and more effective. And no one gripped or censored through the throat.

"We understand *no* from within. Let's sing it again—for ourselves—with the passion of a two-year-old."

They jump in, gleefully aping a toddler's tantrum, but this *no* comes out as rigid and forced.

"Yes, you heard right! Your sound was not as beautiful or free. The human desire to go after something once we have tasted it can cause guaranteeing through pushing, though maybe my toddler image was a little too provoking ...? Either way, let's add in a little swagger. Follow me!"

I stand up and walk across the room while channeling as much John Travolta as I can stand. My weight is dropped through my legs, and my shoulder girdle rolls side to side like the deck of a ship—pectoral muscles and ribcage articulating loosely around my sternum.

"Do you know the meaning of the word *virile*? It starts with the same two letters as vital, vivacious, and vigorous. Things full of life force—*vita*! Potency, power, and drive are necessary for life—important to understand so they do not rule unconsciously and perilously.

"The word *virile* has been linked to a man's life-giving potency more than a woman's. Let's invent a female equivalent. Something more active than fecund. *How about ferile?* Not feral—a domesticated animal gone wild—but a word that brings together a woman's power and fertile creativity. *Ferile!* Maybe new language will encourage soft pelvic undulations to underpin the swagger of an expansive chest—for all bodies. Receive air right down to your pelvis and then feel it ripple up through ribcage and sternum as you walk. Let this subtle spinal wave come to fruition in a malleable shoulder girdle. Flaunt your aliveness!"

I love watching the play in the studio as each person sees just how much self-confident, juicy, full-bodied swagger they can rustle up.

"Please come back to the piano. For *no* to be potent we need strength and suppleness to get to know one another. Yes, it feels sexy. You found it while walking, so now let's find it while standing still. Return your right-hand fingers to the midline of your sternum, lifting your breastbone toward their tips. Stretch your left arm wide and encourage a backward lean into your thoracic spine. Now sing a long tone."

The sound that results from the combination of these opposing actions is strong, flexible, and repeatable—anchored in the chest and supported through the back.

"Fantastic! You are learning to build and tolerate subglottal pressure—the air pressure between your vocal cords and the base of your sternum—without overly hardening the muscles of your shoulders and neck."

Normally when exhaling we collapse through chest and mouth as our lungs release air. A singer's art involves staying expansive and flexible when airways should be getting smaller due to diminishing airflow.

"Let's bring in one more idea with regard to *no*. Let's actively imagine that expressing *no* on your own behalf is a good idea."

This return to my original instruction is still greeted with skepticism and confusion. A self-centered *no* is unfamiliar, taboo, out of reach. Selfish.

"Please tell me some of the things you are trying to say *no* to."

No to overtime.
No to sugar.
No to my mother.
No to lying to myself.
No to my partner.
No to self-criticism.
No to climate change.

With each person's *no* the rest of the group nods in appreciation and support, reminding us that *no* can be an especially good idea for one's physical and mental health.

During Grade Nine my younger daughter cried a lot. It is a difficult time for young women in our culture. Maturing sexually introduces pubescent girls to the subtle inconsistencies and inequalities that adult women are subjected to daily. In addition, Oksana's living circumstances changed when her father downsized, and she and her sister were now with me full time. My partner and his sons had moved into our home, and much as it was exciting, my own stress stopped me from listening well to Oksana. Evening after evening there seemed to be a fresh crisis. I wondered what she had to complain about and wanted the tears and tantrums to stop. One day I managed to step back from the situation. I realized that Oksana should not have to work so hard to be heard. That if her "mad" were more welcome, maybe her "sad" would not have to work overtime. No one should have to be loud to get a fair hearing.

"Now that we have *permission, flexibility,* and *balance* within the *no,* let's invite *ease.*"

Whether large and painful or small and quiet, sharing feelings and experiences needs time, space, and sound. It shouldn't take extra energy to sing a valid *no,* whether in response to a sexist society or a parent's stress.

"The word *no* starts with a *bound* consonant—*nnnnnn.* As you form your *nnnnnn,* note that the front of your tongue presses gently against your hard palate, just behind your upper teeth. How firm and confident that little seal feels! And still, it vibrates like a hummed *mmmmm.* Feel how alive that sensation is as it moves down through your tongue, past its root, along the front of your throat, through your voice box, finally slipping down your windpipe to just behind your sternum. It is a subtle, ephemeral line—but it *is* there. I don't think the easy *bound* feeling of *nnnnnn* is an accident. How many languages start their *no* with this *nnnnnn* sound?"

The group offers *non, nein, nyet, não,* and *ne.* I check online after class and see that 58 of 108 language groups—primarily Indo-European—start their word for *no* with an *nnnnnn: neyn, nee, nenni, nei, ni, nu, nā, nei, nej, nie, naj, nanni, nann, nao, nem* ... The vibrancy of this consonant is a deeply satisfying way to connect with the inner, fleshy sensation of core. It helps us hold our own through simple tongue action; it calms and soothes through its finely drawn physiological line.

"Let's hold *no* as *possibility.* Sing your long tones with space above and below, combined with that little binding just behind the sternum, near the base of your trachea. Enjoy this complex mix of sad, mad, and glad. Don't let your throat constrict by trying too hard, by thinking you won't be heard. As you get to know this way of managing your resources, double-check that your fourth eye is still soft. The anal sphincter understands what you need with regard to grounding and need not become uptight or rigid when you say *no.* So don't brace or apologize when standing your ground."

We sing released, productive tones, eventually leaving the word *no* behind for the vowel *aaaaah.* We cover one and a half octaves from the low D up to the A just above middle C, arriving at the doorway to the *upper passaggio.*

"Just before entering kindergarten, each of my daughters independently discovered the phrase 'You are not the boss of me!' It made me want to laugh, but I didn't, as I could see how important it was for them to push back at their mother, and succeed—try things their own way. And in early adolescence when their *no* became even louder, I thought it a sensible response to the world around them and their place in it.

"At seventeen my oldest had her first boyfriend—a friendly and talented young man who we all liked. As their relationship progressed, she began to feel limited, was afraid she wouldn't have room to grow. Magda broke up with him with respect and a firm *no*, though he continued to haunt her high school for several more weeks, wanting her to change her mind. I picture his athletic six feet towering over her five-feet-four frame.... But she stood her ground."

From the word *no* comes the word *yes*. If I can say *no*, my *yes* is of value. If these words are mine I can make decisions. I can offer and share ... or not.

You can say *no*. I will be able to understand this. I will be able to rise to both your *yes* and *no* with all my heart.

23

Permission to Scream

A GROUP OF powerhouse women come regularly to my Wednesday morning voice class: a midwife, an award-winning jazz pianist, an expert in transformational play, an entrepreneur who manages artists' business affairs, a PhD candidate in voice and community choir, an English professor, and a rabbi. Ba-dum-ba.

We do laugh a lot. But for all the laughing—sides-splitting, tear-rolling guffaws—we are not telling jokes. We are submerging ourselves under the joke and tinkering with the engines that fuel and preserve our lives by messing with our breath patterns. Some of us have decided that the way our lives and bodies have been—*the way we were conditioned to be*—is not good enough anymore: a way of life masking a way of death. Besides being women, we have a few other essential things in common: we are driven, educated, and pioneering. In each class we use our bodies to hold up the mirror to one another. We listen and make sound in ways that feel new.

Sarah has bitten off more than she thinks she can chew. She has a husband, three girls under the age of ten, and a business that recently took up residence in one of Toronto's Centres for Social Innovation, and she still makes time to give her friends tins of homemade holiday cookies or loose-leaf chai. Right now she is preparing a concert of a dozen songs woven with personal stories. The performance, in two months, is the "extra" that is pushing Sarah over her edge. She does not want to give up on this "self-ish" creative challenge but can't imagine juggling it all till the end of spring. She arrives each week on the verge of tears, tired and overwhelmed.

Sarah tells us that this morning she shared a funny moment with her husband when he told her that he needed their vehicle for the day. Tongue in cheek she wailed, "But how will I be able to drive the kids to university, on my own, without the van?" Two of their girls are still in primary school, and the third in diapers. Sarah and her nervous system are used to planning ahead ... at times, mounting a campaign.

For close to ten years, Sarah has been slipping out of the ballet armor she adopted as a child. She is now coaxing herself away from her need to do everything extremely well for everyone else. These ongoing transformations have been aided by her wicked sense of humor and peaceful gray eyes. The softness of Sarah's eyes reminds me how much her voice has melted into her body. Even a Britney Spears tune becomes intimate and soulful in her mouth.

Within the safe culture of this Wednesday morning class, Sarah's long tones match the piano's cues. Her voice shudders and quakes, a messiness that is perfectly productive. Emotional curves call out, mapping animal pitch. I suggest that she follow her bewildered and exhausted voice tone after tone after tone. She backs into the wall, where there is nothing left to do but lean and lean ... and lean some more. Fully yielding into its solid support, she howls herself down to the ground. Crouching, she lets loose sounds that shake my insides. Sarah is a creature in full-blown mourning. She follows her voice way, way up into her soprano without losing the warmth of her chest—intuitively stepping through each floor of her unique, personal vocal house. When she finishes, the air in the studio continues to vibrate.

The other Sarah in today's group looks deeply touched and a little wobbly despite her competent, six-foot stature. Sarah H. is a tenured professor of English and serves on many committees. She has a husband and two small boys and still manages to arrive each week in groovy, idiosyncratic garb. If she were sixteen and I twelve, I would have a crush on her.

At the start of today's class I had been talking about the idea of having each other's backs. I was trying to understand why women are not more supportive of one another, why feminism seems to have failed with regard to fostering sorority. "Why do we remain competitive with one another over the most basic matters?" I had been thinking about a particularly gifted performer who studies with me and wondered why her adrenal glands—which sit on the kidneys—get so fired up when she performs despite the fact that few dancer/singers are her equal. After each performance the ribs in her lower back ache. In my body this is where I feel adrenaline's first surge during *fight or flight* and cortisol's corrosive leak when in chronic stress. I, too, have had achy adrenals at the end of a performance.

I want Sarah H. to step into the fruitful window of her wobbliness. I ask her longtime friend Mary to stand behind her and place both hands at the base of Sarah's ribcage—no pressure, just presence. I witness Sarah H. yield into herself, echoing the first Sarah's use of the wall's external, tangible support. I remind Sarah H. not to lift up through her neck while singing—no striving for pitch. Striving can sound prim, so I describe the feeling of bloom in the female voice, encourage Sarah H. to focus on the back of her body, to take the responsibility of making sound away from her mouth, her articulators. Leaning back, Sarah H. sends forth with her voice, utters undefended cry after undefended cry with each subsequent rising pitch. Her voice's ebb and flow is mercurial. When she breaks into her high soprano, rage and beauty combine unabashedly. The complexity of her over- and undertones is stunning. For the third time in my life I feel my hips unlock physically through hearing a woman scream: not from fear, but in concordance.

Sarah H. says two things when she is done. She tells us of the joy she felt in making pure sound—and how completely different that feels from the precision of articulating words. She also reveals the betrayal and lack of support she has experienced within the academic world—in particular when collaborating with other women.

I respond with a story. "The other morning as I drove past a private school in Toronto, I saw a group of boys celebrate a really good move on the soccer field. Slapping backs and butts, they celebrated each other's prowess and virtuosity. Their happy slapping stayed with me: the sureness of it, the lack of team lines when celebrating accomplishment despite the competition at hand. In my own teenage experience there was no equivalent to these boys' unreserved delight in one another's success."

Queen of the Night

Screaming is an unreserved sound. Its complex texture is molded from a density of acoustic frequencies. I imagine small scraps of flesh behind my nose and at the back of my mouth where soft palate meets nasal passageway, as well as my false vocal cords in the throat rubbing together like vocal folds. When these spaces vibrate simultaneously, ringing through numerous inner air pockets, we produce multiphonics, or multiple pitches. A scream. The intense abandon of screaming is something that an operatic soprano knows, but in her world that acoustic energy doesn't fracture poignantly or stratify recklessly as it does in Janis Joplin's; it stays knit together in a more reasoned and manageable pattern.

Mozart's opera *The Magic Flute* gravitates around one of the greatest virtuosic screamers of all time: the Queen of the Night. Her stratospheric intervals have made it into cartoons, capturing the imagination of kids as well as adults. But the rage within her storied sound is rarely understood or passed down as something to learn from.

When Mozart began composing *The Magic Flute*, the Queen of the Night was envisaged as a good character. Partway through the opera's development its producer decided that the queen should be recast as evil so the male lead could hold ultimate moral authority, thus satisfying his, and Mozart's, shared Masonic beliefs. When the curtain rises we learn that the queen's husband has just died. Rather than passing the absolute power that comes with the Circle of the Sun to his widow, the king leaves it to Sarastro, the High Priest of the Temple of Wisdom. So great is Sarastro's mistrust of the feminine that he steals away the queen's daughter, Princess Pamina, to prevent mother from corrupting daughter. The opera's drama lies in the exiled queen's failed attempts to wrestle her daughter back from Sarastro. As the curtain falls we are given the impression that everything in the kingdom is back in order through the low, majestic ring of Sarastro's final aria.

Between the rise and fall of red velvet, well before the opera's cover-up ending, the queen sings two fiendishly difficult arias. In the first act's "O zittre nicht," she persuades the young knight Tamino to bring her daughter Pamina back home, initiating the opera's heroic quest. In the second act's "Der Hölle Rache," the queen tries to force Pamina to kill Sarastro, who now has Tamino on his side. When her daughter refuses, the queen vows to disown her. That's how angry she is.

The Austrian coloratura soprano Diana Damrau sings this role without reservation. In the UK's Royal Opera House production, the queen's hairline is shaved ferociously high, giving Damrau an imposing, terrifying countenance. Her movements are imperial and certain. Launching into the Act Two aria, energy ripples up her spine as she steels herself to sing with razor-sharp precision.

Mozart was inspired by the incredibly high and agile upper register of his sister-in-law, the remarkable singer Josepha Hofer. Composer Ignaz von Seyfried wrote that on December 4, 1791, five weeks into the opera's successful first run, Mozart—on his deathbed—whispered to his wife, Constanze, "Quiet, quiet! Hofer is just taking her top F—now my sister-in-law is singing her second aria, 'Der Hölle Rache'; how strongly she strikes and holds the B-flat: *'Hört! hört! hört! der Mutter Schwur!'*"* At the end of his life Mozart is not thinking about Sarastro, the enlightened despot† who triumphs at the end of *Magic Flute,* but of the queen and the impeccable rage she is voicing to implore her daughter to kill this thief.

---

* "Hear, hear, hear, a mother's oath."

† Enlightened monarchs embraced the principles of the Enlightenment, especially its emphasis upon rationality. It was implicit that the sovereign knew the interests of his subjects better than they themselves; his responsibility to them thus precluded their political participation.

Mozart has provided a demanding musical container for the high sopranos capable of filling it—resolve marrying brilliance, flexibility reveling in righteous joy. I am grateful to him for not pulling any vocal punches. The queen's incredibly high and truthful tessitura is about prowess. She *should* call loudly on the gods of revenge—retain her power with or without her husband. No woman should ever be put in this humiliating position. Thank you Diana Damrau for sharing your highest little girl peeps—notes designed to competently scream out fear and outrage as well as squeals of delight—reminding all women that we have the means to rage against a thieving old man. That we can do it without shame.

I don't want to kill my father or be estranged from my mother, but maybe it's time to murder the thoughts and energies that imprisoned them and are certainly lodged inside me—thoughts and behaviors that I have passed on to my daughters without ever meaning to. Why not pass on "Permission to Scream"? Offer acoustic backup to my female descendants as support for their evolution.

Thank you Mozart for raising the hairs on the back of my neck.

Pop Princess

Richard Armstrong and I have spent two intense hours working on the vocal lines from Louis Dufort and Tom Walmsley's opera *Julie Sits Waiting*. Now perched with his husband, Steve, around their kitchen island, we are waiting for the chicken to finish roasting, glass of wine in hand. Unwinding with the sauvignon's soft decay.

Steve glances down at his cell phone and inhales sharply. "Whitney Houston is dead! I have to call my mother." He heads upstairs without making eye contact with either of us. Richard and I sit in silence in their Jersey City flat, minutes away from Whitney's birthplace. Two voice teachers quietly absorbing the death of a blockbuster singer.

Steve comes back down to the kitchen. Eyes glued to iPhone, he explains that the loss of any Black performer is a blow to the African American community. Steve was born in the United States shortly after his parents emigrated from Trinidad. He loves British punk bands like Siouxsie and the Banshees. British-born Richard, whose ancestors hail from the north of England, has had a passion for soul music for five decades. My fascination with pop is far more recent, but Whitney is someone we all grew up beside.

For the next several days Whitney's voice dominates the airwaves. Borderless, it catches a ride back to Toronto, suffusing my every thought. Between the following week's classes I watch countless videos of her megahit "I Will Always Love You." A fan has posted footage from Whitney's 2010 comeback tour: the Birmingham concert. Ragged and wild, the once-polished pop princess sings with gusto, her off-kilter vocals and unpredictable pitch matched by the jerky moves of this fan's smartphone. Whitney wheezes, catches her breath; the audience whoops and hollers. When a few individuals heckle she comes to a full stop, yells back, teases hard, flirts with danger, grandstands. Nothing puts her off.

That night I stay up way past my bedtime gathering the threads of her vocal legacy. Whitney's mother and aunt were famous gospel singers. At eleven she took on this inheritance and began to sing as a soloist in her father's church. The rage and joy of religious fervor groomed her extraordinary voice, cultivating a wide range, flexible tone, and impressive ornamentation. Producer Clive Davis promoted a commercial singing style that helped Whitney thrill without threatening. Whitney's pop diva persona and pyrotechnics not only crossed over into mainstream radio; they set the standard for modern R & B singing.

A week has passed and I am not ready to let Whitney go. Her singing of Dolly Parton's "I Will Always Love You" weaves in and out of each morning's early haze. Eyes closed in the comfort of my bed, I picture the original 1992 poster for *The Bodyguard*, her dusky face strategically hidden behind Kevin Costner's white one. Only a few years before, Whitney had been booed at the 1989 Soul Train Music Awards for being too white. That same night she met fellow singer and R & B sensation Bobby Brown, whom she married just before the release of *The Bodyguard*, possibly as a way to reclaim her African American audience. Whitney and Bobby make for a spectacularly combustible couple, and over the years pictures of an increasingly unkempt and emaciated Whitney haunt the tabloids. Her drug use is blamed on Bobby and she falls hard from celebrity grace ... stops singing. This last detail opens my eyes.

What would have happened if Whitney had sung her way robustly through her forties and into her fifties? What would I have learned through witnessing Whitney reckon with herself, come to terms with her story, sing her truth? Did she miss singing during the year the tabloids say she never got out of her pajamas? Why wasn't this pop diva allowed to mature?

I return to YouTube's countless live versions of "I Will Always Love You." In some performances I notice that the chorus sounds very high. What notes is Whitney singing, anyhow? The G, G-sharp, and A. I check them out in my voice and on the piano, and I see that sometimes she sings these lowest notes of her "head voice" as if there is only the "little girl" in them. Pure and angelic ... completely unrooted. Other times those first three notes are all scream, until the word *you*, when she loses her grounding again. She is either disconnected and gleaming or overly tethered and abrasive, unable to integrate through this volatile vocal terrain. She unravels even as she rules my aural sphere.

I want to weep. Whitney does not know how to hold on to core with aplomb in the way women of just one generation before did. Early Etta James never disconnected from her gut, even beyond those notes; she barreled through, using earthy humor as leavening. Aretha Franklin screamed and cooed her dark and light into relationship, no apology for being a force of nature. Going back another generation, Sarah Vaughan negotiated those in-between notes with warmth and flexibility, and Ella Fitzgerald used unself-conscious sass to balance her reliable ballast.

I shape my thoughts about the sustainable female voice while puzzling over Whitney. Another famously gifted singer shares vocal territory with Whitney in this specific range: Billie Holiday. Nearing the end of her career Billie's unanswered "little girl" whines broadcast the thin scratch of addiction. The cracks in Whitney's vocal scaffolding through the middle of her voice, where little girl and strong woman meet, betray how difficult it is to integrate dualities ... almost impossible once substances compromise inner wiring.

Fantasizing a Whitney who sings through the cauldron of menopause, I morph her into a woman capable of holding her own within the pressures of family, race, and celebrity. But I am being naive. Two recent documentary films tell us that her drug use began at the age of ten, well before Bobby Brown. They state that one of her aunts may have abused her, and reveal an ambiguous sexual identity that would have been difficult for a mainstream audience to accept in the '80s. And what if Whitney's voice hadn't been co-opted in church before puberty, and by record executives soon after? I mean, is it even possible for an eleven-year-old girl to survive being groomed by her matriarchal line to turn her emotions inside out in service of her father's house of worship? What if the way she sang publicly had been fully her choice ... and shaped in adulthood rather than childhood? How much commodification can a single body withstand?

It is not easy to sing in front of others. Studies from America's National Institutes of Health point out that female singers are affected more adversely by professional performance than males. I know what these measurable chemical and hormonal "storms and drains" feel like in my own body. Is it the technique we try to adopt: the military chest versus a deeper understanding of how the female ribcage works; the tidying of our upper resonators to make pain and sorrow sound beautiful; the lack of respect for the female pelvis and its essential role, that of birthing breath through receptivity? *Does interpreting male-centric stories through body and breath damage our cells on a deep, generative level?*

The three notes Whitney struggles with in "I Will Always Love You"—the G, G-sharp, and A—are the exact notes that kept vanishing in my own voice when I was twenty-six and going through a divorce. I was dismantling a social structure that didn't serve me and I was alone—none of my other friends had married, let alone separated, and my family was a family that did not condone the breaking of this powerful social and religious structure. I was, in fact, divorcing my parents and their beliefs. Furthermore, without a firm emotional core or a spiritual sense of sustainable light, I was measuring up even while walking away from the measuring stick. Although those notes came back after work with my mentor, Richard, they would not be truly mine until my mid-fifties when I was ready—finally—to integrate physiological and temperamental dualities within a story line of my own imagining.

I wish my mother had taught me how and when to scream rather than how to honor institutions. I believe I would have sung for different reasons. What else would I have done differently?

The Monday after my return from Jersey City my women's choir and I discuss Whitney's inability to save herself despite her adeptness as a singer. As our conversation draws to a close Ciara reveals that she will find it hard to begin the next few weeks without choir; I am traveling to Whitehorse and Regina and have canceled two rehearsals. To soften the blow we sing a short concert, just for us, beginning with "Tom Traubert's Blues" (Tom Waits). We continue through "Motherless Child" (traditional), "Suzanne" (Leonard Cohen), and "Tell Me More" (Billie Holiday). We shine light onto dark terrain while searching for balance in our vocal technique. We use breath to expand the space between hip flexors and sacrum; we flow and swirl through the wet feminine; each melody finds home in our cells. We touch on loss and flare in anger. We bear these stories together and then get them out of our systems. We have each other's backs while doing so. The air between us shifts into the ecstatic. A shared experience as beautiful as the sounds we're making.

24

Joy Is Hard to Own

WHEN I AM *in this body*—primary, potent, and ripe—joy floods in, and with it, the optimism that being fully alive summons. I have not always felt this way. In candid shots from my twenties I am often frowning; publicity photos from that time project a jaded ennui. I am sure this affected tone felt more truthful than happiness, but today I see how distanced I was from myself. I tucked my sadness into mournful material, misused my energetic core by keeping a lid on vulnerability, and armed myself against the world in place of yielding into support.

Pimping out this unintegrated version of my emotions as a performer resulted in "toughness" becoming part of my artistic identity. If I'd gotten past my adaptive response of tightening in the throat to silence crying, I might have felt the relief of weeping. Had I taken the time to feel my own brokenness, identified with its high-keening brilliance, I could have more easily accessed my top end. But instead of welcoming and moving through my feelings, I sang with a low ceiling.

Human sinuses resonate such brilliance that opening them up is risky. The first time a grown man or woman feels these resonators vibrate, he or she may be reminded of things long tamped down: the echo of a baby crying, the inconsolable whimper of a sibling or friend, the screechy top of a mother's voice—sounds meant to jangle the nervous system for good reason. This space may have become habitually boarded up due to humiliation or danger: girls are not taken seriously when they shed tears; boys get beaten up for crying.

A German expression describes crying as "peeing through the eyes." Of course this isn't meant literally. However, loss of control behind the eyes can map through the genitals; a breakthrough into the crying zone can trigger the need to urinate. One of my students remembers standing next to a billowing white curtain sometime before the age of one. Bright golden light poured over her through the open window. She was being toilet-trained and as she began to pee, far from her potty, her mother pricked her finger with a pin to stop the flow. The shock of that pain caused this student to grip throughout her body, not just stop the flow of urine. This story surfaced during a lesson in which we were trying to wake up her upper resonators. Sharing it helped reclaim the upper shine of her voice—allow for its emotional incontinence. There are many good and concrete reasons to avoid parts of our anatomy for fear of self-betrayal or punishment.

How do we lighten the fragile, tender place between our eyebrows—the place that is necessary for tears of sorrow or joy?

Mary, a social activist who uses "play" to provide large-group trauma relief, strides across the studio before bringing her tall, slender body to an abrupt halt next to my piano. She blurts to the class that last week she went home wondering why I had been lifting my eyebrows so relentlessly, why I kept winking at her and cracking jokes. She was certain that she had been reflecting this back to me. When Mary looked in the mirror later that evening to see what her features were actually doing, she saw that nothing was moving under her cap of tight, dark curls.

Muscles on our face can be lifted voluntarily—imagine a faked smile, or forced nod of reassurance. And there are muscles, especially those that soften around the eyes, that are accessed involuntarily, brightening when we feel genuinely delighted, surprised, loved, or loving. Because a person's voice is designed to transmit feeling, the emotional state of a close friend reveals itself in the split second she answers the phone. If she is happy her voice sounds open, vulnerable. Delighted eyes and cheeks verging on a laugh lead to a natural lift of the soft palate and an organic opening of the sinuses. The joyful ring that emerges is the light necessary to access the *chiaro** part of singing. Engineering the cheek muscles or eyebrows into place is not enough. Something fun or funny needs to flit through the frontal lobe to *crack us up.* This is what I was "playing" at with Mary the week before.

I look past Mary and the four other women in today's group. My eyes come to rest on Richard Herman's pigment-saturated painting of a bodhisattva: a wisdom-being motivated by great compassion to achieve enlightenment. Richard's brushstrokes make visible this bodhisattva's noble energetic alignment. I draw the class's attention to the orange and fuchsia rays spreading up from her crown into the heavens.

I tell the group that in my mid-forties I began to crave light. Wishing to release "drama's" intense grip on my emotional makeup I chopped off my dark, dyed locks and bleached my remaining gray hair platinum. Rising up out of each forward bend in yoga class, brightness fluttered about my head. I admitted the fear felt decades before while singing in a class with my teacher Richard Armstrong, repeatedly pealing *Help!* using Snow White's high, piercing tones. I began in earnest to cast aside darkness's deeply grooved furrows by reveling in the upward float of my eyes, cheekbones, and soft palate. While singing, the open feeling in my sinuses became practically orgasmic—partnered instinctually with the growing space in my throat.

I pull out the music for "Good Morning Heartache" and place it on the piano's lectern. It is an architectural wonder of the song world composed by Irene Higginbotham, Ervin Drake, and Dan Fisher, and made popular by Billie Holiday at the end of World War II. Its emotional bones are solid. I sing the word *good* on middle C and the *mor-* of *morning* on the G above. The group sings back this span of five notes sounding neither sorrowful nor joyful but open-minded like the interval itself.

---

* The Italian word for lightness or clarity. In *bel canto* singing it comes from the concept of *chiaroscuro,* a term borrowed from Renaissance painting to refer to the interdependence of light and shadow.

We place *heartache* on the minor third that follows, and trace *old gloomy sight*'s downward melodic pull with the lightest touch. The second line greets *heartache* by lifting the *mor-* of *good morning* up a full sixth from *good*'s middle C. This wider interval asks our voices to ring optimistically within an exquisitely productive part of the female voice. Despite our competence, we teeter between crying and laughing.

The curves of this unfolding melody invite singer and listener into emotion's present tense. Engaging with a song's sighs and inflections processes feeling, explores and highlights the way the human voice expresses states of being. "Good Morning Heartache" cradles sorrow as an integrated part of being alive; it traces recognizable emotional grooves and then moves through them. Today's group releases into full-throttled whining at the peak of each verse, and passes through a solid temper tantrum when singing through the bridge. Fully "expressed" we ask heartache, *what's new,* and calmly invite it to *sit down* on the melody's last two notes.

Many adults grip their facial muscles to censor the tiny muscles around the eyes and across the cheeks that go into fine spasm as the urge to cry arises. The inside of the mouth hardens if we grip behind the nose and eyes to try to control this flood. Lifting the soft palate becomes extremely difficult when upper resonators go into lockdown. The throat stiffens and closes, limiting the free functioning of vocal cords. To mask the choke of crying while singing, auxiliary throat muscles kick in to enforce pitch, preventing our sound from attuning to the truth of our original feeling. To further distance ourselves from uncomfortable sensations, we grip the diaphragm, silencing the communicative capacity of airflow—the shudder of a sob. I have felt this sequence of events in my own body when trying to hold back tears. But singing is crying, in part, and when those feelings arise my job is to keep breathing … let air and water flow.

Crying allows for a naturally calibrated rhythmic relationship between *bound* and *unbound,* similar to orgasm, and thorny because it involves the chaotic, uncontrolled feeling of spasm. A bias against crying means that this ebb and flow can get caught in an inhibited, ashamed loop, no longer remembering how to expand and contract freely. The function of laughing, crying, and orgasm is release, but life has often taught us to override or deny these safety valves. Reclaiming space for light inside the vulnerable tissues of the body takes the sweetness of time, and an equal ownership of mad, sad, and glad as helpful energies.

"You are finding more malleable space in your mouth through softly expanding into your upper resonators, but the emotion arising is causing some throats to stiffen through clinging to pitch. You are right to want to hold on to something, but I suggest that we substitute the grip in the throat with a small grip of self-possession farther down in the chest—the *no* we practice in Slipper Camp!

"Lynn, do you mind if I work with you for a bit?"

I turn to this earthy empathizer, a teacher and actor able to "let down" into difficult and frightening emotional terrain. I receive her nod of agreement. Lynn's early years were heavy with emotional responsibility, and I want her to experience a "letting up." I ask her to choose a colleague from the group who makes her feel happy. She doesn't hesitate. "Jen!" Those who aren't picked collapse ever so slightly; with a wink I suggest they not take Lynn's choice personally.

I tell Lynn we are going to reclaim forbidden feelings, soften fossilized emotions, make room for the sinuses' other inhabitant—joy! And that joy is hard to own. I place Jen behind me and have her smile and wave over and over again at Lynn. Jen's conviviality works magic, and Lynn begins to inhabit *up* by genuinely laughing her soft palate to the heavens, though it feels as scary as the top of the Ferris wheel ride where she and I once got stuck during Regina's Buffalo Days fair. Hope is so infinite it can feel terrifying. Anticipation can so jangle the nerves that it is indistinguishable from anxiety.

I ask another student in the class to burrow the crown of her head into Lynn's sternum to land a sense of containment. Lynn clasps her colleague's head to heart as she sings the last few lines of the song. This gentle *bound* feeling, internalized by her trachea and bronchi, means Lynn can risk the untethered nature of laughter—can even expand around it—without closing in her throat or losing her mind to fear. The final intervals of "Good Morning Heartache" make it clear that the light of sadness lives in tandem with the tenderness of joy—and both are supported by core.

Yesim is watching with considerable curiosity. She is a graphic artist from Turkey, and her excellent English is inflected by a refined musical cadence. She doesn't think of herself as a singer but whenever she opens her mouth I hear the warmth of the blues. In an email she told me that during last week's class she heard something for the first time. "We need *just the right amount* of subglottal pressure for healthy vocal functioning." Similar to Lynn softly inhabiting *bound* in the chest in order to maintain *up*, Yesim needs self-possession—but not too much—to delve into *happy* without losing her rich emotional ballast.

I remind the class to loosen their shoulders, to yawn a little if they are feeling locked. The ability to shrug and soften through scapulae, arms, and neck before becoming firmer through the chest is especially important for women. I point out a specific quality that has become more prevalent in women's voices this past decade. If confidence is not embodied behind the sternum, this can result in a muscular yoke around the collarbones—a ring of audible restriction at the base of the neck. Strangled, compressed, and lacking in warmth, often accompanied by a nasal overtone, or gravelly undertone, this voice betrays the effects of grasping for respect.

Yesim sings a few long notes without me commenting. I want to hear if the warm, free flow of air from behind her sternum and the specific, narrow feeling of subglottal pressure are partnering in her body. She emits a slow sigh on a single tone; it oscillates between *bound* and *unbound*. She glows with excitement at having accessed last week's new feeling by herself and tells us that the gentle pressure she feels, just behind her sternum and well below her throat, is the size of a small, hard pebble. She also confirms that it is easier to attain subglottal pressure when she is accessing the right emotional feeling—without overstating it!

I agree: "What was particularly beautiful about your tones was that you did not sacrifice either Upper or Lower Fluff, or your ability to release through the chest while pursuing subglottal pressure. Your singing reminded me that women have been too often told that we need to be more confident. The way we use the word *confidence* in this culture brings to mind a puffed-up and held chest. This exaggerated posture is not renewable. It borrows energy from the masculine that is difficult for me to fully inhabit, at least in the way I see men stiffening their chests. So, let's pull apart the word *confidence* starting with *confide*—meaning with faith or trust. I think singing with confidence means expressing honestly while trusting that you will be heard."

Petite, fiery, intelligent, Yesim glows with even more excitement—"Yes! Yes!"—and sings a stream of long tones with the delight that singing *with confidence* brings. She combines self-possession's understanding of subglottal pressure with the brilliance behind her eyes … fosters joyful, righteous expression. She relaxes into the promise of being heard while judiciously juggling several states at once.

Most artists who come to my studio are highly motivated, hard workers, but overworking and joy can be at odds with one another if balance and care are not part of the picture. Ntokozo is up next. She is an accomplished performer and pioneering creator who, like her forebears, has contributed immeasurably to the Toronto arts and culture ecosystem. In the past four weeks Ntokozo has been especially committed to letting go of old habits and has been coming to both Slipper Camp and Group Class each week. This is her eighth session in a month. Like Yesim, and Lynn before her, she is lifting her soft palate as consciously as possible; however, the resulting sound is nasal rather than sparkly. Ntokozo tells me that the nonnasal sound is so unfamiliar to her ears that she is having a hard time trusting and repeating it. She also says that if she can maintain the yawn space from the beginning of class, she is often able to avoid excess nasality. I agree that this is what I have witnessed too.

I remind Ntokozo that when she began to train and perform she was still in her teens and, like all humans, only two of her four sets of resonators, or sinuses, were fully developed. Due to her youthful appearance, she is still asked to play much younger roles, and this will have continued to affect her use of her resonators. One of the late-to-form sinuses—the

sphenoid—is key to freeing vocal sound through partnering head resonance with chest resonance. I encourage her "yawn" space to get to know
emotion by thinking a delightful, sustainable thought—reclaim the idea
of "happy" as central to her technique. I suggest she imagine a tiny swing
set above her hard palate, or a miniature cat sitting on her tongue and
batting at the line where soft and hard palate meet. This makes the whole
class giggle. Ntokozo is ready for these prompts, and as she lifts into joy
her tone becomes moving and repeatable, note after note.

She laughs through her tears. "How do you do this for a living!?" I
answer with a smile that I am *almost* over my hang-ups about *glad* and
sad. I invite Ntokozo to sing part of a song she knows well, "Ain't No
Mountain High Enough." The first three notes of the chorus—G, A, and
B—are right where a woman's head voice begins. They will benefit from
her current exuberant fluctuation between laughter and tears. Ntokozo
takes this feeling into the lower notes of the verse as well, reminding
every single pitch to be joyous, remembering that the motion of emotion can be playful. Her singing sends shivers up my arms, and I tell her
so. Ntokozo beams.

The last singer to work today is Jen. For almost a decade she has
been unearthing her emotional inheritance. This diligence has revealed
a vast vocal landscape. Jen is the most "advanced" singer in the group
and her impulse will be to live up to this; and waiting for her turn will
have been anxiety producing. Jen is also the adult child of an alcoholic.
As a little one there was not much space for her own fragile upper resonance, her younger self's needs and tears.

I ask Jen to launch in. As she sings I follow her on the piano well
up into her high soprano, where she softens into joy. Her insightful
and diligent taking on of each of her classmates' positive physiological
changes has kept heroism, and the need to be perfect, at bay. Jen radiates well-earned, nongrasping achievement, and her beautiful sound
shines upward like a bodhisattva's halo. Suddenly she bursts into tears;
I ask what they mean. Jen tells us that it feels wrong to be able to do
something so well without suffering, and that she is afraid to share her
success with the group.

The other women respond quickly: her singing made them feel ecstatic; they experienced it as a torch lighting the way; it inspired confidence in their own body. Jen is helping them to go further through privileging the inside of *her* body, inviting the others to identify with their newfound lightness using confidence. The class's generous comments show me that empathy, cultivated through weeks of getting under one another's skin, has eased jealousy and suspicion away from these women's learned body/brain maps.

"Female joy remains a challenge despite our craving it. After decades of pleasing others, or using manufactured delight to sell objects, it is easy to lose track of this feeling's purity. Trusting that we are allowed to reveal joy on our own terms through expressing subjectively risks a radical return to true nature. Moving out from under the shadow of sexual abuse, or racism, or a parent's alcoholism, or religious repression, or a nation's political instability asks for confidence—a confidence that partners reliable core with freshly expressed joy. As we sing the following notes together, imagine that something good might happen today."

We move into collective sound, sharing long tones. With each ascending pitch we reestablish gentle resilience behind the sternum and bright optimism around the eyes. Five female voices shimmering in front of my bodhisattva's flames ... floating toward the heavens.

———

Later in the day Mary sends me this email:

> *On the way to work after class today, I saw a man on the sidewalk collapse to the ground. He was having a seizure. Three people got there before I could: one knelt down, putting his hand on the man's feet while whipping out his cell phone. Another knelt down, took off his coat, placed it on the man and lay down, awkwardly spooning him. The third, a woman, put her hands on his head. It was this gorgeous moment of strangers holding—not gripping or pinning down—and simply being with someone in their pain. What an unexpected, powerful moment of community. Something REALLY good happened today!*

A touch of bodhisattva-enlightened grace.

25

Slipper Camp Seven—
Oooo Slides

I'VE CUT IT close after rehearsal with Peggy Baker's dancers, and despite biking home in a fury from the National Ballet School, I slide into the house alongside my Slipper Campers. Heading back to the kitchen to grab a sustaining cup of milky black tea, I pass an accomplished actress whom I remember first seeing on the Stratford Festival stage in 1986. She is talking with B'atz', an emerging actor and theater producer of Mayan ancestry, recently graduated from Humber College, where I teach. B'atz' is committed to shaping diverse and equitable practices in Toronto's burgeoning theater scene. Full mug in hand, I come dangerously close to tripping over Ronit as I enter the studio. A mindfulness instructor and master's candidate in Environmental Studies writing about "self as the site for social transformation," she is lying on the floor with her legs up the wall. Yesim yawns extravagantly near my bodhisattva painting, leaving her graphic design work far behind. The room fills until eleven bodies ring the space, with three more glowing online.

"Disa Sauter's research at the Max Planck Institute for Psycholinguistics in the Netherlands has determined that there are two nonverbal human sounds that everyone on the planet can interpret. In other words, they are not learned emotional displays but fully instinctual responses, common to our species rather than specific to culture. What might these be?"

Their answers bounce across the airspace above my piano: "Crying?" "Screaming?" "Orgasm?" "A yawn?"

"Nope!"

A lone student ventures, "Some kind of sigh?"

"Very good! Specifically the sigh of relief. This sigh is understood by all humans."

According to Ms. Sauter, laughter is the other nonverbal vocalization we all know. Anger, disgust, fear, triumph, and sadness have been influenced by family and culture and are no longer universally recognizable. No wonder human animals often misinterpret one another when sad or mad.

The long tones we use for "What the fluff!" borrow from the sigh of relief. Upper Fluff uses the lift of laughter. Using both relief and laughter as the basis for Double Fluff opens singer and listener to the positive sounds we all share—encourages us to feel in sync with one another. To marry "sigh" with "laugh," the flow of air from behind the chest is coordinated with head resonance. Double Fluff sounds free but on the "airy" side and needs productivity in the right part of the body to refine its tone. A judicious amount of "mad" energy planted behind the chest while singing a long tone integrates the sigh's gravity with laughter's levity. Singing the word *no* can re-create healthy containment within airflow.

Ms. Sauter's study might help explain why an unadulterated human *no* is trickier to produce and interpret than a laugh or sigh. From what I have seen, most of us have unconsciously altered our relationship to sounding the word *no* since we were quite young. I want to see if my class can investigate anger's *bound* propriety with as little individual and cultural baggage as possible.

"Let's replace the *no*'s firmness with the narrowness of the *oooo* vowel. My first voice teacher said that an *oooo* was '*like medicine, baby …*'" I channel Maria's smoky, opulent Italian vowels. "Lounging on her couch, she'd ask me to sing one more '*for baby Jesus …*'"

Laughter aligns the group.

Maria first invited me to sing an *oooo*, but it was Neil Semer's pedagogy that put the *oooo*'s sophisticated meeting of efficiency and release
to good use in relation to melody. Neil used the *oooo* to slide judiciously
between pitches. Through patient, persistent practice I learned that
"ease" and "containment" benefit one another.

"Watch me carefully as I demonstrate."

I chart a perfect fifth on the piano, playing the B just below middle C,
then the F-sharp five notes above, returning to the B. I shape my lips into
an *oooo*—as if nursing, or blowing a kiss—full of vulnerable desire. I flow
air from behind my sternum without any thought to controlling pitch
from my throat. Beginning with the lower note, I slide the *oooo* vowel up
to the F-sharp and back down to wherever my airflow takes me, letting go
before I get all the way back to the B. As the pitch slides slowly upward, I
melt into my body, loving all the unnamed notes that sit between the piano's black and white keys, imitating pennywhistle or trombone. I include
the back of my body in this downward yielding action so that the slide
seems to rise of its own accord—gravity birthing levity.

"What did you witness?" The room is really quiet. No one moves.

"Yikes! Don't worry about having the right answer! Moving from
long tones on an *ah* to *oooo* slides is a bit like going from a seated hatha
practice in yoga to a vinyasa flow class, or from the ballet barre to movement across the floor. There is so much more to track. Watch while listening, and then say what you have seen and heard, whether it is simple
and obvious ... or unexpected and a little mysterious."

I re-engage with the *oooo* slides, invite class members to jump in
with their observations.

"Your lips were pursed in a very round *oooo* shape."

"The slide was so smooth that I didn't hear any separate pitches."

"Very good! What else did you see, hear, and *feel*? Shall I model
another one?" In response to their nodding heads I slide through
another fifth, this time from B-flat to F. I exaggerate the softening of my
neck and back muscles toward the earth, wanting them to see and identify with the lack of physical lift, despite my pitches moving upward.

A young woman squeaks out, "You looked like you were melting?"

"You are right!" She relaxes visibly as I continue: "While the pitch slid upward I melted downward. This is confusing because I seem to be lying about 'up'—but physiologically, pitch is neither 'up' nor 'down' when it comes to the vocal cords. Most of you missed seeing the melt because we have been conditioned to think that singing a high note requires us to *do* 'up' with our throat muscles, but all this does is squeeze the pitch out.

"It is worth trusting the *oooo* vowel. Its long and narrow shape traces a line from forehead down to the base of the sternum: a resonant imprint that easily vibrates upper resonators while accessing sensation in the chest. The *oooo*'s tube of gently *bound* vertical vibration integrates head and torso. Its consistent, manageable passageway allows us to melt our 'big body' downward without bottoming out acoustically, which can happen when using the more unwieldy *aaah* vowel.

"Underpinned by a feeling of release in my body, I let the rising of pitch during the slide be governed by my vagus nerve—consciously resisting a desire to 'help' by lifting in the throat. This fosters a partnership between height and depth that is tangible, easy, and repeatable. Healthy."

Pitch and resonance function differently from one another. Whereas I can "do" things physiologically to open up head and chest resonance, it is best to leave my vocal cords alone. For higher pitches the superior laryngeal branch of the vagus nerve instructs the cricothyroid muscle to alter pitch by elongating the vocal cords to appropriately increase tension. It leaves them short and thick for low ones. When my vocal cords match pitch intuitively, vocal range easily widens, and tone and texture become freer and more generous. I discover that "release" is fundamental within "work." If I tighten up through my neck and throat, push my chin forward, or frown for a high note, vocal cord elongation is restricted—and the only option left to guarantee pitch is the strong-arming of my voice box. Melting through the *oooo* slides avoids inadvertent lifting or squeezing around the larynx in order to achieve height.

Inhabiting pitch as a horizontal, collaborative process can affect belief structures. Conceptually I am flipping pitch upside down … upsetting the hierarchical relationships that dominate Western thought and behavior. Because the speech roles of our vocal cords are so familiar—creating identity, explaining reality, shaping story, defending ideas, convincing others of our truth—they need an attitude change to allow singing to be elemental and equanimous.

The fifth's span of five notes is wonderful for this paradigm shift because it is wide, but not too wide. It is also the most foundational interval after the octave—true to the natural harmonic series. Both ancient Greece and Egypt, encamped on either side of the Mediterranean Sea's teal blue shimmer, honored the potency of the fifth. The fifth weaves through most every musical tradition around the globe, as well as pop, rock, blues, and lullabies. It is so stable that Western classical music refers to it as "perfect." Its lack of prejudice isn't only cultural; it is emotional—it can anchor both major and minor chords. The fifth is fundamentally open-minded.

Sliding through a fifth sets a reliable template for engaging intuitively with melodic structures. Passing through all of its inner pitches in a deeply egalitarian way allows the upward and downward curves of a "sigh" to become the flexible emotional architecture of song-making.

Still, it's hard to believe that we don't have to make pitch. It takes faith to step out of the vagus nerve's way, especially now that we are sliding between notes. Intentionally hiking up the vocal cords can make a singer feel more deserving of the resulting high note than accessing pitch in a way that feels less overtly intentional, less like striving. Thankfully *oooo* slides provide an opportunity to undo ingrained physical conditioning related to overwork and self-worth.

"I want us to start by singing these slides down around our speaking range, which is called the lower bridge or *passaggio*. The first two slides—from B to F-sharp and from B-flat to F—make it easy to feel all the resonant areas in the voice at once, chest, upper throat, mouth, and head. The narrow binding of the *oooo* teaches these resonant spaces how to rely on each other while moving over a range of pitches."

As we move through our slides, I see that some students' lips are not fully *oooo*-like. I blow kisses and pout outrageously to remind everyone of the *oooo*'s precision. Still, two of them hang on to a stiff upper lip.

"What is a boudoir?" I ask.

Answers spring quickly from around the piano.

A room full of cushions and rich red silks.
A place for romance!
A large closet where women dress.

"Close! The word *boudoir* comes from the French verb *bouder*, which means 'to pout.' A boudoir gives pouting—and other sensitive feelings—a safe space. What else do my *oooo* lips make you think of?"

A kiss!
A baby nursing!
The French language!

"Yes. All sensual things—and potentially vulnerable-making. Don't be shy! Reveal your 'need,' and slide again!" Everyone's lips articulate the *oooo*'s fine shape.

"That was excellent. To make clear how important this shape is, try an *oh* on your next slide and see what is sacrificed." Everyone hears and feels that the *oh* fails to reach into the chest or register behind the eyes.

"The *oooo* is deeper and higher all at once; it encourages a conversation between light and dark. It grows a fine, resonant root behind my sternum, while at the top end, a vanishing point hovers above my sinuses. This vertical column of vibration provides a narrowness within which vocal sound can thrive, especially if we retain our sensuality.

"Let's *oooo* slide over a series of fifths focusing on sensation and resisting internal comment or question." Everyone does what I ask: lips true, knees unlatched, backs melting.

The nuts and bolts of this exercise are getting clear in my students' bodies. However, many of them are not allowing their long tone to "run out of air." They are pushing or squeezing to extend breath. In the early days of singing, running out of air is a *good* thing, even though a singer might panic about never being able to finish a phrase. We have to stop grimly doling out our last dregs of air; this stinginess usually costs us freedom of expression and beauty of tone. Breath will extend naturally once a vocalist is ready to introduce efficiency and economy.

"For now, I'd like us to risk more freedom when it comes to airflow within this activity. The *oooo* is providing a long, narrow shape, and now I'd like you to stop thinking of it as an exercise and let it become a practice. We so easily make mastering a skill a miserable experience— let's start by pretending you like this exercise."

Following laughter's release, everyone *oooo* slides again, and, indeed, acting as if we like what we are doing softens our eyes, making our overtones more fruitful. "Yes! Your *oooo* slides magnified in the room. And your lack of caution meant that many of you ran out of air, which is the first step toward figuring out exactly where and how to extend your exhale.

"To create more productive airflow, imagine a tiny, ruthless trader or a small, shameless bully behind your sternum. I find a petite, evil witch's energy useful when it is placed 'just so' at the base of my trachea. Similar to embracing my 'inner airhead' for full head tone, accessing my 'inner witch' helps me galvanize a darker part of my psyche for chest engagement. These emotional 'homeopathic remedies'—a minuscule dose of poison, one for light and one for dark—keep us out of the throat by honoring our full archetypal range. Accessing less comfortable, dark terrain shows me where my overly protective witch is and how she's doing … makes her less dangerous."

I listen to each student in turn. It's challenging to do an exercise that introduces "productivity" to the chest without trying to "get it right." The third student to sing—a gracious, brilliant yoga teacher—makes almost no sound despite her good intentions. A scene from a film I saw in my early twenties pops to mind.

In provocative film director Ken Russell's 1969 adaptation of D. H. Lawrence's *Women in Love,* Alan Bates and Oliver Reed wrestle naked in front of a fireplace in Edwardian England. Two risky, accomplished British actors making flesh-to-flesh contact: intimate, powerful, and erotic.

Despite any discomfort the actors might have felt pushing against the mores of the late '60s film industry, or of their Edwardian characters' imagined propriety, the sensual aggression of this filmed tussle is fully committed.

I ask Yumee to place the image of two men wrestling naked just behind her sternum for the next *oooo* slide; it serves her well. The sound that tumbles out is juicy and engaged—no longer rigid or quiet but full of surprise, and the possibility of more surprise. The others in the group smile and nod their heads. We never tire of someone else's growth; it brings hope.

The *oooo* slides, as much as they are a task to do well and learn from, need some drop and swing in the chest—a little wrestle or swagger. Finding this spot is tricky for women, as it is unfamiliar. We have armed our chests and shouldered too much responsibility in order to survive a world that does not know how to welcome our ever-more-visible prowess. A swagger is loose, sexy, and beautifully "full of itself." It comes from within, is not driven or diligent. The female need to be "nice," or to placate, can entrench this feeling's illegitimacy. The "nice guys" in the room might also think this sensation is not for them.

"See if you can find Alan Bates and Oliver Reed on YouTube tonight. See if the scene is as passionate as I remember. I think you will witness transgression and commitment, violence and eroticism—the feelings we want to awaken right where our airflow originates. This weaves *fight or flight* into *rest and digest* in the exact spot where sound is birthed, where moans and groans and even grunts keep us grounded and real—especially useful when singing gets more challenging."

We slide our fifths for another few minutes, retreading our downward path, semitone by semitone, from the *lower passaggio's* B to F-sharp to D to A below, then painstakingly up again to arrive at the D to A one octave above. Contacting each and every pitch within this vocal range through gentle intention and open resonance calms and invigorates, massaging vocal cords to life while touching on a broad and balanced emotional spectrum. Fostering attitudes that allow for up and down to feel less hierarchically valued, and for *bound* and *unbound* to relate harmoniously, leads to change; not only do vocal cords become less managed, that whole human becomes less reactive. This change is not accidental or coincidental ... it is devotional. Integrating flow with accuracy in the *oooo* slides replaces defensiveness with self-possession.

To quote Maria, *"It's like medicine, baby ..."*

26

Slipper Camp Eight—
Ease in a Tight Spot

"IN LAST WEEK'S Slipper Camp we focused on *oooo* slides in the lower part of your voice. The narrowness of that vowel in combination with the slide's relaxed diligence were our guides. Today we will finesse the *lower passaggio* before taking on the *upper passaggio*."

I can see that some of my students are wondering what a *passaggio* is!

The Italian word *passaggio* translates as "passage" or "passageway" and refers to the two major transitional zones in a singer's voice. In English we use the words *break* or *bridge*. In the female voice the *lower* one is roughly from the B a semitone below middle C to the F-sharp above, and the *upper* one is roughly an octave higher. Men are an octave lower than women for each *passaggio*. Renegotiating the voice's relationship to height and depth as we move through these regions is crucial. If we maintain an either/or proposition in relation to "high" and "low" when traversing these breaks, it will feel like a "ceiling" locks in place despite "wanting" to sing higher notes. To move through each *passaggio*'s volatility with grace, it is necessary to embrace and regulate contradictory energies, stay present to each moment.

To work with the whole group I will use starting pitches that are more or less right for most singers. In the *bel canto* tradition, each vocal category—bass, baritone, contralto, mezzo, and the many tenors and sopranos—begins and ends each *passaggio* on a specific semitone. As a singer becomes familiar with what healthy access to the *passaggi* feels like, she refines the exact note that is her entry point, and roughly a fifth above that, her exit note ... personalizing her bridge. Sorting out these transitional zones not only makes the voice's complex passage-way between chest and head easier to move through; it helps orga-nize the feeling of weight, or engagement, above and below each note. The entire singing voice becomes more integrated—whole—once we befriend both *passaggi*. But this is all theoretical till we meet them in the flesh!

We review last week's *oooo* slides beginning as usual with the fifth that starts on the B right below middle C and ends on the F-sharp above—straddling the heart of the *lower passaggio*. We find the right shape for *oooo* by saying the word *who* as in "Who is at the door?" I shape my lips while looking toward my front door.

"Vowels are unique in shape and size. They hold and manifest a wide array of sensations. How that feeling became codified into the building blocks of language is an evolutionary mystery. Singers slow vowels down, swim in their emotional waters, experience their sacred wisdom. The *oooo*'s narrow gift is found in the word *blue*: feeling blue, singing 'the blues.' Its vertical compression accesses loft behind the eyes at the same time as sensation in the chest—crying mixed with the fleshy tug of heartache."

We sing a second draft of *oooo* slides through the *lower passaggio*, down to low D and then back up through middle D to the A above. Thanks to the word *who*, a gently aspirated *h* breath is flowing authen-tically from behind each person's sternum.

"Great! Your vocal cords worked easily through the *lower passaggio* because you let the vagus nerve do its job of tracking pitch in motion. Because the *lower passaggio* is an everyday, relatively flexible part of the voice, it does not demand the high-wire precision of the *upper passag-gio*. Still, I believe that the *lower passaggio* can be the most treacherous or misleading part of the voice. As 'home' to our speaking voice, it feels familiar, but it is often tied to ego in ways that we can't see. More grooved than groovy."

Each of us has strong unconscious opinions as to how the human voice should sound—especially our own. "Polite," "masculine," "in control," "intelligent," "warm," "acquiescent": a long list of survival modes. We are able to shape a vocal identity for our speaking voice because of the almost unlimited play in how head and chest resonance can mix in the highly suggestible *lower passaggio's* range. We can talk using a tone that is thick and heavy, or airy and light, or incredibly brash and edgy—even extremely nasal and guarded. Timbral options are exciting, speak to our needs, and, as we free the voice, are important to explore.

I sing a long middle D—the fulcrum note in my *lower passaggio*. I morph the shape of my mouth and change the pressure behind my chest, as well as the availability of my sinuses. Resonance and tone shift as the balance between light and dark alters dramatically—each note's texture seems endlessly mutable. The *lower passaggio's* flexible fake of almost any color that strikes our fancy is problematic in several ways. A sound that is repeatedly forced on the vocal cords usually limits range. Bending the natural functioning of the voice out of shape limits timbral options. Imitating someone else's sound can disconnect your voice from a true sense of self. I believe it can change who you think you are as well as how others perceive you.

We are not only born with specific vocal equipment; we pick up the use of that equipment from hearing a parent's voice. Sometimes we inherit the emotional state that comes along with it. A forebear's traumatic life experience can bias their child toward restricted or reactive vocal patterning. Approaching the *lower passaggio* with devoted equanimity offers the opportunity to become aware, and then ask the voice to be true to itself through enjoying all of its colors without prejudice.

It is fine to have aesthetic preferences, but it is also important to understand that a preference can become an emotional bias with vocal consequences, and equally, a vocal bias can have emotional consequences. It is dangerous when our preferences box us in, limit our choices, like an algorithm that thinks we still want to buy the jeans we just purchased or decided against. It is important to welcome all sorts of textures—allow the voice to reveal color through a variety of communicative styles.

I conclude, "To engage with freedom and discipline in the *lower passaggio*, it is important to map maximum ease and flexibility for each of its notes. This means finding an unmanufactured—or better yet, non-egotistical—relationship to phonation while moving between notes."

I demonstrate two *oooo* slides. They are radically different from one another, meaning different from the root on up. In the first one I "walk out of the room" with regard to accomplishment. To give my mind something to do, I think of the slide as horizontal, not vertical. The movement between my pitches stays easy, neutral, and unopinionated. During the second slide I try to ensure that I do well. Simply thinking that one thought causes me to engage with a little more muscle than necessary; I ever so slightly resemble a tube of toothpaste being squeezed through the throat. I ask the class if they saw and heard the difference between my two *oooo* slides.

Heads nod.

In the second one your neck muscles got tighter.
Your tone lost height.
I felt my whole body squeeze upward in empathy.

"Yes. All I did was change my thoughts, and through that I got in my own way. I am going to give you something to do on the inhale that will give your mind a helpful focus.

"While I play the next fifth on the piano, I want you to feel the top and bottom of this interval in your body and head *while* air pours into your lungs. Shape your face and mouth in relation to how pitch registers in your acoustic physiology, making sure to hold resonant space for the higher note at the same time as the lower one."

I show my students what I mean, and it is clear that when I inhale silently and spaciously I am hearing the availability of both notes' resonance in my full being. Before I even utter a peep, that capacity is visible in my face because the inner architecture of my head is now more ample. Following input from their mirror neurons, the group around my piano takes on the potential of both pitches' physiologically sensed space. Their look of exuberant relaxation while inhaling makes me want to laugh out loud, but their next *oooo* slides up and down as a horizontal, unbiased journey. Sound that is fresh, refreshable, and refreshing.

"That was excellent. You encompassed both notes the entire time that you slid that *oooo*! You were so busy being open while holding oppositional thoughts in balance that you had no time to restrict yourself through the throat ... the area accustomed to our deeply held personal speech patterns. Language can promote lying in order to ensure survival. But, oddly enough, it is the purity of nonverbal vocalization that we've stopped trusting as grown-ups. Just now you banished the egotistical physiology of the *lower passaggio,* a physiology tied in to speech habits that defend, explain, or prove. That ego-free singing must have felt good. We restore ourselves by re-centering tone."

I turn to Dani, a willowy, raven-haired singer. She is an excellent producer who brings her Italian heritage to life through various musical projects under the umbrella of her company, Espresso Manifesto. "Dani, in an email last week you quipped that you had better get back to your *oooo* slides so your teacher would not be mad at you next class. You know that I never want you to do an *oooo* slide just for me. I want you to love the physicality of this action and the beauty of the perfect fifth ... and I'd love you to stop being your own toughest critic."

Dani smiles and shrugs. I have not offended what she can't yet help, *and* she seems curious about what is coming next. "Breath blowing through the vocal body without censorship promotes enjoyment. It is the sigh of relief. Dani, that equation has been your most recent big *aha* and something you now access reliably. The pleasure of airflow is a great tool for developing internal bearings—whether musical or emotional. Enjoyment allows us to listen and evaluate—step aside without threat—*even when we are doing something difficult.*"

I want our high-level skills to be in line with how the body works by nature. Discover feelings of personal agency without having to overwork.

"Dani, do you remember when you found it difficult to straddle your *lower passaggio*? Sometimes your voice flipped chaotically from chest to head resonance without rhyme or reason. The relationship between head and chest seemed either/or. Now with airflow coming from behind the sternum, and not from your neck, your throat muscles are negotiating the *oooo* slide's pitches intuitively—leaving the vagus nerve to do its innate and nuanced job. Your attention to maintaining upper and lower resonant space within the narrow *oooo* vowel has resulted in a calm productivity. Your notes no longer crack or squirm as you move from one resonant floor to another—they no longer seem pigeonholed. I'd say that negotiating the *lower passaggio* is now a piece of cake for you. Enjoy this piece of cake because cake is enjoyable, not because social media says we should have our cake and eat it too."

With Dani's recent success in mind, the whole class slides pleasurably from the B to F-sharp and then proceeds upward without peril until, four slides later, we come to the fifth that spans E-flat to B-flat. A number of faces look somewhat alarmed by what they feel when passing through the B-flat, our most recent slide's "top" note. As the students slide through the next fifth, from E to B and back, more eyes light up with slight panic when moving through the top note.

"The looks on your faces show me that you felt something change. Those top notes are the doorway into your *upper passaggio*. You were doing such a good job of inhabiting top and bottom at the same time that you could intuitively feel the natural functioning of your voice and its need for something to morph as we got near the *upper passaggio*. On the B-flat and B-natural you could feel your acoustic head graze a ceiling. A more intense part of the voice is revealing itself. It's time to include sounds more in line with openhearted whining as well as your soft palate's elevated laugh zone."

This ceiling is not something a student can blast through. It is necessary to narrow even further, in the right place, to move into this range. An unforced, open-throated whine slips sound into our highest resonators while holding the feeling of ache behind the chest, leading to a precise, and more intense, narrowing in those two places. I ask my students

214

to pinch the finger and thumb of their right hand together while reaching that arm forward at eye level.

I continue with my instructions: "Take the fingertips from your left hand and press them vertically along your sternum. When you arrive at the B while singing the next E to B slide, employ the finger pinch in your right hand while looking at it, and press your breastbone into the fingertips of your left hand; ease away from both the pinch and the press as you slide back down."

The group follows my instructions, and the sound narrows and threads through to an even finer upper resonance than their Upper Fluff had previously allowed. A current of excitement runs through the group as they realize how easy that "high" note was.

"I know the pinch is an odd action."

About twelve years ago I was teaching at Humber and getting frustrated with a class that could not figure out the entry into the *upper passaggio* through the *oooo* slides. It was not their fault—this skill took me almost two years to figure out during my studies with Neil, and I had not clarified my own pedagogical language around it. I had these students for only one term and wanted them to have something to hold on to. Hand gestures help us navigate the invisible in the voice; a specific gesture can accurately alter inner experience. I said to my young theater students, "Just pretend you are picking a cherry from a tree at eye level." I wanted a small action right in front of the frontal and ethmoid sinuses to wake up their acoustic imaginations—and it worked.

I conclude my story by telling the Slipper Campers, "That little pinch, in conjunction with pressure behind the sternum, has made the *upper passaggio* easily accessible to hundreds of students since then. Enjoy how a refined feeling of subglottal pressure in your chest partners with increasingly brilliant tone ... without undue stress, thanks to placing your fingertips vertically on your sternum."

Most of the class falls in love with the little pinch as we move further into the *upper passaggio*. But as we arrive at the fifth that has D at the top, I begin to see some strain and lift.

215

"You are not imagining it. The *upper passaggio* feels more limited, and becomes more difficult, as we near the fifth that spans A to E. To not feel excessively trapped, we need to remind ourselves of two things: ease in the back of the body and space in the mouth at the top of the pharynx. So, along with finger pinch and fingertips to sternum, 'have your own back' by softly leaning into the back of your body. Trust that when things get more challenging, this does not mean they are bad or wrong. To deal with mouth space, continue to physically imagine how the pitches will resonate in your upper pharynx *while you are inhaling.* Your soft palate will feel as if it is unfolding right up to your skull, possibly reminding you of the internal magnitude of a scream; use the comfort of your back as counterpoint to this lift of alarm."

I ask Jen if I could work with her in front of the group. She agrees, though I know she does not like being singled out. Her *oooo* slides are exemplary, but her attitude hasn't yet aligned with her ability. Witnessing Jen's growth process will help the group understand both the complexity and achievability of this skill.

Jen does all the right things, but her *oooo* struggles a bit, *sounding* pinched rather than *using* the pinch. Her desire to "help" the sound is pernicious, especially with peers watching. So, even though she is experienced, she is lifting the muscles of her neck just a fraction.

"Well done, Jen. You really understand the map of the *oooo.* But engineering—as helpful as it can be when keeping track of all these actions—is not the reason we go up into this part of the voice. You tell me what the *upper passaggio* is for."

Jen replies with a sassy laugh that it must be for pain and suffering because it is so difficult!

"Not far off!" I reply. "But let's be a little purer in how we regard the emotion in that space. Let's trust our right to want, to whine, to cry—think of it as beautiful. For this feeling to thrive we actually need to push less and allow more. Bring the backs of your fingers to either side of your neck while sliding up. This will encourage your neck to stay soft, which will release the engineer from her desire to do well and will allow the 'place that knows how to whine' to do its job. But first, think of whining as legitimate."

Even though they are not making any sound, a number of students place the backs of their hands against their own necks, encouraging Jen while learning how to promote their own softness. I take Jen to a slightly lower interval, she sings the E to B, and it is good.

"Jen, that was an excellent shift. On the next slide simply trust that a narrowing airflow knows how to access this space without excuse. Allowing a whine to be beautiful rather than hopeless is worthwhile because this whine believes it will be answered."

She traces the F to C, roping B-flat, B, and C into the narrowing.

"That was another good pass! I know you are focusing very carefully, and I want you to make sure you are relaxing with each inhale, not rushing to get this over with. Embrace the lean in your back and the compression behind your sternum as a 3-D notion of subglottal pressure. This will provide ample counterbalance to the increasing height at the back of the mouth and acoustic narrowing in front. Employ the scream of delight's upper-chest amplitude."

The look on her face says, "You've got to be kidding!" but she does exactly what I ask and the sound is both narrow and easy from the F-sharp to the C-sharp, with a clear plumb line through her torso.

"On the next inhale, Jen, double-check that you are imagining the upper and lower pitches of the fifth within your face and neck even as you drop your belly. The high, young, female sounds in your head need to have the safest of environments in order to stay fresh and undefended, to cry and whine when they need to. I want your sound to glint like the silver thread in the gray cap you wore to class today—become a silver lining for all sorts of emotions."

There is so much to remind ourselves of as we take on the *upper passaggio*. She juggles it all, and the G to D slide sails out beautifully.

"Wow, that was easy, Jen! I don't feel like the inside of your throat is getting in the way by being too helpful. But there is one more thing I'd like you to take note of."

I turn to Lesley, who is standing next to Jen, and ask her what she is feeling in her own body—can she sense what is ever so slightly amiss in Jen's? Lesley is a gifted craniosacral therapist and I am pretty sure she will spot what I mean. Very accurately, she touches her chin; she has seen and felt a small quivering.

I go to Jen and slip my left hand under her jaw, gently touching the soft flesh that could become a double chin. I remember my first teacher, Maria, telling me that a good singer, even a young one, always has a double chin. Finally, after almost four decades, her comment registers fully as I note this flesh's connection to the ease of the tongue root and front of the neck.

"Lesley, lightly touching Jen's hyoid bone, just above her voice box, might help the muscles of her chin—which are part of this free-floating bone's suspension—to soften through touch."

I have felt Lesley's gentle hands on this part of my neck during bodywork, and the resulting release was mind-blowing. She takes over with Jen as I return to the piano; we continue, marrying subtle craniosacral touch to *bel canto* technique. I remind Jen that her chin is allowed to quiver, that this release might allow for emotion to surface.

On the next slide Jen lets herself wobble just a bit in her upper resonators, as well as softening through her tongue. The sound is buttery soft: no tension in her neck; soft tethered connection to depth; and loads of mouth space for the E-flat's upper needs. Arriving at the top, she hits a sweet spot and her eyes well up. Why? Because this is where crying resonates. Her open-throated whine has blossomed. These tears were triggered by the simple honesty of how the sound feels within Jen's autonomic nervous system.

"Jen, you are on the cusp of crying. I want to slow this moment down, let it become granular—not be afraid of its goodness. Even if it makes you antsy—like the ant crawling over my big toe at this very second—is there anything you would like to say about what you have just experienced?"

Jen laughs, and I silently thank the ant. She tells the group that she'd have loved to escape to the bathroom, as she hates feeling "under the gun." She often feels this way at the start of an *oooo* slide, whether she is in front of a group or home alone. She reveals that feeling and accepting emotion, in all its uncomfortable glory, is her current personal challenge. She is on the verge of "balanced emotion" and "technique" becoming "one" through trusting resonance, and resisting the over-work that micromanaging feelings requires. She explains that the work behind the chest today felt more like "healthy resolve" than defense, and this might have been why her chin and hyoid bone could "be them-selves" and function naturally.

I love the way Jen has articulated her experience. She lived in the *upper passaggio*'s tight space without overcompensating or bolting. Doing so in front of a group means this breakthrough is thoroughly hers. I am also proud of the group. Though this is a Slipper Camp, and we usually don't focus on just one person's growth, their thoughtful, body-centered witnessing supported Jen's growth. The quality of the group's listening will have altered their own understanding of "ease in a tight spot"—which is exactly what the *upper passaggio* demands.

27

Slipper Camp Nine— True Economy

CAN YOUR BODY have its way while your mind is engaged? Can they be on the same page even when they appear to have different tasks— and possibly even different opinions about how to get things done? If they are on different pages, can they still make the most evolved choice—collaborate? I don't think I have ever seen true political democracy, but I have occasionally felt democracy in a group or relationship. I hear it in the human voice when an inner physiological economy allows body and mind to balance and integrate.

In last week's Slipper Camp we had worked with *oooo* slides in the *upper passaggio* to foster "ease in a tight spot." We sought balance by marrying the concentrated drive of anger with the spontaneity of joy and the release of sorrow. Erasing negative biases around these emotional constructs made it possible for us to access each feeling's primary gift. Our resonance filled in and rounded out.

This week we are going to return to the *lower passaggio,* as well as the notes between the two *passaggi.* I tell my students to remember that this low to middle range seems especially malleable, and because of that they will be tempted to sing these notes any which way.

"Consciously integrate all that you know—the breath, the fluffs, and the *no*. Recall the feeling of containment you found in last week's *upper passaggio's oooo* slides. Decide on a fair balance of light and dark and a just amount of air pressure."

Thought and feeling coexist in a democratic relationship; I direct my students to give them equal voting power using "economy" as a guiding principle. The origins of the word *economy* are Greek: *oikos,* meaning house, and *nemein,* meaning to manage. Our body is our home. To renew our physical and emotional resources, we need a fair distribution of effort in each of our resonant rooms. We need to feel and balance each pitch's needs.

"Gather together all your skills and then make integration your priority. I can remind you of the necessary bits and pieces, but I cannot 'give' you integration. *Only you can integrate.* 'Wholeness' is something we find for ourselves, within ourselves. It is what the human brain/body—your brain/body—desires.… It is in our design. Homeostasis refers to a physiologically maintained balance that abides between interdependent elements, or systems. Allostasis is the process the body uses to regain homeostasis when stressed. By managing your emotional vocal house, you will learn how to 'hold your own' with equanimity. Use the conscious compass of self-ish-ness to coalesce."

Glorious sound pours forth from today's five students as we patiently work our way through the *lower passaggio,* long tone by long tone. We concentrate on economy and integration—while open to height and depth—leading each note to hang three-dimensionally in the space around these students' heads. Though their mouths are open, their voices seem to emanate from their whole being. What a sweet spot—the human voice free of ego drive, and deeply attractive thanks to balance. These humans are not singing louder than they need to. They are not competing with one another. Like the birds, they are not *too* sad, or *too* mad, or *too* glad. Each feeling is represented, leaving room for each one to work its primal magic. Emotions as comrades.

My eyes move past the group and come to rest on the bodhisattva image I used in chapter 24 to illustrate joy's upward energy. The canvas is large—four feet by five. Emerald green banners frame both sides of the bodhi's figure. Vibrant red, fuchsia, maroon, rose, green, orange, and teal blur together to give her an out-of-focus quality, as if channeling a TV screen from another dimension. The specific placement of color that Richard Herman has used to bring this bodhi's body to life maps other energies useful for singing. There is a dark smear of maroon around her throat and up through her left ear; the vagus nerve's collaborative, intuitive functioning manages hearing as well as voicing. The same red cradles her midsection—the diaphragm—intimate with asymmetry and involuntary impulse. A little below my bodhi's diaphragm, a teal blue line traces her transverse colon, hinting at the calm of *rest and digest*. Her upper chest is tender pink, ribs fanning heart out toward her shoulders ... which don't appear to be shouldering too much. Down the center of her sternum, gently galvanizing her core, Richard has placed a vertical line of deep forest green. Above her head flames rise and evaporate, and behind her benign face and unruffled neck a golden disk unifies head and body. Its glow makes visible how my students sound right now.

I didn't even know what a bodhisattva was when I bought this painting. I had no understanding of the energetic dimensions she was balancing on her flat canvas surface. A bodhisattva's compassion achieves enlightenment on behalf of all sentient beings, not through the heroism of doing for others but by finding inner balance ... internal economy. Her life's purpose is to practice *sattva*. This Sanskrit word translates into English as harmony, balance, joy, peace, serenity, intelligence, and goodness. I started calling in the bodhi/body's energy in 1991, before I could even name it. Almost thirty years later, listening to my students' economical—but not budgeted—sound, I *feel* the meaning of *sattva* through *hearing* it.

What they are doing is not easy. It is transformational.

In January 2015 I experienced an intense depression that lasted eleven weeks, something I had not gone through since before my daughters were born. All of 2014 had been hard. I lost my voice twice, once while singing for Richard Armstrong in Banff in the early summer, and once again when pushing myself to demonstrate an aggressive chorded sound for a Humber student that September. I was out of balance within my life's circumstances. Lacking the courage to express myself cleanly, I had twisted myself out of shape, and instead of providing helpful bearings, anger tied up my throat muscles. When depression moved in, my lowered immune system made me susceptible to a viral laryngitis contracted while working on the *3 Singers* project in Chicago. I worked through my illness, gave more than I had, and lost my voice a third time.

Telling this to my students, I add, "Fighting for proper crediting for the vocal creation was also upsetting and exhausting. No wonder the *Chicago Tribune* praised the vocal lines for their feminist jolt! I was sparking out!"

Everyone laughs.

"With the help of that laugh, let's sing through the vocal wilderness that lies just above your *lower passaggio*—G, G-sharp, and A." The class does its best to mix light and dark, but some are carrying too much weight, while others are detaching from their ballast.

In March, two months after my burnout induced laryngitis, I flew out west to write at my friend Julie's place on Lummi Island. My voice had not fully restored. The lowest stuff was sort of there, and the *lower passaggio* too. But those few notes between the *lower* and *upper passaggi*—the ones the class has just sung—were a disaster. It felt as if I didn't even *have* notes there. By the way, those are the same notes that vanished just after my first divorce, when I was twenty-six—and the same notes that Whitney Houston crashed her way through in concert as her life unraveled.

What I noticed while out west, and could not understand, were brand-new squeaks up in my soprano range. These little peeps seemed to be some kind of residue from the laryngitis. I was not happy with them, as they were unfamiliar and vulnerable. I tried not to hate them for their fragility. I had a role to sing in the upcoming months, as well as a recording to finish before then. I had no idea how these strands of girlish sound could help.

Each day I went to Julie's beautiful Steinway piano in the big house. I gave her a lesson. Guiding another person almost always ups my compassion. I reminded myself that if I could teach her, perhaps I could show myself enough respect to listen fairly to my own voice. I started working with those three notes—the G, G-sharp, and A above middle C. I nurtured my patience. I listened very carefully to what the squeaks—the light—had to tell me as I sang those pitches. I vowed not to negate or overwhelm what was fragile. I let their gleam hover over-head. I promised these gossamer sounds safety and support through providing a modest firmness behind my chest. I focused carefully and nonjudgmentally … grappled with my identity, my ego, my maid-warrior. I tried not to predict anything. As much as I had work to do, I tried not to hunker down.

Over the first few days my sound was pretty dreadful: crackly, unsure of what it should hold on to, or how. But each day it began to fill in, ever … so … slowly. I continued this painstaking work after return-ing to Toronto. I did the usual Slipper Camp routine for myself, taking extra time and care over the G, G-sharp, and A. Eventually the sound *became* itself—a slightly new self. I felt the fulcrum of my voice sit just a little higher than I had previously allowed. Surprisingly, my depth was not only still there; it felt more relaxed … fathomless. I realized that the joy I'd been "employing" during the previous, difficult, year had been slightly frenetic and engineered. This left me trying to integrate feelings that weren't genuinely glad with the mad I'd been denying—no wonder my sad had turned into depression. I had lost the tools for wholeness.

To preserve this renewed feeling of little girl delight and the well-being that came with it, I had to promise myself, with each inhale, not to overwork … to maybe even court "underwork"! If there was a sound that was taxing to the upper squeaks in my voice, I needed to listen to that information carefully and either "gentle" my approach, or say *no* and stop. I had to honor the little girl* and her needs within my voice, body, and psyche.

"Each of you," I tell the class, "has a version of this story when it comes to the part of you that tries to take care of everything and the part of you that needs to be taken care of. They need to build a respectful, intimate relationship with one another for health and balance to be cultivated within your body. Taking the fragile part of my sound into account allowed my depression to lift."

Today's Slipper Camp is small in number, and they are all quite advanced, so I decide to work one-on-one. I ask them to map each of their colleagues' individual work in their own body in order to stay engaged with today's theme of economy.

"Feel these two ideas in your body simultaneously: 'caring for' and 'being taken care of.' Find a transparent place for a collaboration that feels balanced and effortless—democratic, fair, and just. It will take discipline, but it will be worth it."

I turn to Yesim. "When we are put on the spot, we panic just a bit and batten down our hatches. This pulling down of the soft palate results in a cloudy, low-ceiling sound. I know you think you are 'not a singer' and that voice is a relatively new skill, but your composure is great and your low voice reliable. Recently your relationship to height has come along beautifully! I am asking you to sing alone first for all of these reasons. Let's start with the newfound height in your voice—the opposite of battening down the hatches—and descend in pitch from there."

Starting with the A so recently restored in my own voice, we descend semitone by semitone. Her sound is delicious when innocence is alive and well.

---

* In the cis-gendered male body, this shimmer is related to the "falsetto." Pre-puberty, its tenderness typically hovers above spoken and sung notes with integrated ease.

"Each and every pitch requires this intense identification with light, even as you seek the purchase behind your chest."

She does this, and we sail down through the *lower passaggio* and right into her basement. Yesim's almost imperceptible moans and groans provide an interesting friction, or traction, in her chest, support the light in her darkness. The whole class is wowed.

"Great, Yesim! You let go of your allegiance to how your vocal basement felt in the early days of renovation. You've finished that hard work, and now—through integration and economy—you can live in the lower regions with grace, ease, and honesty, thanks in part to the propriety behind your sternum. That took me years and years to manage, and you have found it in eighteen months! Brava!"

We all sing a few long tones, taking on Yesim's process and progress.

I make eye contact with Denise. It is a little daunting to be "up next," and I see a mixture of excitement and dread in her eyes. I smile and nod; we both relax. "Pretend you don't know anything even if you are trying to intelligently balance three or more ideas." Denise attempts knowing and not knowing, and the sound is quite good, but it goes on and on forever, getting a little grim near the end of her exhale.

"On a scale of one to ten, how well do you want to do?"

Denise announces with a generous grin, "Eleven!" We all laugh. Most of us register anywhere from nine to eleven, no problem!

"Drop it to three and let what wants to happen, happen."

Denise drops her desire to succeed to three while minding her tasks. Thanks to her change in intention—the clutch between knowing and succeeding newly eased—the length of her notes is no longer tense, dutiful, or desperate. When chest, chin, and resonators stop pushing forward, healthier alignment allows for freer airflow.

"That's right, Denise, you have to risk a slightly shorter exhale. We are so used to thinking a long breath is superior that we don't even question it. Achieving a grim long note or phrase can make us feel noble and successful even when the sound is pushed or constrained. As adult artists we like to think in long thoughts, because we can, but expressive sighs are all sorts of lengths.

"I want you to take this lovely, more emotionally available note and ease into a series of gentle leans into your mid-back, right where your bra strap is, while allowing the next pitch to *flow* out of your mouth."

Denise's sound elongates without duress, as expected. By dipping into a malleable body that understands resource, she no longer has to stingily budget air to prove her prowess. The class relaxes while hearing her note, appreciates that this is a sustainable sustain.

"Releasing into elongation demonstrates that true economy—energy in sync with environment—provides long-term sustenance. Denise's resulting sound is tasty and nourishing. When we sing to 'keep up with' or 'please' someone else rather than in our own sweet time, a tendency to elongate the note by unhealthy means creeps in. Speaking of 'own sweet time' …"

I turn to Doug. He cocks his head slightly, but the eyes below his questioning brow retain their sparkle.

"Doug, I want you to choose the most 'just' moment you can imagine to start your tone. Evaluate your inhale *while experiencing its pleasure,* in order to find the exact moment when it wants to 'turn around' or 'reverse' into an exhale. Enjoy the transit of air through your body, its natural ebb and flow, its unassailable understating of transition."

Doug jumps right in, and an easy, integrated tone emerges.

"Now I want you to enjoy and imagine the idea of 'middle' as you flow your air. You might want the soft yields that Denise found through her back to enjoy 'middle.'"

His tone elongates just a bit, making us all want to "hang out" with him.

"Finally I want you to imagine that the end of the note is a tender, optimistic goodbye. Not a *full stop* but more of an *au revoir … see you again.*"

His next tone begins because it is the right moment, continues because it wants to, and transparently takes its leave when it is done.

"In an exercise, it is easy to become accomplished but perfunctory. If we find the pleasure of one, hello; two, accompaniment; and three, taking our leave, each note can become valid and interesting from beginning to end … while 'practicing technique.' Let's all try this."

Several engaging long tones later, there are still two students waiting for individual attention—Ntokozo and Jen. I ask them both the same question: "What do you feel your greatest challenge has been most recently within this approach to voice?"

Jen answers quickly and easily, "Allowing emotion to run a little wild."

Ntokozo announces, "Keeping my mouth really open!"

"Excellent! I could not have put it better for either of you. I want you to sing your long tones at the same time. Use the challenge you revealed as the tangible ingredient to aid integration—not the impediment—even if you feel this challenge rear its head as an 'issue' while vocalizing.

"Ntokozo, you have told me how much yawning helps you open your mouth in order to achieve the vertical tube that allows for both fluffs to coexist. As you know, the Upper Fluff is a by-product of the Lower Fluff. Unfold your mouth as you would in a yawn, and at the same time try to be self-possessed behind your sternum—while resisting rigidity. As for you, Jen, you know what you are doing but need to remind yourself that there is no need to engineer your body's actions as if you were responsible for 'getting it right.' Do all those little things just for you. *Be yourself* while making sound."

They sing simultaneously, and I almost buy it.

"Why have I asked you two to sing together?" They are a little stumped, so I open the question to the rest of the group.

Doug suggests, "So they don't compete."

Denise says, "So they can't hear themselves and judge."

Yesim adds, "To feel that they are not alone."

"Each of you is right, and each of you is expressing something you want for yourself! It is true that I want this tandem singing to foster common ground, shared responsibility, and friendly companionship. It is a challenge for two slightly perfectionistic and driven, more than capable professionals to stop caring about their sound. But, more importantly, I want to feel you care together about your process. Collaborate."

Jen and Ntokozo grin at one another and nod their heads. "*Aaaaaahhhhh ...*"

Returning to the next long note, their complicity is contagious. "Holding your own" side by side invites integration to be fun rather than grim—something for everyone, not just the special few. The democratic practice of integration gives each of our energies a vote from within. Working judiciously in all the right places returns the body to a belief that singing is about allowing—that it is easy and organic. Through healthy repetition, this refines a new relationship between *fight or flight* and *rest and digest*. Eventually it feels fun, collaborative, and natural. *Real.*

I address the class. "Thank you for telling the simple truth based on what you see and hear and feel. Thank you for being surprised by ease and contradiction and playfulness—holding each of these things while working effectively. Thank you for doing this so openly, and together. Singing is often such serious business, and my wish for you is that you become as free and integrated in your sound-making as you were when you were an honest and vocally productive infant."

There is no question in the baby's mind about making loud, purposeful noise; or random, soft sound; or squiggly, indirect sound. Sound for the sake of sound as well as sound that has clear meaning and intention. Sound that gives voice to the feelings in the body. Why else would we want to sing any interval, phrase, or song?

―――――

Class ends and my front door closes one last time. I sigh out a ragged puff of swirling, shifting air. Memory floods back in; Richard asking us at the beginning of a workshop, in Toronto or Banff or France, to describe our relationship to our voice. Each time my heart would pound, palms gather sweat. I usually crackled, "We have a love/hate relationship." The sound of my voice betrayed a lack of wholeness.

I was raised to be honest, but I don't believe I was raised to tell the truth. I was told that I could do anything a man could, that I was of equal worth. But the social structures I grew up in—religious, familial, educational, economic, sexual—did not need me to say how I felt, or what I thought. It is hard to feel integrated within structures built on fundamental lies that reinforce binary thinking. Women still do more housework and child care; equal pay is not legislated in Canada. It is through singing that I learned to refigure this emotional arithmetic—from sums that never added up to a calculus I can understand and live by.

Navigating the *upper passaggio* offers me the opportunity to develop agency within a tight spot. The only way through is narrow, verging on claustrophobic—a bit like the chafing rules that can exist within family or culture. Through this *passaggio*'s demand for precision, self-possession is fostered over reactivity. But without genuine leeway and joy, that propriety can sound monochromatic ... dead.

The *lower passaggio*'s infinite range of vocal color reminds me that from very young I was able to quietly bend myself out of shape to fit within many situations and relationships. The flexibility required to "make things work" can be helpful, but, like a tight space, too much compromise can lead to feelings of entrapment. Taking the *upper passaggio*'s balanced containment into the *lower passaggio*'s endless possibilities brings choice, or consent, into play through equanimity. A good thing, as jeopardizing those nine semitones can undermine an entire voice.

Each *passaggio* has something concrete to offer so that *bound* and *unbound* can communicate productively with one another. The practice of the *oooo* slides invites a mastery of difficult, seemingly opposite energies. Its prowess rests on refinement and balance—helps me "see" and "hold" myself. Returning to homeostasis I believe that I could play first fiddle as well as second—a co-creator rather than reactor or accommodator. A partner.

Just after 2015's depression, while channeling the voice of a mermaid onstage, I had a flash of "How the heck did my voice do that?" in the middle of a very precise, and brand-new, texture. It was not only the sound of my voice that astonished me; it was the idea that I could discover something new in front of friends and strangers during a "performance."

231

Just before singing this role I had recalibrated the fulcrum of my voice through respecting its tender Upper Fluff needs despite my depression … or maybe as a way through it. I identified with an undefended part of myself that I would have rather kept hidden. Listening to the full resonant range of my voice with care and respect kept me true without having to hold the reins too tightly, or use my spurs unnecessarily. My voice healed itself through mind and body collaborating in a way I was finally ready to welcome.

Economy is integration is wholeness.

PART III

Women and Voice

28

Commodity del Arte

IT IS 2013 and I have just come across an old TV clip of the preteen, pre-celebrity Britney Spears competing on *Star Search*. A big black bow pulls back her long hair. Her demure party dress has a fluttery skirt perfect for twirling. The slender straps of her patent leather Mary Janes crisscross small arches. A ten-year-old girl contained by pretty things. Britney's singing of "Love Can Build a Bridge" is unaffected and accomplished and, although the song's theme feels bigger than her pre-Ophelia years, it is not provocative. In a brief exchange with the show's avuncular host, Ed McMahon, she explains that the reason why she doesn't have a boyfriend is that they are mean.

There is a moment in Britney's performance that I never want to forget. At the start of the chorus she holds the word *love* for six full beats. As her glorious tone unfolds, her prepubescent, pre-"packaged" body melts right down to the knee. The length of her spine swoons. Her voice thrills her own insides. A miniature masterclass in vocal inhabitation. I never thought I could be touched by Britney Spears, but 1992 Britney is not the "Princess of Pop" who recorded "Baby One More Time" in 1998.

When my girls were four and seven I did not welcome the sound of Britney's sixteen-year-old, pop-sensation voice spilling out of the car radio. I did not like the tiny, grasping grunt that started each of her exhales, nor the whiny timbre that filled in her vowels. She sounded pleading and artificial, desperate to be nice even when behaving "badly." In passing, I heard that a door's creak had been digitally wedded to her rasp, post-recording, in order to amplify its seductive qualities. Huh? I am not seduced: door, or no door. I hear a young woman aping the *grrr* of female orgasm without inhabiting its wisdom: the body's intelligence reduced to a marketing special effect.

Sixty percent of human communication is nonverbal; this includes physical gesture as well as vocalization. A grunt, whine, groan, or holler is a powerful, immediate conveyor of feeling. Words codify feelings into agreed-upon emotional constructs. An adult can use language to say that she feels like crying while showing no sign of it. Though a grunt or whine doesn't lie, a singer can overwork any prosodic vocal fragment—render it inert. Emptied of original sensation, it becomes a calcified, far-off memory. Reducing a vocal sound's impact might be safer for both singer and listener by providing communicative short-hand, but this kind of singing is not a chemical-changing, transformational experience. I call Britney's relentlessly repetitive *grrr* a vocal "relic." Now imitated by countless other pop sensations it minimizes the authentic power of our animal body. To my ears it sounds like an orgasm's remainders.

I surprise myself the week after my young Britney epiphany by asking the Thursday class what they remember of her. Despite decades of personal troubles, spread far and wide on supermarket magazine racks, she is remote to this group. I remind them that Britney Spears was gobsmackingly famous, with ten chart-topping hits and millions of album sales worldwide. I demonstrate a version of her *grrr*, locating mine well below my vocal cords behind my sternum, thus leaving out the neediness of her whine. The class recalls Britney's signature sound and looks at me expectantly, wondering where I am going with this.

"Think of the words *grunt* and *groan*—they conjure sound and feeling low in the body. There is a little violence in their grip, in the growling part of the sound. A dog threatens with this sound, keeps danger at bay using the little *grrr*. There's no need to go all out with this economical hint of anger—the traction of a soft growl feels good in the chest.

Orgasm brings together *fight or flight*'s arousal with the safety of *rest and digest*. Taking note of an orgasm's parameters can help develop a conscious, collaborative relationship between the *sympathetic* and *parasympathetic* functions of the autonomic nervous system—essential for a singer's craft. The orgasm's renewable creativity models how to engage with *work* and *release* at the same time."

I ask my class to try out Britney's *grrr*. It does not go as I had imagined, maybe because her "relic" is too remote to conjure feeling. Eventually we pass our own *grrrs* around the circle. Sourcing this small slice of an orgasm's acoustic from our own bodies forces us to hold desire and satisfaction in equal proportion. As relaxation and activation ally we discover that the *grrr* is embarrassingly transparent in its present-moment, unbridled pleasure. I describe young Britney's full-bodied swoon on *Star Search*—the vocal readiness that the music industry toned down while still capitalizing on her *grrr*. A pimped-out promise of physical pleasure emptied of respect for the female orgasm's essential potency.

The class's four women are now accessing the *grrr*'s dual nature with ease. They sound as if they are satisfied while still wanting more. But our lone man struggles. I tease Sebastian, saying that it must be easier for women to balance this contradiction since we are wired for multiple orgasms. Sebastian laughs and tries harder to feel deeply sated while still exhibiting need. Through trial and error he finds this delicate balance. I witness the same thing in other classes; it is easier for women to find this sound—once they have jumped over the hurdle of propriety—but the men either release fully into satisfaction, or restrict themselves by pushing for what they need. When their voices finally find this tantalizing mix of pleasure, longing, generosity, and joy, I am reminded of Tom Jones's virile resonance.

I wonder what Britney's mature voice would have become if it had not been minimized by her producers, eventually reduced to an unanswerable whine. I wonder what would have happened if her father, Jamie Spears, had not been granted conservatorship over her life after her very public mental health breakdown in 2008. Her financial empire—and even her use of birth control—fell under the shared purview of Mr. Spears and a lawyer named Andrew Wallet.

On June 23, 2021, Britney spoke forcefully and movingly in public about how angry and traumatized she'd been for thirteen years despite getting onstage night after night to perform. She could no longer fake her happiness and asked for the conservatorship to end. It took five months and multiple legal hurdles for Britney to gain her independence.

The grim fairy tale I tell of Britney and her *grrr* underlines the importance of owning one's full self during childhood, adolescence, and into adulthood. It does not speak to the range of pressures a celebrity like Britney has to juggle well before a human being's physical, mental, and emotional landscapes have fully developed. I cannot imagine the coping mechanisms she might have used to hold on for dear life.

I would have loved to hear Britney grow up without losing her prepubescent vocal swoon and swagger. Witness her become her own woman through retaining her full resonant self. I miss the Britney who did not happen, the Britney whose orgasm was stolen.

———

Hannah, hardly off her horse, is now stuck in heavy traffic on the way back from a day in the country. She and her two friends keep me posted via text—"Can we start late?" "We're almost there!" "We'll pay the full amount!" They arrive in high spirits from the riding and the drive. We breathe together, settle into long tones, and soon Hannah is ready to sing.

Since childhood Hannah has been told that she can't carry a tune. Exploring her voice in my studio, she often opts for loud, brash sounds: tight, guttural frustration in the midrange; high, piercing wails up top; and low groans plunging down to earth. This raw, cathartic exploration has brought the validity of nonverbal sound to her attention and increasingly her pitches connect to the ones I offer on the piano. When this happens I point out that her autonomic nervous system is doing its job, whether or not her mind can tell.

Through this series of classes Hannah's colleagues have witnessed her voice increase in expressivity: range and texture. Last week I asked her to "groom" one of the other women while singing, as if she were handling her horse. Connected to her equestrian self she found a creative, caring focus for the female body, which brought her into relationship with pleasure and wholeness. Her competent actions soothed her own nervous system while identifying with her friend's and this opened her entire being to a more expansive vocal palette. Moving past simply getting her feelings "out of her system" or "off her chest" Hannah was able to be both inside and outside of herself, increasing her capacity for self-awareness and, through that, communication.

Today the sound of Hannah's voice is very particular. There is a slightly "caught" quality at the start of each long tone. This small amount of friction sits right behind her chest; I map it in my own body to see if it will cause trouble. Her air is flowing freely, and so rather than correcting this below-the-throat "catch," I follow it through the low, medium, and high ranges of her voice. Partway through it dawns on me that each breath has a hint of orgasm's deep pleasure—not the performative sound that Britney uses but an energetic feeling of owning herself.

I ask Hannah to stop for a moment. Her friends are thrilled with what they have just heard; their comments celebrate her singing's clarity and ease. Hannah announces with a wide grin, "I did my homework!" Her voice is vital, naughty, and triumphant. She asks me if I remember what it was. "Yes, of course, the fifth piece—orgasm!"

Two decades ago, when I first suggested investigating orgasm in relation to singing, it was in order to experience freedom of breath and voice during an *unbounded* moment. In recent years neuroscientists have charted the complexity of orgasm. Brain scans indicate that females access both pain and pleasure centers as we come. Is this because both *fight or flight* and *rest and digest* are woven into an orgasm? I note the idea of "arrival" within the expression "to come." Coming into the room, into relationship, into oneself.

Last week when I suggested orgasm as homework, it was because Hannah had revealed that she was in a strong and supportive relationship. Trusting my body and voice within intimate and connected sexual activity has spilled over into having physical agency while singing. I believed that Hannah's physiological intelligence could guide her voice too.

What I marveled at when Hannah sang this week's juicy long tones was how nonreactive she was in her body, without any loss of potency. She was neither a pushy extrovert nor a collapsed introvert but an ambivert—true to herself and available to others. The "stuckness" I sometimes heard in her throat when she worked in the wrong place to match pitch was replaced by a little useful friction down behind her sternum. Her mature *grrr* grounded her voice's expression.

Hannah no longer needs an external object to groom. She has recalibrated the work of singing through partnering a physicalized attitude of caring with a small dose of orgasm's genuinely unabashed aggression. Instead of *fight or flight* and *rest and digest* arguing, Hannah can now value, balance, and synthesize a range of sensed energy as she sings each note. Her sound reveals a reclaimed relationship to self and pitch based in presence and trust.

This morning I need to tell my choir that one of our members, Maja, has cancer and that she will be missing today's session for her first round of chemo. The news comes as a shock to the seven women gathered in my studio. Maja has seemed happier than ever in recent months: touring two successful one-woman shows; delighting in a growing brood of grandchildren.

I watch the news of her cancer land, ask the women ringing the piano how they feel. "Sad." "Queasy." "Surprised." "Tender in the uterus"—where Maja's cancer has taken up residence. We go to work. I ask each singer to find a position, anywhere in the studio, in which her back feels especially soft and exposed—maybe leaning forehead to wall, or in "child's posture" on the floor, perhaps draping arms on the piano, or resting forward onto the couch. The women prostrate themselves. I ask them to drop their bellies and then shift focus to the back of the torso, becoming intimately aware of sacrum and back ribs by allowing these areas to fill with breath. The image of these women spread around the studio, engaged in intimate inner exploration, is terrifyingly vulnerable. I suggest, "Stay where you are for the long tones and see if you can sing from your uterus." The sound is gentle, conscious, and caring—a moving communion I've not heard before.

Afterward I ask the women what singing from their uterus felt like. Niloo comments that her uterus became the base for her spine. Lesley shares that singing from her uterus offered a powerful doorway into her autonomic nervous system and that this organized her voice and body from the inside out. Nadine found that singing from her uterus made her feel that she did not have to take things personally and wondered if this is why she feels *so* emotionally great in those first few days after her period. She had thought it was because the pain of her cramps was over with, but now she wonders if it is because she is feeling "personality" free. We all laugh as she explains, "Believe me, there is a lot of excess personality in the days leading up to bleeding."

I play the introduction to "Tom Traubert's Blues" on the piano—our choir's moaning song. Tom Waits is naming the wounded masculine, acknowledging his part.

Wasted and wounded—it ain't what the moon did—I got what I paid for now ...

We sing in our lowest register—more than a whisper, but shy of grunt or growl. Those sounds have too much purchase for what we want to express. Our sad, spirit-soaked voices hold the news of Maja's cancer. I have never heard the group sound so unforced, so inside themselves, so transparently available.

At the end of the first verse Natasha's face streams with tears. Roula says she wishes she was less strong, that she is breaking down her excess strength through singing this song. Chris's face is flushed; she tells us about a woman giving birth to a stillborn baby ... her own story.

We arrive at the chorus, which has lifted its melody and words directly from the Australian song "Waltzing Matilda." In response to each verse's painful unraveling, Tom Waits asks Matilda to dance with him. Besides being a woman's name, Matilda refers to the bedroll carried by itinerant workers from ranch to ranch in the Australian outback. At the end of a long day these homeless men cradled their bedrolls while dancing around the fire … holding loneliness at bay. I have played several homeless women but never thought to dance.

But who'll go waltzing Matilda, waltzing Matilda, you'll go waltzing Matilda with me …

Lesley tells us that the tenderness of the man's descent touches her at her core. For her, Matilda represents a sex worker. She pictures the man escaping into the arms of the feminine, his desire to be soothed, to not be judged, to enter into the experience of his animal body uncensored. She comes to a full stop. *"The female uterus must have absorbed so much rage through the ages."*

A *hhhhhhmmmm* runs through the choir. A PhD candidate, a bodyworker, a retired air traffic controller, a midwife, a writer, an actor, and an event manager—common women talking uncommonly about the deeply private responses of our most private parts. Maja is "cancering" and we are using our singing senses to identify with her illness. *Trying to make sense of the world we live in.* Any woman with good sense would be "cancering," shoplifting, drowning her children, keening in front of parliament, asking for equal pay, for a say in how things are run—or barking at the world like Heracles before us.

We leave the deep moan of Tom Waits for Anonymous's "Motherless Child." An African American spiritual, it unites the feeling of being orphaned, bereft, and homeless with that of faith. Virginia Woolf wrote, "I would venture to guess that Anon, who wrote so many poems without signing them, was often a woman." In this case Anonymous includes men, women, and children—whole communities of believers conspiring its beautiful bones.

Sometimes I feel like a motherless child … We layer our feelings, singing as mother and as child. *Sometimes I feel like a motherless child …* Four duos overlapping until four lines run in canon with a slow, underlying pulse that has arisen from our swaying pelvises. *Sometimes I feel like a motherless child …* We sing with enormous light in our collective tone, making room for each voice while partnering with the gravity of hip and thigh. As the high point in the melody bubbles up—one duo after another—we become the spray from a gentle waterfall, the pealing of bells. *A long way from home* … Through not competing with one another, we create acoustic spaciousness. *A long way from home* … We keep each other aloft. *True believer, a long way from home* … As the song stills, we stay grounded in our pelvic organs—close to Maja's cancer.

We talk. Out of the burble a clear thought emerges. We have each felt motherless moving into our professional lives. We have also felt motherless in our private relationships. There haven't been a lot of female models to help us make sense of this new world. No matter how much our mothers loved us, patriarchal structures made open intergenerational expression between women difficult. We are a long way from home.

When Britney Spears came back after years of tabloid scandal and mental health challenges, she gave a performance at Billboard Music's 2016 Awards. Her medley began with a song called "Work Bitch" from her Las Vegas show *Piece of Me*. In the TV clip Britney's eyes and face look terrified, her pelvis stiff, frozen in fear … no swoon in sight. "Freeze" is something we humans do when we are threatened and can neither fight back nor flee. Something a woman might default to when her *grrr* is stolen or silenced—either the *grrr* of anger or the *grrr* of sensuality.

When a woman is sexualized according to the prevailing male fantasy, she becomes a commodity. Without first-person agency she is compelled to compete with herself and with other females in ways that limit healthy, important conversations. Conversations that could teach us how to support one another in this time of rapid relationship change. Conversations that could support important social change related to gender constructs. Conversations that could return the *grrr* to every body, strengthening give-and-take … ebb and flow. Relationships within each human as well as between bodies.

29

No Defense, No Pretense

LITTLE MORE THAN a century ago the last passenger pigeon fell off her perch in the Cincinnati Zoo. Drawings of her migratory species show a refined bird with subtle, elegant coloring. I wish I had known Martha. I would have liked to witness her ancestors congregate in one of the three large airborne colonies that flew nomadically over North America in the late 1800s. Only forty years before her death a single convoy of 2.5 billion pairs of beating wings took three days to pass over Chicago: creating a cold downdraft, darkening the sky, deafening human ears below.

One bird, one perch, one zoo. Who could have imagined this ending? We hunted, made pigeon pie, tore down the trees that made up these birds' habitats, and despite their vast numbers and competent, intrinsic life skills—flocking, foraging, and reproducing—they could not survive. From instinct to extinct.

Several times this year I have flown over Chicago's suburbs, alighting on the Midway tarmac. I am working with Erica Mott and Ryan Ingebritsen to co-create an opera-installation about migration and unjust labor practices in America's early 1900s garment industry. To create the vocal energy necessary for protest, I first have to teach three young vocalists that a person's voice is emotion laid bare, that it comes from the autonomic nervous system, that it is the perfect instrument of self-betrayal, of transparency. With each warm-up I seduce these women out of their tensions, their desire to measure up or become someone they are not, invite them to drop learned vocal habits. In place of pleasing others I want them to feel pleasure when they sing ... stop fitting in.

Giving voice to moan, groan, sigh, whisper, whine, screech, and holler will help these three performers taste the fineness of their own nervous system. It will encourage them to de-commodify body, soul, and sound through consciously identifying with the fullness of their music-making, from beautiful to terrifying. It is time for these women to stop being their own lovely product, learn the "ugly" in their voices. Erica, Ryan, and I agree that working creatively with birdsong will set a template for the female voice to protest without apology or pretense.

3 Singers is only one of two performances I have been developing this year with birdcall at the core of the vocal creation. Trying to produce sound like birds do has been humbling. Humans have a single voice box that houses two vocal cords; when they vibrate against one another, this contact brings forth sound—gentle gauges of feeling. Birds have a syrinx, low in the chest instead of the throat. The syrinx's two sides can be controlled independently to phonate harmonically unrelated pitches. This is why bird sound is so complex, so hard to approximate; a human would need two voice boxes coordinating at lightning speed.

Through identifying with various birds' high and agile song I've become hyperaware of how small they are. Their heartbeat and breath rate are much faster than a human's, their tiny syrinxes vibrate more quickly than our cords, and their resonant spaces shimmer an impossibly fine gleam. It is natural for them to spin out stratospheric melodies. But if I gradually slow down a recording of a birdcall, its incremental pitch drop eventually settles into my much larger human body with tones and timings I can identify with and through that feel fully.

My growing respect for birds is offering a way to play outside of the "rights and wrongs" associated with female sound. I wonder about behavior—ask myself how a woman's sense of self might intersect with or differ from our species' strong social instincts, often visible through her traditional place in community. Stepping outside of known boundaries through taking on birdsong, I hope to find new wilderness for female expression and interaction. But the more deeply we delve into creation, the more differences I discover between the birds and my experience of being a woman. I can't get over the fact that a bird uses 100 percent of its air when making a sound. Far too often I have held some breath in reserve, hedged my bets, been stingy with my sigh, not spoken from the heart—not fully inhabited my voice like birds do.

The garment industry's first female workers—most of whom were in their teens and twenties—were charting new territory when they took on employment outside the home. Despite their youth and inexperience, they stood up to factory owners who were not providing decent pay or a safe environment. I ask my three Chicago singers to risk vocally by using an improvisational structure that will elicit discovery and transgression within their performance bodies.

Beginning with individual birdcalls tailored to each woman's voice, I ask for these cries to transform into sounds that contain both vowels and consonants (fragments of human language) while retaining "birdyness." Next I ask the singers to stretch these brand-new musical building blocks into longer *complaint phrases* in order to convey something they are currently compelled to fight for "just for themselves" using sung and extended sound. Finally I want these *complaint phrases* to transform, on the fly, into one of the slogans used by women demanding control over their work lives and their bodies in the early 1900s.

The three stages of this improvisational structure invite an evolution from *bird* to *siren* to *woman*. Or maybe *bird* to *female* to *siren*? For two full days the three singers commit to their body-led transformations. The low, throaty moans of Lara's rock pigeon transform into a sexual abuse lament, then a string of *nos* that reclaim spirit and self, finally arriving at a divine slogan, more aria than chant, "No gods, no masters!" The high, brilliant shrieks of Jenna's blue grosbeak fracture into one of union leader Clara Lemlich's speeches, ending in a metal-shredded "Eight hours for work, eight hours for sleep, eight hours for what we will!" No gendered vocal decor to distract us from her urgency. Our third bird starts with a tuneful little hook full of good cheer. Maggie then funnels her version of a ruby kinglet—all flap and feather—into a driving rap about the amazing resources a woman has, the beauty of her sex, her moon-led rhythms, and her fecundity. She fully embodies "Bosses beware: when we're screwed we multiply!"

While I wait to disembark the homebound flight from Chicago, the plane's speakers spit out a song at low volume—innocuous orchestration, bland soprano voice, a regurgitated message that has been sung for longer than I have listened. The lyrics try to convince women to hurt for the sake of love, as if it was our job to suffer, stand by, and repair. Trapped in the aisle I remember that dumbed-down music—Muzak—was created just over one hundred years ago to keep factory workers productive and placated. Pumped-in music in place of human work songs.

It took a full century to complete the list of primarily Jewish and Italian immigrants who perished in Manhattan's catastrophic Triangle Shirtwaist Factory fire. Only eighteen months before, these same workers had returned to the Asch Building in Greenwich Village from strike action that had protested long hours, unfair wages, and unsafe conditions, and even though their hours and wages had improved, they had not bargained successfully for their safety. Doors to stairwells continued to be routinely locked to minimize unauthorized breaks and theft; and elevator capacity remained insufficient in case of emergency. To avoid being burned alive as fire broke out on the sewing floor due to the highly flammable fibers floating in the air, 50 of that day's 146 workers jumped from the eighth, ninth, and tenth floors. The force of their landing bodies imprinted the sidewalk while the company bosses escaped from the top floor via the roof. The women who died that day had been unsafe on the job in more ordinary ways for years; foremen commonly forced their female employees to trade sexual favors for thread.

The last strains of music masquerading as love come to an end as I step off the plane into Toronto's early-morning gray. I am so full of rage I could choke.

It is September 2014. Boreal birds are beginning to fly south, and I am flocking with the women of *A Mourning Chorus* for a repeat performance of our endangered and extinct bird project, this time at the Royal Ontario Museum. Sara Angelucci is an ingenious producer as well as an excellent artist; she has managed to get us included in the events accompanying a new exhibition, *Empty Skies: The Passenger Pigeon Legacy*. Singing beneath the gold and blue mosaic of the ROM's rotunda, we will be the *amuse bouche* for an evening of lectures from passenger pigeon expert Joel Greenberg and de-extinction maverick Ben Novak.

All of us songbirds are excited to try out the acoustic of the golden-domed entrance to the museum, honored to be in such a beautiful and respected institution, glad to be together again. But I am worried. Making this piece about birds and extinction kicked up so much volatility for me last time in relation to women, instinct, and voice. Grappling with the all-too-recent death of my father while deep in the heart of menopause has left me with severely depleted resources. My inner forest is picked bare and I don't feel up to rehearsing and performing. I'd like to quit.

I tell all of this to my friend Eve on one of our late-night walks. She says, "You can't quit." But I am not certain that my voice can handle being in public right now. It takes weeks to build performance stamina and I feel hopelessly introverted.

Eve is right; it would take more emotional work to quit than to show up. So I show up small and tidy, with nothing to spare. And, like a sparrow, I try not to worry. I "mark" the first few rehearsals, singing so quietly that I am not really singing at all, indicating what I am supposed to do at the right time and in the right place. I resist the heroic—drop any hawk from my squawk. I walk slowly, I move slowly, I laugh a little, and I work on friendly. Friendly and fragile are oddly easy; the other women in the group know how to throng around it. I end up enjoying pulling my own weight and nothing more.

I have always resisted identifying myself as "sensitive," but this summer I have been humbled by the porosity of my skin. Daily, hundreds of hot flashes reveal exactly which subjects irk or scare me. These flares are not only illuminating; they are burning away the things I thought were mine, the things I cannot handle, the things I no longer need. Every step of the way I am being tempered by my own fire. Refined.

Teaching is starting up full force at Humber College, as well as in my home studio, but all I can focus on is the pain I feel throughout my body: in my joints, under my skin, in my gut. It is from holding too much, in too many areas of my life. I don't know how to discharge my sense of responsibility ... all I want to do is cry ... let go. I take a deep breath, wonder if small and tidy, friendly and fragile might help with this too.

Returning to teaching after even a short hiatus is typically a period of growth and synthesis for me. Despite my trepidation over feeling depleted, I learn that over the past few months I have become more discerning in how I see and hear. A new level of experience has settled into my bones thanks to this year's challenges; empathy, understanding, and language entwine.

A number of new students have asked for lessons. They stride expectantly through my front door and into the studio. Some of these young Amazons know they are fighting a battle and some don't. Regardless, the war wounds their bodies bare in lesson after lesson share similar physical truths. An epidemic of women straining, damaging, or losing their voices. I can't remember ever seeing it this bad.

Are women on an endangered species list?

In that first week of September I work with two women who were abused sexually when they were little, as well as four more who are completely cut off from ease and delight in their bodies for less overtly traumatic reasons. They are bright, focused, engaging—capable and direct by our culture's norms. Their vocal injuries include: a paralyzed cord, a baby polyp, a small blister, and a burst blood vessel. They need help handling what feels urgent and scary for body and soul. Not all of them are professional singers—but they are women with voices, unique identities, interesting careers, creative pursuits ... some have children. All of them want to be heard.

I say that I have not heard the unmediated female voice. Let me clarify. I have rarely heard my own unmediated voice. I have almost always used my voice to rally myself, to bolster, to take it all on. This is the "news" for me this morning ... my realization ... my story. I am ready for these damaged Amazons. I have been prepping for years, and having so recently released into my own vulnerability, I know exactly what to offer.

One of the women who has experienced abuse tells me that she has had addiction issues most of her life, though she has been clean for four years now. During the course of her lesson I notice how her alcoholism resonates with my own workaholism. The clarity she has about her own life journey invites me to stay true to mine. I decide to work very slowly with her at a speed I can handle, with a load I can bear. My body's flaring guides me, and our needs attune. I remain soft, unheroic, while dealing with her trauma—within myself and within my instructions to her. Together we discover how to access the heart of her issues without re-traumatizing.

Within this forest of emerging stories, a longtime student arrives first thing on a Wednesday morning, full of terror. Mirian is recording a demo of five of her songs in only two days. Her manager wants to shop her around, but her voice is tired—exhausted, in fact. She uses the expression "vocal fatigue." That is the polite way we singers put it.

I know Mirian fairly well. She was a student of mine for two years at Humber College. Alex Fallis, Heidi Strauss, and I created a large inter-disciplinary piece for her graduating class. She was also in a play by Maja Ardal based on Marina Nemat's *Prisoner of Tehran*, for which I created vocal material. As well as coming to classes in my studio, Mirian was in my women's choir for a time. There is water under our bridge.

I ask Mirian to tell me more about what she is feeling—how she is experiencing herself right now. She says she can't soften down to her pelvic floor when breathing. I ask her what is going on in her life, why she might be holding her breath. She tells me she has just moved in with her boyfriend and is really happy about this, but finds herself breathing shallowly in their new home. I tell her this is not an unnatural response to a big change. She may be getting used to mundane, yet surprising, habits. She might not yet have a room in which she can thoroughly "let down." And, of course, it is also possible that the grip through her pelvic floor is telling her something more, about her choice to cohabitate, or about her reaction to the civil war that has just begun in Syria, where her family is from. Regardless of what is causing her to feel distanced from her pelvis, something can be done if she listens to herself and expresses what is going on. What is certain is that her breathing doesn't feel deep enough, and that her body and brain have some collaborative work ahead.

Starting with the dropped belly breath, I gently coax Mirian to relax, inhale after exhale. The many waters we have shared remind the fluids in her body to ebb and flow without my saying much. The solid structure that appears to be her becomes more permeable—available to air, and the conversations this awakens. I breathe alongside her, my pelvic floor receiving, just as hers is. Air floods in through each of our upper mouths as our lower ones release.

The quality of my body's interaction with today's air is different from last year's—softer and more liquid. I feel not only the malleability of genitals, perineum, and anus, but the space around my sacrum swells wide. All along my spine, right up to my skull, muscles sway and bow, making room for air to slip into the deepest recesses of my lungs' alveoli. Even the pleasure in my throat and mouth is more intense than before. I share these sensations and thoughts with Mirian, encourage the parts of her that can be heroic to do even less.

When Mirian sings her first long tones, I hear a deep tiredness; her cords sound sluggish and a little swollen. I remind her to believe in her pelvis and trust that its soft receptivity will reintroduce ease into each exhale. This helps her pull back from a cathartic but re-traumatizing force applied upward through shoulders, neck, and chin when singing. This lift can be a coping skill to force the cords together, but it isn't sustainable. As Mirian steps away from the ego-need to "achieve" regardless of how high the cost, she stops bullying her vocal cords.

Being tired will cause a singer to push in order to get her material—*herself*—across. I suggest that we work on the first few lines of each of her songs, set simple templates for doing less within each melody's emotional landscape. My own need for slow gentleness provides an antidote to her worry. Nearing the end of our session I ask Mirian what she observed internally while going through her songs. She says that bit by bit her whole upper torso softened and eased, and that she feels energy now in place of exhaustion. Finally, her breath has dropped.

Finding love for my own body—meaning my actual state of being—encouraged my comments and insights to be broad-minded as well as specific. With ease as our guide, each of Mirian's songs became manageable, and I learned something new about who she is, and who I am as well. We can make ourselves real using both of our mouths and like the birds stake territory, we can call for a partner, protect offspring, sound the alarm, migrate, make meaningful community, thrive at work, effect change in parliament, and sing for the sake of song-making ... all without push or apology.

30

A Mouthful of Stones

THE RADIO IS on. A young woman is telling the story of her rape in a voice hardly out of its teens. Her gentle, halting, average lilt compels me to stop all activity and sit down—leave the dishes for later. She shares extraordinary and intimate details: how small and quiet her voice sounded to her, how it cracked when she said *you have to leave* just before the young man, also a freshman, ripped her baby-pink shorts down past her hips. She said that she knew she should be screaming but couldn't, and after the rape she asked if he would like to stay the night. In response he called her crazy, and after he left she felt that indeed she *was* crazy for the way she had accommodated his violence.

Guilt settled in. She stopped washing her clothes and caring for herself. *The secret of rape is too big for one body to hold.* She told a counselor, who suggested the college's mediation process. In his statement her attacker simply denied that they had ever had sexual intercourse. That put a stop to the conversation, as the young woman was not prepared to take it to the police. Partway through the year her attacker was moved, by the university, into her residence, and they shuffled her off to a cinder block motel for "her protection." Instead, she left school and set off on a pilgrimage to reclaim her body, walking from Mexico to Canada along the Pacific Crest Trail.

A young woman who comes to me for a first private lesson worries that if she opens her mouth too widely she will be raped, but the opposite is true. Women who come for singing lessons, regardless of the surface reasons, have a need to reclaim both of their mouths. Women's mouths and vaginas have been conflated and disrespected for millennia. In the studio I hear a rape story every few months.

The word *rape* made it into the English language by the end of the fourteenth century. It means to seize, prey, abduct, or take by force. Though rape happens one woman at a time, it is not something that happens to just one woman. You do not have to be raped to experience vocal fallout in a culture that normalizes the wielding of power by one group over another—that is bent on taking rather than exchanging.

Aviva has come for a lesson. She is a professional singer who moves easily between Ladino, Yiddish, and Sephardic melody. In her cantorial role, she openheartedly engages large groups in worship. We have not seen each other in several months and she is here for a tune-up. I notice familiar tension patterns as she sings her long tones, in particular when we arrive at the notes right above her *lower passaggio*. These pitches lie just above the top end of a woman's speaking voice.

A vocal imprint comes to mind. It is Lucy DeCoutere* speaking on the radio in the hours after she was pulled apart on the stand by Jian Ghomeshi's† defense lawyer. Lucy had told the court that she continued

---

* Lucy DeCoutere is a training development officer for the Royal Canadian Air Force. She also played the role of Lucy in the maritime mockumentary television series *Trailer Park Boys*. DeCoutere, along with seven anonymous women, publicly alleged sexual assault by Canadian Broadcasting Corporation presenter Jian Ghomeshi in September 2014. She was the first to publicly identify herself as a victim of his violence.

† Jian Ghomeshi was a popular Canadian personality who co-founded and hosted CBC's cultural magazine Q from 2007 to 2014. Kathryn Borel, the show's producer, reported to her union in 2010 that Ghomeshi had sexually harassed and emotionally abused her at work for three years. Once when she yawned in a meeting Ghomeshi allegedly said, "I want to hate fuck you, to wake you up." She was told by her executive producer that this "was the way he was" and she needed to "figure out how to cope...." Ghomeshi was charged with seven counts of sexual assault in 2014 and 2015, including overcoming resistance by choking. He was fired by the CBC. In February 2016, at his trial, Ghomeshi pleaded not guilty, did not take the stand, and was acquitted of all charges. In May 2016 he apologized in court to Borel, acknowledging that his "conduct in the workplace was sexually inappropriate." His words do not count as a legal admission of guilt.

to communicate with Ghomeshi even after he had hit, choked, and hurt her, without permission, during intimate sexual relations. This admission contradicted earlier statements in which she said that she had not had any further contact. For this Lucy was deemed an unreliable witness and the case was dismissed. My acoustic memory of her voice during the post-trial interview lifts the muscles at the front of my throat, hamstrings my larynx. Losing its grounding, my voice box mirrors the strained, insecure sound of Lucy justifying her hard-to-explain behavior.

I say to Aviva, "Let me try something, please." I take the fingertips from both my hands, place them across my collarbones, near the midline, and pull down firmly, drawing flesh over the raised bone between my clavicular and jugular notches. I feel instant relief through the tender strap muscles that support my larynx; they release right up through my jaw hinge, and past the front and back of my ears. I take a breath and sing a long tone. The sensation is amazing; my throat feels absolutely clear and spacious. The physical adjustment provided by my fingertips anchors my voice box, making it impossible to push, apologize, defend, or explain.

I ask Aviva to put her fingers on her collarbones. She pulls down gently and firmly while singing a long tone. Her eyes light up as her vocal cords relax away from justifying themselves. The feeling is foreign and delicious … curious. Over the following week I use this technique with all my female students and am stunned by how unapologetic it makes each of us sound.

When the allegations against Ghomeshi became public, I was in Poland for the 3 *Singers* premiere, coaching the show's three performers to stand their ground vocally through using forbidden female sound. Each night in my hotel room I went online to keep up with the news back home, but it was through emailing girlfriends that I engaged with the story. We shared intimate tales with one another about sexual relations and behaviors that had not been good for us, whether on a single night or over nights that went on for years.

Lucy DeCoutere took a huge risk when she opened up the conversation about consent in Canada in 2015. In contrast to Scheherazade's storytelling tactics, she did not tell a man's story to please him or to stay safe from punishment, but rather voiced her own experience—an experience that was at odds with his. Lucy's reveal became collective; women spoke out in newspaper articles and on the radio about nonconsensual sexual experiences they had had as teens, in their twenties and thirties, within marriage, after divorce. We shared that we had been acting in ways we thought we had to, hiding uninvited, humiliating, and sometimes even violent experiences. Not giving voice to our stories had isolated us from one another. Lucy stepped out of everyone's comfort zone by speaking frankly about something disagreeable. She risked being shamed for her sexual nature. And women learned that we could start having each other's backs. A female *no* took shape. A *no* that predicted 2017's #MeToo and #TimesUp hashtags, galvanized in the wake of Harvey Weinstein's predatory behavior, brought to public attention, coincidentally, in the weeks right after Hugh Hefner's death.*

Has it really taken a thousand years to rescue Scheherazade?

When we don't press the pause button during the part of the story where all the virgins are married and murdered one by one, we tacitly agree to make women completely disposable. Like Scheherazade, I told numerous little stories through both of my mouths to stay safe: a *yes* that wasn't always *yes*; a *maybe* that sometimes meant *no*. When we don't tell Scheherazade's father to take care of his own business, or the king to control his temper, we normalize their emotional failings. Our silence makes violence untraceable. A woman's consent has no weight in such a world, and tension is woven right into her sound-making body.

In this day and age it should not be an act of courage for a woman to use her voice to tell us that she has been harmed during sexual relations. But to quote Lucy, "There's something missing in the way that

---

* The stars being as they are, I was in Chicago teaching a voice workshop not so far from the original Playboy Mansion the day Hefner died. As I demonstrated the *dark breath* to a new group of students I had the sensation that a larger-than-life staple was being extracted from each of my hip flexors through the course of the exercise. My psoas muscle had never felt so free of threat, my breath so easy. It came as a complete surprise and was utterly sensible.

women are being heard.'"' It is hard for women to talk about sex when both our mouths are intrinsically linked, when our sexual natures are seen as suspicious, dangerous, untrustworthy, shameful, and—most grievously—owned by someone else.

I was born as women's liberation and the sexual revolution took seed, but I was not raised to speak about my sexuality without apology or defense. In the shadow of second-wave feminism I learned more about competition with other women than cooperation, and found it hard to let down my guard. Without language grounded in sorority, I missed out on the possibility of support from other women. But after Lucy opened her upper mouth to speak about what had happened in relation to her lower mouth, honest conversations about sex began within my circle of friends. When we voiced our unarticulated, unevolved experiences with men, lamenting our isolation from one another while negotiating our generations' tricky heterosexual terrain, I understood that I had more in common with an abused woman than I'd ever thought possible.

We have a hard time properly recognizing and understanding stories that weave violence with intimacy. Successful sexual encounters depend on a physiological fabric that integrates *fight or flight* with *rest and digest*. This messy, necessary entwinement of perceived dualities can get in the way of developing nuanced language around sexual engagement, romance, and love. Growing up in a culture that is judgmental of human sexuality—that does not appreciate the human body's inherent wisdom—makes integrating sexuality into identity extremely difficult. In this climate it is hard to chart the line between excitement and comfort, or between abandon and respect, for any body.

The young woman whose baby-pink shorts were ripped down past her hips didn't want to feel crazy; she wanted to feel whole and connected after an experience that tore her in two. When an abused woman behaves in mystifying, self-protective ways—ways that

---

* Interview with *The Current*'s Anna Maria Tremonti, CBC Radio, October 20, 2014.

appear to justify or cover up the abusive partner's behavior—we have to remember that we are used to language that pairs "losing your mind" with "falling in love." It is normal that Lucy continued to communicate with Ghomeshi. Seeking reassurance from the perpetrator of hurt or shame in an attempt to make things right, to regain self-worth, does not defy logic. Any lawyer who has handled domestic violence cases knows this. A lawyer with this specific experience should have had Lucy's back.

For a woman to give consent, she must know that she owns her body. She must cultivate a refined understanding of what her body is saying in a variety of situations. She must have access to her voice in a way that allows for self-expression, especially when it's at odds with the dominant culture. She must override fear to say what she means. Each woman who speaks through one mouth to tell the story of the other helps all women attest to their lived experience. Difficult when power is involved—physical or otherwise.

In the public sphere, women's sexuality has been pimped out to sell cars, vodka, sports magazines—a literal spreading of our legs for the benefit of capitalist culture. The more open sexual climate of the '60s and '70s co-opted women's bodies before we could fully reclaim ownership. This surprising outcome of second-wave feminism occurred because women had no economic or political power to speak of…. We weren't in the system.

Just after the Ghomeshi story became public, Canadians learned that male dental students in Halifax, Nova Scotia, used a private Facebook page to discuss the female colleagues with whom they'd like to have "hate sex"—echoing Ghomeshi telling a work colleague that he'd like to "hate fuck" her. I had to ask a young man in my college class not to use the word *slut* to describe how he felt in a moment of vocal yielding. He is a decent young man, but he couldn't compute that a woman releasing within a sexual context does not make her dirty or slovenly. These are costly exchanges that reflect our ongoing inability, or refusal, to value women.

A short story has resurfaced recently from my childhood. I always knew it was there but never dwelled on it or its ramifications. When I was four years old I played with the much bigger boy next door. We roamed all summer long through six or seven backyards with the gang of kids who lived in those houses. One day, with the help of some of the others, he pinned me to the ground under the hedge at the far end of his yard. He pulled down my underwear and shoved pebbles and dirt into my vagina. Somehow my mother knew I was in danger (maybe I called out, maybe another kid told her): she found me, grabbed me by the hand, and yanked me home. Though she saved me, I experienced her adrenalized anger as directed at me. *I had gotten myself into trouble.* She carefully picked out the debris from my tender, pink flesh under the glare of the bathroom light. Running water flushed the evidence down the drain.

I was too young to make sense of what had happened. When I brought it up with my mother shortly before her death it was too late. Her mind skipped back eight decades to a childhood story about a four-year-old neighborhood girl who was a show-off. I wish I had asked earlier. Was it before or after I was photographed singing freely on the picnic blanket with my Aunt Fides? Did this violence affect my voice? Like the stones inside me, our society's shame around female sexuality is something I've never invited.

Con + sensual = together + felt.

After hearing about Ghomeshi's acquittal I crawled into bed and held myself—traced my sexual history and redrew the line around what I would now call consent. That this cultural conversation did not happen when I was in my teens and twenties is an immeasurable loss for not only me and my generation—it will have affected my daughters and their partners.

Last spring I coached a young Toronto-based student via Skype while she recorded her first album in New York. Anna's husky-hued voice doesn't shy away from the darkness of cultural or familial inheritance. Its timbre makes palpable the complex struggles of first love

261

with aching acuity. Poetic lyrics wed well to the simple surprise of her melodic hooks; acoustic traces circle my mind long after a lesson ends. A few minutes into our first Skype session, I hear that since her last in-person visit to my studio Anna has started to whisper her songs. Her voice sounds passive and the poetry no longer makes sense. I remind her that she is the artist and that it is her full-bodied expression of desire and longing that the world needs to hear; she does not need to censor herself even if she is the only woman in a studio full of men. She confesses that she chose to restrict the sound of her own voice, that minimizing herself began in her adolescence when she quieted her singing so that her dominant older sister wouldn't hear her through their bedrooms' shared wall.

I guide Anna through the Slipper Camp exercises, speaking to her artistic soul with each piece of technique. Over the next thirty minutes she reconnects with herself and the story she has to tell. Color and range return to her voice, and her songs become compelling once again. Months later we debrief this experience and she shares how important it was for her to see this familiar habit of quieting herself when performing under pressure for men, and then correct it through feeling supported by an older woman.

Maturing in our lopsided sexual belief system is next to impossible—especially when older women are called "unfuckable." But let me tell you a secret: menopause has left me unable to remember what men are for, at least not in the way my body once assumed. The bleeding away of my breeding impulse has been accompanied by a glorious settling that won't let me settle for less when it comes to intimacy. Sensing newfound weight in the line that runs from shoulder blades, down past sacrum through the backs of my legs to my heels, I feel an even deeper love for gravity, for Mother Earth.

When I invite a woman to lie on the floor of my studio and access the depth of her sound—her own gravity—she changes. The sound flooding from her upper mouth reminds her that she owns her lower one. There is no one to please or take care of within this unmediated, potent, personal experience. The sounds emerging from her body are based on receiving air fully. Slowing down, she renews her relationship to her pelvic floor, becomes a woman listening to herself.

Women need female support for the health of our nervous systems. Confidence is built when what we reveal is heard and believed. Women listening to women. Women supporting a woman being listened to by one man—or a full society of men. Together we can develop the aplomb required for the telling of difficult stories and the creation of new ones. No more "Love Hurts," "Hit Me with Your Best Shot," or "Hit Me, Baby, One More Time." Would our species mature erotically if we sang about love in a new way?

31

Don't Be Afraid

EARLY JUNE AT the Banff Centre. Massive evergreens cocoon my cedar cabin; the mountains behind hold everything in place. My fingers crush sound through the piano's big, hard body … chord after chord, a relentless, numbing, insistent rhythm. The weight of my shoulders smashes through humeri and into forearms. Dry, spindly wrists lock slightly, channeling burden through knuckles, jamming each fingertip's individual swirl onto the ivory keys. Knitting together one minor chord after another, I descend into a blackness I cannot change. I am she—the she of massive complaint. Over the top of my playing I complain hard. Sing. And Sing. And Sing.

But is this singing? This she-complaint I am stuck with, and stuck with, and stuck with … again, and again, and again?

I want to stop.

Stop the relentless banging of these painful, needy piano chords as my voice careens over and under, and all over the place. I don't know how to take care of myself as I unburden heart and soul.

Can I please stop?

How long does a woman have to scream to be heard?

The neural circuitry in an addict is so gouged and grooved by the pattern of that particular stimulus—upper or downer—that nerves become less sensitive and have to be hit harder and harder by the substance itself for the addict to get relief. The partner of an addict—be that addict "workaholic" or "alcoholic"—needs to yell louder to get through.

I am yelling, hollering, screaming my truth. Out-Joplining Janis, out-shrieking the jonesing we all feel for the thing that might save us ... or at least put us to sleep, knock us out ... out of conscious misery.

I want to stop playing, stop hammering these keys. *I've gotta stop grinding vocal cord against vocal cord.* It is a desperate feeling. Slip-sliding cords trying to spill truths I can't yet articulate.

I see my teacher out of the corner of my eye. No, I don't. But he is there, seated to my far right, and I am blocking the real him while she-the-banshee sings me in the way his early-teaching-self first guided. I cannot tell what is going on here. A voice in my head says, "STOP!" But I sing on, grinding and grinding and grinding out a pain I have known for too long. This path of destruction is set deep in my bones.

Is he bored? Does he hate this pop tune? Is it on his list? Why am I so disconnected from my body? Why am I singing this painful crap? Who should hear this? My partner? My father? Why do I care so fervently about what Richard thinks? I wish I was singing for a woman, for any women, for all women ... for my friend Katherine.

I keep singing. I sing four more songs. I hurt every step of the way. I hurt as I try to forgive. I hurt as I say I'll be there through thick and thin. I hurt as the old-style love I was raised to give—to want—chokes and crushes and ruins my mind and my heart and my voice.

This fairy tale has no godmother.

The problem with catharsis is that it is shortsighted. It can become the addictive substance—gouge deep grooves of dopamine-filled satisfaction. Addicted to drama. Mine. My family's. My man's. His family's. We build a new empire of little people playing out the same sad story. Or angry one. Or faked, "perfectly happy" one.

Here I am—foot hardly out the door—frozen on the path to freedom and health, punishing myself again.

Ban her. Ban she who disturbs the peace. Banshee, a fairy creature wailing as if someone is about to die. Keening at a funeral comes from this blessed Irish, or Scottish, she-thing. The best keeners are in high demand. O's and

Macs—native Celts—plying their special gift ... and curse. I celebrate my own Mac heritage ... raped by Vikings, to be sure. My palms own this as tendons twist and retract now that I am nearly sixty.

Irish folklorist Patricia Lysaght points out that a banshee dresses in white or gray—runs a silver comb through her long pale hair. Combs are part of a mermaid's allure too. Steal this symbol of beauty and power, left by either banshee or mermaid, and risk being spirited away by a dangerous-voiced woman.

The screech of the barn owl, the siren's song, the bloodcurdling shriek of a banshee, keening—sounds that terrify and warn—these are part of my chosen artistic inheritance as well as my bloodline. I have learned to manifest these vibrations through body and voice. It was not hard; they were clamoring to be released from my vocal treasury. Now I need to understand them ... retain their feelings in ways that cost me less. Sing their truth with equanimity.

Can I return to the trashing of my voice now, please? It is the story that has had the most meaning for me for more than two decades now. So full of feeling. So much information. I am used to its pain.

As Richard watched me sing, I adjusted myself to what I imagined as his gaze. What did he want and need? Was I doing well enough? His sadness has always touched me, reminds me of my father, of the lovers I have had. How in touch is he with his dreams and his losses? He is so sensitive and works so hard. *I need to make it better.* This is what is burdening my mind while playing these chords, screeching these tones— thinking and thinking and thinking these thoughts.

Getting back to my voice ... and one of the secrets I am holding ...

My teacher is the man to whom countless people owe the owning of body and voice. *I do.* His wisdom slays me and yet I am not sure he owns his own.

Getting back to my voice, again ... but, wait, here is one of my father's secrets ...

He wanted to be rich. *Nice guys don't win.* He sacrificed his gentle, creative soul to money and control. He sacrificed love and family ... and then his brain exploded.

And getting back to my voice, again ... No! One more secret ...

All my men/lovers/friends/directors/composers/husbands have been drinkers, or "holics" of some sort. Holy frolickers. Gifted and beautiful ... struggling to land well on the earth. I wanted to play with them. I thought I needed that. I wanted to be the Mélisande to their Pelléas by wandering into dark woods *together.* No straight lines. So much to discover. But the way I feel now is nothing like how the story was meant to go, and just this morning the cells of my body told me how washed out, dried up, puffed, misshapen, and hurting they have become. They—we—I can't punish myself like this anymore.

And back to my voice ... my choice ... again, another secret ...

There is a little white patch on my right vocal cord. Dr. Osborn tells me how closely he needs to place the probe—practically touching its gleaming surface—in order to see it. The long wire of the tiny camera has been carefully inserted up a nostril and through my nasal cavity to curve down past the back wall of my mouth, into my throat past false vocal cords, finally reaching my larynx. Dr. Osborn has talked me through the procedure each step of the way. I am breathing slowly and calmly and don't feel any pain at all as he locates the best route through my nasal passageways. Earlier, when I told him that the scrape of the camera usually leaves me with cold-like symptoms, he coated its wire with gel to help it slip down easily. There has been no disruption to the delicate material lining my pharynx either. My mucous membranes have been left in peace.

The tiny white patch is a sign that damage was done when I was singing in that cedar cabin for my friend and mentor, Richard. Singing tired. Singing emotional. Singing confused. Was it a blister, a burst blood vessel, or an abrasion from those abrasive Joplinesque sounds? Neither the doctor nor I know. I tell him that it felt blistery to me. He is clear that it does not require surgery and says if I am careful in the next few months it should heal fully.

That is what I want.

I no longer want to be a siren for pain.

As I sang those five songs for Richard in that mountain cabin, all I could think was: "Surely I am past this. Surely I am past self-abuse, anger, bad choices … this bullshit inheritance. Surely I know enough, have felt enough … have seen enough options."

I have.

But to be a clarion for health … that will take composure, self-possession. Ownership.

Where will I learn this?

Look inside. Integrate.

I will not forsake my anger and drive, or let them get the better of me. I will calm my confusion, let go of my habit of doing someone else's work, of taking on too much responsibility. Lift my foot off the pedal just the right amount. It might feel like I am coasting rather than driving.

Who is my example?

Lie on the ground; the muck of decaying leaves sticks to skin and hair. Soften and swell through your belly and pelvic floor. Feel the earth hold you and breathe with her. Slowly, slowly mother and daughter spin through time, holding one another. Gravitational pull reorienting the stately alignment of our heavenly bodies. Cells mutate, heal, shift, transform.

The pain in my heart is outrageous.

Don't be afraid.

32

Cassandra Is Tired

MY FRIENDS AND I are listening to each other with unprecedented care and focus. We talk and laugh in peri- and post-menopausal ways about the physical and emotional realities of our aging bodies. Very little feels muted within, and very little is censored between us. We are reclaiming our natural ability to have each other's backs while negotiating a change as disruptive as puberty.

It is immaterial whether we had children or not, whether we are still in a relationship. None of us is now tethered to deep-seated breeding impulses. In fertility's silent aftermath we have no patience to fake, please, or make up for much. This biologically enabled emotional freedom is worth the cost of achy joints and dry eyes. There seems to be so much less to protect, or defend, and so we say what we think and feel ... and listen deeply. Maybe this is the unmediated female voice I have been longing for.

I love to look at women's bodies. My daughters' and my friends' ... my mother's. We move through the everyday clothed, but I can see how unique each person is underneath the cut of her skirt or jeans. Body Blitz, a women-only water spa, used to have a clothing-optional policy. When I relaxed there with my closest friends, we'd forgo swimsuits, trusted the hot water to peel away remaining surface differences. Our talk came alive under the skin. Moving from pool to sauna to steam room, I absorbed an abundance of shapes, sizes, and skin tones. So many ways of walking, of sitting, of slipping into water. The intimacy of the baths impressed upon me how full of life we are, as well as the fullness of our lives, so much etched into our beings. It is affirming to see a woman at home in her body. Safe. Gravity has tugged on my flesh long enough that I have no choice but to let go.

Over the course of my lifetime, women's bodies have become more and more exposed, used to advertise just about anything through slack-jawed, blank-eyed, ready-to-please, compliant images. We don't look self-possessed. We don't look *in* ourselves. Our cultural idea of beauty looks nothing like what I or other women say we feel. We are so much more varied and interesting than our commodified images, than our "measuring up" voices—voices we are judged for, whether demure or demanding. How little schooling there has been for us to learn how to trust what we have to say.

The title of one of Mozart's greatest comedies, *Così fan tutte* (1790), is translated as *Women Are Like That*. The 2014 Canadian Opera Company production, directed by Atom Egoyan, was sumptuous and detailed. Though the reviews ranged from slight outrage to full-on embrace, I know his vision was successful; my stomach started to hurt before the end of Act One.

Librettist Lorenzo Da Ponte's story begins simply: Two young sisters are betrothed to two young brothers from Naples. Bowing to Da Ponte's original title, "A School for Love," Atom's production is set in what looks to be a private school. Reminiscent of Britney Spears's plaid kilt in her "Baby One More Time" video, the sisters' uniforms land well above the knee. The narrative line begins in a biology classroom equipped with human-sized "specimen pins." While the brothers sing about Fiordiligi and Dorabella, their wonderful, faithful fiancées, their trusted mentor, Don Alfonso, listens in. To prove his world-weary wisdom he places a wager—their fiancées will surely cheat given the chance. He then manufactures that chance. Guglielmo and Ferrando pretend to go off to war before reappearing in disguise—apparently a mustache and turban are all it takes to fool these girls. Don Alfonso and Despina, the maid, encourage the sisters to attach themselves to the wealthy "Turkish" strangers, saying that it is unlikely that their future husbands will return from war alive. These new men present secure marital options. End of Act One.

I understand that this is supposed to be funny—witty, even—but I can't get past the cruelty. Girls at that time had so few choices: they could stay at home forever under their father's roof and their mother's dominion; or marry someone in order to run their own home; or become a nun and live under the protection of the church. A woman with a bank account was well over one hundred and fifty years into the future. Credit cards didn't yet exist, but who cares?! It wasn't until the '70s in Canada that a woman could get a Mastercard without her husband's permission. As for jobs …

My eldest daughter was an au pair in modern-day Italy the same winter I saw *Così*. During her stay she was shocked by the gender dynamics of that culture. Her directness in speech and presentation, and her interest in having platonic male friends—not just a boyfriend—weren't understood by either the young men or the young women. When she went to a bar alone she felt mistaken for a sex worker. There is a wider range of acceptable behavior for women in Canada, but the social underlay is not dissimilar to the one Magda felt in Bergamo, directly descended from Da Ponte's more than two-century-old libretto.

To find out if anyone else is upset by *Così*'s story, I go online. In reviews of various productions the story and its current sociological resonance is not examined, just how it is dressed up and played. A few in-depth articles about the work itself state that its "misogyny" is "a given." Occasionally tensions between the libretto's plot and Mozart's music are pointed out. Despite the story's dismissive treatment of the sisters' emotional lives, he has given them deeply affecting melodies, just as he highlighted the Queen of the Night's impeccable rage through her virtuosic arias in *The Magic Flute*. In both operas Mozart does his best to bring women's voices to life within impossible circumstances.

In Act One of *Così* when the two women bid farewell to their fiancés, their outpouring of love is rendered true with every pulsing breath. In the second act when the trickery is well under way, the older sister, Fior-diligi, sings a sublime aria that lays bare her distress over the feelings she is developing for the "Turkish" stranger—though she hasn't yet succumbed to his requests. Mozart's exquisite music does not change the fundamental objective of the narrative, which is to prove that all women cheat. Under the weight of Don Alfonso's desperate need to win his wager, Despina's jaded advice, and the strangers' pleas and threats, the women are betrothed unwittingly to each other's fiancé.

Da Ponte's libretto was considered modern and fun in eighteenth-century Europe, though partner-swapping stories reach back centuries thanks to Shakespeare, Boccaccio, and Ovid. Because of its humor it is an example of *opera buffa,* a theatrical form that thrived parallel to *opera seria.* In the latter, gods and heroes act out serious themes and are played by high voices: sopranos and tenors. In *opera buffa* lower male voices became more important by providing a moral compass within the hilarity either through meddling or bombastic pronouncement: a mirror of Sarastro's function in Mozart's *singspiel The Magic Flute.* The noun *buffa* refers to a comedic actress or clown and comes from the Latin word for toad. Why toads? Because a jester puffs out his cheeks as part of his comedic display—rolls his eyes at the end of the "play," shrug-ging off everyone's actions. But the verb *buffare* translates as *buffet*—to be knocked about—like the sisters in *Così.*

Così ends with the men's ruse exposed. Low-voiced Don Alfonso excuses his manipulative behavior by explaining how helpful his edu-cation of his male charges has been; they now know how vigilant they must be, given what they are marrying. The girls are emotional messes because each one discovered that she preferred the other's beloved, and now must return to her original match. As for the brothers, they have lost more than a bet.

I ask Atom—a close and valued friend—about his staging choices for the final sextet in which all the characters sing of their return to "reason." He tells me that the libretto's words are open-ended enough that a director could choose to partner the sisters any which way, but he returned each sister to her original fiancé as most productions do.

Fiordiligi and Dorabella—finally self-aware—can't change their plot. Putting my sick stomach aside, I pay attention to the muted affect of each singer in Atom's finale; neither male nor female has escaped emotional flattening. Thank goodness for the eighteenth century's shorter life expectancy.

I play opera director and re-stage the piece in my mind. I consider dressing the sisters in fundamental religious clothing in Act One—after any of the three great monotheisms—and throughout Act Two have them gradually remove these coverings as they experience their true feelings and explore their options. I picture the women paired in that final tableau with whichever suitor they choose, wonder if this coupling could change each night according to what the singers have felt while performing the opera. I mean, if we are fickle, why not be *really* fickle? Or maybe *flexible,* and include the maid Despina and trusted mentor Don Alfonso as possible partners, despite age and class differences. Let the characters surprise each other, the audience ... even themselves. Make it harder to wrap up male and female relationships; resist the urge to jam the social status quo back into place.

Così tripped me into forty-eight hours of acute distress. My feathers more than a little ruffled, I alternated between swallowing feelings of deep disgust and complaining about them to anyone who would listen. My squawk was that of a chicken plucked raw. Henny Penny crying, *"The sky is falling, the sky is falling!"*

One tired Cassandra.

It is sickening that lies about women continue to be shoved down our throats: that we are seen as untrustworthy; our feelings weightless; expected to "settle" at the end of the day under someone else's rules. For weeks I write my way out of this turmoil, shoving food down my gullet all the while. I remember the bulimia I struggled with in my twenties, only this time I am leading myself through the inconsistencies of this culture. Less buffeted, I don't need to vomit to find relief.

What drew me to opera on a deep, fleshy level was the intense fusion of scream within its decorum. But can female truth be revealed from within opera's overly cultivated wilderness? When women sound good singing about our troubles, what does this tell an audience? If a director doesn't illuminate a work's relevance today, why is it being done? It is not enough to be a songbird in a cage, colorful plumage on show. Through uncovering my personal scream, I have been able to see that opera's scream is a tidy scream that works for men. It is not okay for a fancy song to plead and excuse a woman's case, all at once. This is not the way reform happens.

I saw *Così* during the development of both the Toronto and Chicago bird projects. I used these creative homes to work with women's voices as honestly as I know how. I hoped that our unmasked vocal sound could counter the dangerous limitations placed upon us in the everyday. I began to think of this creative work as fighting female extinction. My bird-self screamed: *Where's my path?! What's my path?! Who can I trust?! What can I trust?! Where is my partner?! Who is my partner?! Must I partner?! And if I am still compelled to partner, how ...*

I don't want language to mediate my potential for directness. I don't want to dilute my physical sensations, the rawness in my bones. I want to follow the trail of my wilderness, allow for mistakes when relearning instinct. Are there even words for what I want to do and need to express?

Even with bird cries as inspiration, these avian art projects were fraught with the challenges felt in a Western woman's body when trying to override sounding pretty or singing politely. The Inuit throat singing I learned in the Arctic during my twenties leaps to mind as an antidote. Exhales honking like a goose, air exploding into my lungs— pitch and resonance, high then low. *All nature in my chest;* my chest *is* all nature. Sore ribs the next day, extrinsic and intrinsic intercostals worked beyond their cage. I picture a bird's wishbone and my ribs unlock. No more opera. No more dirty corset.

On most of this planet our treatment and contextualization of women is based on inequality; it's our everyday, mundane, psychosocial food—threatens to slip down my gullet by the hour ... drown me. I can track my culture's effects on my well-being by noting the lack of ease with which actual food slides down my esophagus—the muscular tube that lies behind my trachea, passes behind my heart. In medical diagrams the human esophagus looks more like a bird's trachea than the short cartilaginous windpipe that connects a woman's voice box to her bronchi.

The windpipe and the esophagus are our lifelines, transporting crucial nourishment, either air or food. They track each other; if the windpipe is tight so is the esophagus, and vice versa. As a student accesses sound, expanding their trachea, they often burp, releasing pressure through finding space.

Così premiered more than two hundred years ago, and its values could be dismissed as outdated. But we do not have to look terribly hard today to find women who have been judged in the same untruthful light as the sisters for their sexual nature, their desire to choose with whom to partner, or their need for justice after having been hurt physically by a man in an intimate context. Women casually made fun of for being true to themselves.

When I sing the melodies a man writes, steeped in a tradition bound by males, and act onstage in ways that keep the male story central, I risk damaging myself. Throughout my twenties I worked on one of the *Così* sisters' arias for hours in practice rooms at various institutions. I sang them in audition before juries of men. Through linking my breath and resonance to Dorabella's, I incorporated the confusions she felt, the things she thought she desired. And it seemed normal, in line with how I was raised ... so I thought nothing of it. But singing old material in old ways entrenches old stories in a performer's cells; and hearing these tales does the same for the bodies and minds of those listening—regardless of gender identification.*

Encoding emotional falsehoods through art interferes with a woman's self-knowledge. It can even prevent her from feeling what she is

---

* Human experience is so dependent on what we have already constructed that when a participant in a controlled medical research project is told they have a hereditary gene that predisposes them to a certain disease, they are likely to manifest the symptoms of that sickness without actually having it.

feeling. It encourages her to mute how she expresses her experience, forces her to do backflips to protect others from her honest-to-goodness story. What means are needed so as not to lose track of ourselves in order to express difficult things? I need to believe that telling the truth will not result in physical punishment or psychic death. I need faith that my truth is worth expressing—that "self-betrayal" won't lead to ridicule.

Women have been seen as overly emotional creatures throughout history. Dishonored for this capacity. The inner movement of chemicals and hormones—this ability to be moved—is what keeps human beings connected to our bodies. But the female molecular response to life has rarely been affirmed, believed, or trusted. Understanding and valuing mad, sad, and glad equally marries a woman to her true nature. Charting our feelings in an unbiased way fosters the human ability to connect with self and identify with others. Clarifies expression.

Human design allows us to hear emotion in the tone of a person's voice, to see it in the unconscious movements of the body. I am hungry for the science that is charting our neurobiology in a way that brings "feelings" out of the closet ... the science that honors our animal makeup. The less we think of emotions as good or bad, the less likely they are to be misunderstood, reviled, blocked, or twisted. It is time to stop thinking that a benevolent dictatorship of mind over body—over "matter," or "what matters," or "is the matter"—is a healthy relationship.

The body's many systems are designed to self-regulate, to heal whenever possible. We have more than enough immune cells when not chronically stressed. When we pay attention, the body educates through encouraging us to listen to ourselves; movement and feeling turn easily into sound and word. The ability to soften my anal sphincter while in *fight or flight* permits me to breathe easily; once this becomes habit, I can undo a lifetime of limiting structures in one second flat, partner softness with my urge to hit, run, or freeze when under emotional threat. When the body and mind collaborate, representing the whole human, the sublime and direct link between physical feeling and thought processes thrives. This is nonpartisan, internal democracy. Not trusting the female body—with the exception of idealized, unrealistic forms—preferring the sound of the unloved female voice (the pop music whine that begs to please), reinforces a sorry legacy of unembodied behaviors for everyone.

I gained respect for my own in-the-body reality through giving birth at home; undiluted pain and joy reimagined my insides. I found perspective and range through witnessing my daughters' trust-based relationship to their own carnal needs and capacities. They were perfectly in tune with themselves, and through this I became proud of "being a girl." Mothering began my true education, taught me how to recalibrate my worth internally through valuing theirs. When I am inside my body without shame, when I track my feelings without judgment, I process reality so much more reliably. For any woman, our manifest rhythms and cadence, harmony, and undertow are essential to life on earth not just because we might have sex or make a baby. The agency that comes directly from owning our bodies and having them respected raises a personal sense of virtue so that the fullness of our lives and the truth of our stories become as valuable as those of men. Who we are is more important than who we have, or have not, had sex with, or who we are no longer having sex with. I am thinking of Mozart's demoted Queen of the Night right now ...

Very few female mammals live beyond their breeding years: orcas, narwhals, short-finned pilot whales, belugas, and humans. In the case of orcas, older females are often the leaders of their pods in a matriarchal clan system that sees generations living together under the same waves. These grandmothers often live past the age of eighty, whereas males die in their fifties. Adult sons of older mothers have longer life spans than those whose mothers have not survived. Scientists posit that orca grandmothers go through menopause so as not to compete with their daughters in the breeding cycle. They also note that grannies help rear their grandkids. What I find interesting is that older female orcas are most likely to lead their communities when times are tough. They know their underwater geography and have decades of experience foraging for food.

I've decided to act like a whale. Pretend that my leadership is valued. Open my mouth. Fully through the grand climacteric, I picture myself more Tiresias than Cassandra: gender fluid, inner eyes wide open. Generalized sexual interest in men is gone, evaporated along with my body's familiar monthly surges. I wonder if any heterosexual woman can understand the full effects of cultural objectification before she has stopped bleeding and no longer needs to be "picked."

As for *Così*, I am angry with Despina for not giving the young women useful advice—and with Mozart and Da Ponte for capitalizing on her hurt and anger for their own comedic pleasure, while safely staying on their side of the relationship bed—though the virgins in this opera fare better than those in *The Arabian Nights*. Like revisiting Scheherazade's marital situation, the experience of seeing Atom's accomplished 2014 *Così* stoked my outrage, made the three and a half years between his production and September 2017's #MeToo and #TimesUp hashtags long and aggravating. It is now clear to all of us that consensual sex is radical, as is a woman opening her mouth without fear.

———

Dancer Kate Holden has her back to us. She walks upstage left to face a massive canvas suspended on the diagonal. The taut fabric has been gashed in three places. Kate extends both her arms, presenting an invisible orb to the otherwise blank surface. As her hands cup the air, she hums a note, fills the empty space between her palms with warmth and resonance. She walks away from the canvas only to return to it once more, back still to us, mouth invisible as her hum refills the space between her hands. This time she slides her pitch up by one full tone. She pauses for a moment before letting gravity swing her left arm back and down while expiring a gentle *sssssssssssss* …

Has she asked a question? Is it about possibility? Has that possibility been deflated?

Kate walks downstage right and reaches toward the audience as if to touch something or someone in the empty space right before her. In between the gestures she creates a small, fractured melody. She carries her sound with care, and her gestures are full of expectation. John

280

Farah's musical accompaniment begins, triggered by Kate's desire and imagination. She dances virtuosically for fifteen minutes. Throughout, her vocal repertoire includes the very private *sssssssss* we have already encountered, chest-imploding *guhs* colored with the dull thud of grief, and high-pitched coloratura bubbles. At one point she races toward us repeatedly on all fours, growling and barking out a to-do list of epic proportions. The hairs on my arms stand alert. Kate's sounds range from fragile and intimate to the loud, piercing shrieks of a bird as she spreads her wings—arms ripping voice wide from sternum up beyond crown.

As her story builds she unfolds fully and wholly in body and voice, charting the stage in a grand circle, vibrating sound from head to toe. She finally carries us downstage to the spot where her first small melody unfolded. As John's now massive instrumental music pours through her, she fills the theater with one long ecstatic high note—an exquisitely balanced scream. *Hers.* Kate returns to the blank, torn canvas and repeats her opening gesture, holding the same invisible orb. The hum from the beginning of the piece is now replaced with a warm-toned vowel. We can hear that her mouth is open, and when she turns to face us we see its gaping shape.

Women are learning to talk about what is unspeakable. We are supporting one another in this act of courage. The torn, blank canvas is huge, but Kate's open mouth offers me hope, her back reminds me of sisterhood, and sisterhood is richer than what I once believed.

33

Digging the Mermaid

GIUSEPPE DI LAMPEDUSA is in love with a mermaid. In his short story "The Professor and the Siren," he draws on nature to describe the sensuality of her voice: "It was a bit guttural, husky, resounding with countless harmonics; behind the words could be discerned the sluggish undertow of summer seas, the whisper of receding beach foam, the wind passing over lunar tides."* He can't resist its elemental pull.

Playwright Richard Sanger wants to adapt this story for the stage and has asked me to be its siren, Lighea. I resist his invitation to incarnate the animal and the divine because I can't imagine a composer who could do justice to a mermaid's voice and tell him so. I also say *no* because my boyfriend at the time makes clear his jealousy; he is a writer and does not like imagining another man's words in my mouth. I don't share this with Richard. Despite being in my mid-forties, a feminist, and the mother of two outspoken teenage girls, it takes me a little while to admit that this is a problem. When I do we break up.

Richard asks me once again if I would like to be part of his mermaid project. This time I ring out an enthusiastic *yes* and, having just heard Nik Beeson's CD *Howlings*, I tell him that I have found the perfect

---

* Giuseppe Tomasi Di Lampedusa, *The Professor and the Siren*, trans. Stephen Twilley (New York: New York Review Books Classics, 2014), 37–38, Kindle.

composer. I can finally imagine a hybrid sonic-theater style that would give my body enough space and support to inhabit a siren's voice.

Richard, Nik, and I talk endlessly about mermaids. The men get so fired up that I have to remind them that sirens aren't real—that they spring from our collective human imagination. They nod vaguely in my direction before slipping back into talking about "our mermaid," as if she were flesh, blood, and salvation. My men seem to need and fear the siren's call as much as any lonely sailor … any man trying to find his way back home.

We are all at sea when it comes to grounding ourselves in the feminine.

In ancient Greece mermaids flew and sang before they swam. It is said that the first sirens requested wings so they could search after Persephone, who had been stolen from her mother by Hades, ruler of the underworld, before he raped and then married her. Persephone becomes the great agricultural goddess in Greek myth, regulating the seasons … fecund and imprisoned. Some versions of the myth say that the sirens, having witnessed Persephone's horrific tale, asked for wings so they could remain virgins.

Despite their original ability to fly, the power of the mermaid's voice is not drawn out of thin air. Like Bella and I imitating birds in Basunti's lush North Indian garden, or our singing flock at the Art Gallery of Ontario, or the women in the sweatshops of any garment district raising their voice in protest, or actresses recently calling out sexually abusive male behavior in the workplace, mermaids issue female sound that has not been cultivated or controlled. Resonance that thickens air.

I decide to make our siren a stepping stone toward female instinct … use her for myself. The word *ferile* is perfect for my mermaid: a female virility that doesn't necessarily lead to fertility, or being fucked. I mean, mermaids' legs can't be spread. *Ferile* is potent, captures the dangerous promise held in a siren's high-pitched song. Many a captain has wrecked his ship on treacherous rocks while distracted by a mermaid's captivating cry. (Is an imaginary woman being blamed for a real man's bad navigation?)

During our conversations with Richard, Nik and I arrive at concrete ideas for vocal improvisation. I sing along with recordings of wolves and whales. I imitate their sounds, and I let myself be wild through ululating, howling, and shrieking. When I listen back to the improvs, I hear that I am equating elemental only with aggressive. Though mermaids threaten death and destruction, I wonder if they nurture life too. Wombs and watery graves … seaweed, roots … the basement. My uterus has sheltered at least two female embryos. The *vi* of *vita* opens the door to life, the shape of the first letter consonant with the shape of a woman's fallopian tubes—her vulva too. I recall the word *pudendum*, another term for a woman's external genitalia. The word's musicality seduces me until I learn that it translates from the Latin as the "part to be ashamed of."

I try to conjure our mermaid "unashamed" by expanding her range of feeling beyond the mundane, well past my earthly imagination. The element of water guides me to sounds that are *unbounded*—undomesticated and undomiciled—charting an expansive range of dynamics, soft shimmer to deep swell. Breaths spill and splash and caress. My vocal "house" pulls free from the expectations I have tied to "home"—to the work of making a home for others. She tows me under, follows me to bed.

In sleep I become a mermaid; not ours, but a garden-variety siren. I dive down to a most extraordinary color-scape of subtle, washed-out blues and greens and stay beneath. I must be fifty or sixty feet under. While studying marine biology at Pearson College, I learned that colors are absorbed one by one the deeper you dive—reds and pinks vanish, then oranges and yellows, and finally green, leaving only blue before going to black.

The next morning I can't shake the feeling of my mermaid hands. They were unusually fluid: fingers longer than a human's and unjointed; flesh semitransparent, jellyfish-like. My digits rode through the water, floating like seaweed, more a part of the ocean than I ever felt while scuba diving in my teens. The lyricism of my sea hands makes it clear that there is a wealth of power in a mermaid's ass, in her tail. How extraordinary not to use your arms to get around underwater ... the best kind of fishy. A mermaid's engine is below the waist. No shame there.

Walking into my kitchen to make the day's first cup of tea, I have a bracingly fresh thought. I have been using my own life with men to calibrate the mermaid's sensuality and emotional spectrum. But she is outside of this experiential paradigm, not of the twentieth or twenty-first centuries: no neuroses, no feminist struggle, no separation agreement to determine who owns what. No fear around *no* or *mine*. No backtracking or apology. A mermaid is less parceled out, less pulled apart than I am.

But still, I have to use this body—my fleshy digs—to give her voice.

The story we are bringing to life begins when Paolo Corbera, a young journalist, is dumped by both his girlfriends. He goes to Turin's Via Po to drown his sorrows. In the darkness of a dive bar we name "Bar Hades" he recognizes the distinguished—and phlegm spitting—Italian senator, professor, and retired classicist Rosario La Ciura. Rosario asks the young man which Corberas are his progenitors, thus situating Paolo's fallen aristocratic status next to his own peasant origins, underlining that, first and foremost, they are both Sicilian.

Sicily is a monster of an island: skin parched and brutal, bristling against the ever-present threat of Mount Etna's volcanic eruptions. Repeatedly conquered by everyone from the Greeks to the Normans, it is a place of reckoning. Over drinks the retired classicist and the former skirt chaser remember Sicily's exotic scents and its extraordinary sea life. The men begin to bond.

Against the backdrop of Mussolini's growing pre-war power—horrific to them both—the seventy-year-old professor eventually reveals that the repulsion he manifests toward women is the result of a tryst he had with a mermaid when he was twenty-one. Rosario was declaiming ancient Greek verse one splendid afternoon off the eastern coast of Sicily when a mermaid rocked his boat, quite literally. Lighea easily seduces him, starting by gently correcting his pronunciation. Rosario revels in her salty, oceanic odor for three full weeks, but doesn't dare accept her invitation to dive into the deep. When she swims away he withdraws into academia, specializing in the classics and ancient Greek. He confesses to Paolo that "She *was* a beast and a god!" and, since then, the mortal flesh of women smells putrid to him. Rosario's inability to get over Lighea has calcified; he clings pathetically to an unrealized, outmoded relationship with the feminine … his misogyny most likely a hatred for his own suffocated muliebrity.

——

Richard wrestles Lampedusa's short story into a clearly structured play with sparkling dialogue. His use of poetry—his and Homer's—makes room for sung and extended voice.

On the final afternoon of our first development workshop, led by director Ruth Madoc-Jones, the two actors, Jordan Pettle (Paolo) and David Jansen (Rosario), and I are poised behind our music stands for a full read-through. Musically we are going to tackle the climax and the denouement: a storm's epic sweep coincides with Rosario's inability to follow the mermaid in his youth; and a lament marks Lighea's enduring feelings for Rosario.

A full read-through at such an early stage is a daunting, unpredictable journey for performers and creative team alike. We have mined so much through conversation and research, and are dying to bring all of it to life. At this stage we haven't practiced anything, but the script and our imaginations will guide us through an inhabitation of the piece if we let them. I have no idea what will happen when I open my mouth; I need to be available, utterly unpredictable, and yet somehow achieve agreed-upon qualities and timings.

To conjure the storm I will use the full textural range of my singing voice to improvise with Nik's electroacoustic piece *Howlings*. I will imagine the call of my siren sisters who are begging me to rejoin them under the waves—allow that to influence the energy of this climactic moment. I will explore the mermaid's emotional landscape when she realizes that the young Rosario is unable to follow her into the deep. Finally, I will improvise a solo lament to welcome the much older professor into the ocean. Best not to be timid while searching for the vocal stuff and muscle of my mermaid.

We start.

Richard, Nik, and Ruth sit on the far side of the creative team's table only a few feet away from us three performers. I feel a little naked and hollow standing in this cold, white, midwinter rehearsal hall. Hands resting gently on the ledge of my music stand, I soften into my viscera. I quietly grab a chair and lift one leg up onto it to disturb the ladylike status quo of my stance, feel my pelvis hammock toward the floor. Gravity warps time and space. I become endless with regard to inhale and exhale … ebb and flow. As each breath drops into my torso, my diaphragm expands to its outer limits … watery … oceanic … immeasurable … renewable. I connect to the ancient, in-the-mouth pleasure of the Greek text.

deur' ag' iôn, poluain' Oduseu, mega kudos Achaiôn,
nêa katastêson, hina nôïterên op' akousêis.[*]

Homer tells us that Odysseus has been invited to stay his ship and listen to the sirens. Why not!? They are praising him! Richard Sanger has woven these lines throughout the piece so that the long ago Greek word *akousêis* comes up time and time again. Homer uses it as a verb, a command. *Listen!* The English word *acoustic* comes from the ancient Greek *akousêis*. For a singer, an *acoustic* is something to suffer or enjoy. Does the room, theater, or concert hall have a "good" acoustic or not? Will it make my job easier or harder? Will it "drown" me or "dry out" every sound I make?

Following the modern noun *acoustic* back to Homer's verb "to listen" completely changes my idea of singing. An acoustic provides a place to listen—to listen deeply—a place for expression, free of pushing. Too often I have felt the need to fill a room or overcome the accompaniment, and have worked way too hard rather than simply *living within the sound limits of a space … within my own limits.* Somehow an acoustic has always felt like my responsibility … something to make up for, to rise to…. But the ancient Greek reveals to me that there is a role for the listener too.

---

[*] This transliteration of the ancient Greek is from www.songlyrics.com/christopher-tin/seirenes-sirens-lyrics/.

Like Mozart subverting text I give my own voice something worth singing about; I stretch out the *oooo* vowel, make tangible my invitation to "listen." As the mermaid, I am offering time and space to the male characters so they can go back and retrieve something important ... something deep inside. To do this they will need to listen to themselves without emotional prejudice. And maybe I can ease up, be more direct ... trust I will be heard.

I call out to Rosario, ask him to come with me into deep waters. I engage with tangible, fleshy pleasure in my breath and sound. I do not censor. I improvise melodically and look for the divine and the animal in tone and pitch, and when I realize that my mortal lover cannot come with me—*cannot leave the safety of dry land*—I let sorrow fill my chest, shredding its way expansively through my mouth and up into the small crevices behind my eyes.

I sustain a many-stranded sob and lean into the beautiful sounds Nik's recording offers, making a song out of what is broken and ecstatic. I pound the sound down into my chest and let it chord into rage and regret. The tape's sounds meld with my foundations, spur on my feelings. The storm abates and I fall into the lament, stepping delicately through a series of half-voiced chromatic pitches. I play with the microtonal shifts that a morphing vowel allows. A gentle, off-kilter lullaby delicately creeps its way out of my body. The hollow shimmer of depth and height in my voice on the final *akousêis* transforms the rehearsal hall air.

We are the ancients.

We decide to make our mermaid a composite of all the women in Lampedusa's story. I am to play a dumped girlfriend, a pastry shop waitress, a barmaid, a housekeeper, and a wizened fascist. All these characters will flow into my characterization of the mermaid, carrying both men forward on an estrogen-rich current.

But despite our careful shaping of Paolo and Rosario's "mermaid ride," Lampedusa's piece is misogynistic at heart, true to its pre–World War II Italian sensibilities. At a table reading mid-process—the summer after Jian Ghomeshi's dismissal from the CBC—I am struck by how offensive the story now sounds. Since the cracking open of our collective smoothing-over of sexual harassment at work—and our naiveté around sexual consent after hours—Rosario and Paolo's coarse beliefs about women burn way too hot. But need, pain, and fear float just under the surface in our times, too. I can only hope that by giving these characters the space to voice freely their mistrust and mistreatment of the feminine, we might make obvious what everyone pretends has changed. From wage gap to sexual devaluation, each day's news seems to have at least one story that betrays our true feelings about a woman's worth ... a glut of online crime series start with a mutilated female body.

I find new entry into our piece by honoring the young journalist's persistent interest in the older man's inner life. I cherish the intimacy that develops between them thanks to Paolo's ability to identify with Rosario's frailty, loss, and regret. When the older man unearths his long-buried story, admitting to the strength of the mermaid's pull and his weakness in the face of her uncharted creative power, I begin to appreciate his existential struggle.

Lighea's invitation to enter her oceanic element—the wild and the divine—was beyond Rosario as a young man. He could not follow his heart ... his own inner muse. He had neither personal tools nor cultural permission. Academic and political structures fail him, aren't meaningful enough despite his eminent status within them, and he lives out a dried-up, bitter existence. Through admitting his secret to Paolo—giving shape to the strength of his own feminine through conjuring the mermaid and her voice—he transforms. Age graces him with the confidence to join Lighea in her watery depths. On his way to the World Hellenists' Congress to give the plenary address, he jumps ship.

We call our adaptation *DIVE*.

It takes five years to bring our piece to full production, and my body and voice age. I think frequently about the mermaid, how she is shaping my personal journey at a root level. Mid-development we stage a salon of the music, with narration, in my home—four shows over two weekends. It is time to make our collective imagining public.

During one of the salons I chance upon something brand-new. The May night is hot and humid; there are twenty-five people seated in my studio, faces glistening with sweat. We are near the end of the showing and I am standing on the piano, howling the ceiling open at the climax of the storm, melding with nature. When Rosario does not follow me, the sound of fascist jackboots presses my body down to the piano's closed keyboard. Ass settled on the edge of my well-tempered "rock" I utter my final words before slipping into the ocean: "I know in the end you will come."

Countering the weight of lost intimacy with the sheen of a seven-hundred-year-old mermaid's optimism, this last line comes out with an astonishingly bright gravity. I have never heard my voice descend to such well-lit gravel. Caught in the glare of tonight's shiny faces, I think, *I sound just like Lorne Greene!* The warm burr of his voice on TV's *Bonanza* is exactly how this new vocal sound feels in my body: fully undefended in my throat; rough-and-tumble ready behind my sternum. If I could talk through the *grrr* of an orgasm it would sound like this. And yet it is not "sexy." It has authority. Is authorial. I thought "digging in" vocally would bring me depth, but now I realize it is not necessary to dig.... I just have to settle. Settle with my levity intact. So much closer to pleasure than work. Has Lorne Greene just become my muse?

While Lorne fades into the background, mermaids, muses, and women's mouths mix and mingle.

The women of ancient Greece were not full citizens; they did not have the vote, could not own property. Within Athens' walls they were mandated to speak in pleasing, dulcet tones; *unbounded* voice was equated with a vagina's leakiness. To make unrestricted sound women had to leave civic space. What a way to guarantee that your sister, wife, daughter, or mother not offer her opinion, her creativity—not have her own her voice in public. Out in the suburbs, closer to nature, women were allowed to engage with a ritualistic sound known as the *ololyga*. This high, piercing female cry would have functioned cathartically, a communal blowing off of steam. A prophylactic *tarantella*.

My mermaid, Lighea, is the daughter of a muse. A muse is amuse is amused is used is abused is … *Use* uses three of the muse's letters for its own purpose.

Muse (myōōz) (*Free Dictionary*) *n.*

1. *Greek Mythology* Any of the nine daughters of Mnemosyne and Zeus: Calliope, Clio, Erato, Euterpe, Melpomene, Polyhymnia, Terpsichore, Thalia, and Urania, each of whom presided over a different art or science.

2. muse
   a. A guiding spirit.
   b. A source of inspiration.

3. muse A poet.

The *New Oxford Dictionary* is more explicit: "A woman, or a force personified as a woman, who is the source of inspiration for a creative artist."

My character is descended from the biggest muse of all: Calliope, who reigned over eloquence and epic poetry. Ovid referred to her as the chief of all muses. Wow, the mother of all muses! Calliope was celebrated for the ecstatic harmony of her voice, and is believed to have been Homer's muse for the *Odyssey*. The meaning of her daughter's name—spelled Ligeia in Greek—is soprano, or clear toned. No little mermaid whine for her.

———

I make my entrance opening night, bob on the waves, tug on the professor's boat.

I am Lighea … the daughter of Calliope … a mermaid, a siren …

Lighea has an animal's sharp little teeth. She licks them clean with her tongue after eating, and when offered wine, laps it from the professor's hand. To speak my lines I flow the air from behind my chest as I imagine a wild dog would. I practically bark; I do not let the shape of the words—the consonants—hold back my air. The vowels tumble and eddy and froth. The effect is jarring and uncanny … undomesticated.

Don't believe the stories they tell … we never kill, we only love.

With the exception of Ariel—the little mermaid Disney introduced my daughters to—I imagine all sirens and silkies live somewhere outside of human rights and wrongs. Lighea is not immoral but amoral. Preparing for the allure of her voice, Odysseus lashes himself to the mast so as to keep good boundaries. Not because he is afraid of cheating on his wife, Penelope—his philandering was sanctioned—but because an intact core is necessary to stay alive, and he doesn't have one.

Meanwhile Penelope stays home, runs the state, and remains faithful to her husband despite a steady stream of suitors. She doesn't spread her legs for some twenty years, while being shushed publicly by her son for opening her other mouth. Though a mermaid can't choose to spread her legs, unlike Odysseus's wife she can make any sound she pleases—including dangerous ones ... ones that can sway powerful men from their course.

I am reminded of Aristophanes's play in which Lysistrata invites all the women of Greece to join her in withholding sex from their husbands as a way to end the Peloponnesian War, which had been going on for more than three decades. She envisioned women on all sides of the conflict closing one mouth with the hope that the words coming out of the other would be heard and heeded. This strategy has been used in modern times to protest violence and corruption in Nigeria, Kenya, Togo, South Sudan, Liberia, the Philippines, and Colombia—with the goal of effecting change. Why was I not taught, as a young woman, about the collective power of owning our private parts this thoroughly?

When I first learned to sing I felt the need to hold on to something; I would imagine hugging a tree while opening my upper mouth. It was not until I could settle into my pelvis and clearly voice *no* for myself, without reactive stress and strain—feel it in my chest while gleaming behind the eyes—that I began to reclaim self-possession. This reminds me of Odysseus and his mast. It took time for me to learn how to vibrate my inner mast, to feel my resonance integrate as core. Identifying with Lorne Greene's entitled rumble is a stepping stone, but it is my belief in the value of a woman's pelvic basin that supports my mast—and my right to open my mouth.

The Greeks are correct that there is a relationship between a woman's two mouths—controlling what goes in and out of either is crucial. However, it is a woman who must own both of her mouths, have them in her possession, use them as she sees fit—exchange the verb *goes* for *come.* A mermaid's power lies in pairing full ownership of her lower mouth with unabashed permission to make unsanctioned sound. This is the opposite of what we have been told to do, subtly and pervasively, for generations: to spread our legs—or sometimes, hold them way too tight—while making only the right sounds, or none at all … during sex, while giving birth, straddling a Corvette, or speaking truth in parliament.

Feminine life force—the muse—is something we all have … to contend with, to mine, to mind, to honor … and, in my case, to own and sing. Through breath I tend this creativity, plumb my inner resources. Singing inspires me—imagines wholeness by telling me who I am. It allows me to feel the curves within the sacred space of my body … where I lay claim to my poetry. Do men miss this *unbounded* relationship within themselves? How deep is a man's mistrust of emotional incontinence, of his voice's upper "falsetto" … of (absent) tender tears? Does this fear underline all gender constructs?

A mermaid crawling onto dry land is part of my evolutionary process. She is a stand-in for the parts of me not yet fully present, for the parts of me I have learned to hide because they seem dangerous or shameful to society, to men, and even to other women. This is not because the sounds I am making are inherently rough or aggressive or potentially murderous; it is because they're real, unfettered, and precise.

When young Rosario is unable to follow his muse into her element, Lighea storms and laments, and then lets go and slips back into the water, joins her sisters to swim in what is current.

Maybe that is enough for now.

With a Full and Happy Heart ...

My studio has been blessed by hundreds of students over the decades. I thank each of you for your wholehearted entry into what has been, in practice, a living lab. Your transparency has taught me so much about vocal transformation. To those who appear in the book, thank you for granting me enthusiastic permission to use your name, or an alias. I do not take your trust, generosity, and courage for granted.

I would like to thank the dozen apprentices who shadowed my work over the years for your many questions about the whys and hows of this practice. Your curiosity and commitment refined my teaching.

Maria Meindl, Deanna Yerichuk, Sheridan McCarthy, Heidi Reimer— beautiful midwives, meticulous editors, unflagging inspiration— thank you!

The first draft was supported by a Chalmers Foundation Fellowship that I received through the Ontario Arts Council. I thank the jurors for the gifts of confidence and time.

The research of Dacher Keltner (*Born to Be Good*) and Stephen Porges (*The Polyvagal Theory*) supports what I witness in the studio. Their kind responses to my several emails gave me courage to say what I see, and thus evolve my pedagogical approach.

Very early versions of several chapters were published by the Canadian journals *Descant* and *Poiesis*. Thank you Karen Mulhallen and Stephen Levine—inked words ignite courage.

Gracious friends who provided quiet space to escape everyday responsibilities include Ginger Farley, Dennison Smith, David Smith and Denise Richard, Julie Robinson, Caroline Benjo and Carole Scotta, the Doody-Dickson household, Richard Armstrong, the Fletchers, Sheila Goldman ...

There have been many thoughtful, reflective readers along the way: Maggie Kast, Roger Peplar, Alex Fallis, Katherine Bruce, Traci Foster, Richard Sanger, Carmine Starnino, Aviva Chernick, Ciara Adams, Louis Laberge-Côté, Katherine Duncanson, Athena Colman, Danielle Wilson, Atom Egoyan, Natalie Klym, Katie Mazzini, Laura Taler, Shelley Craig, Duane Prentice, Susanna Hood, Ezra Cake, Georgia Webber, Diana Belshaw, and Trenton MacKenzie-Armes. Every chapter counts.

Of invaluable support during the many, many drafts: Eve Egoyan, our walks and your airplane read; Joanna Mackie, your generous, scribbled notes; Julie Trimingham, safe harbor and a turning point; Caroline O'Brien, synchronous paths; Niloofar Hodjati, cottage time, herbs, and feedback; Linda Hutcheon, intellect, body-based knowing, and cultural passions; Theo Dombrowski, unbridled enthusiasm for all things voice; and finally, Richard Armstrong, I was terrified of what you might say, and yet—and, of course—you tricked me into further following my voice.

Tessa McWatt taught me how to sit and write with rigor and pleasure on multiple retreats in Wales, India, and Corsica. *The Flintstones* theme sung at the top of your most magnificent lungs in a mountaintop kitchen only one example of the shared laughter that buoyed this process.

My artistic collaborators from this last decade have underpinned all my impulses and thoughts while writing: the women of URGE, no longer active as a collective but active within my psyche; the artists of Peggy Baker Dance Projects; Nik Beeson, Richard Sanger, Heidi Strauss, and Alex Fallis of the Mermaid Collective; and the dancers and musicians who brought *In This Body* to life.

Kimberly Grey, how extraordinarily kind of you to allow me to use "Poem for My Ribs" to open the door to breath, body, and image for this book's readers.

My father, my brothers, male friends, and beautiful former partners: outright mysterious collaborators in the messy stuff that made this book important for me to articulate.

North Atlantic Books, your invitation to publish came as my mother was dying and made it possible for me to relax into the final months I had with her. Thank you to Alison, Susan, Keith, Janelle, Adrienne, Sylvia, Ashley, and Jasmine for your compassion, clarity, and professional expertise.

My mother never read this manuscript. By the time I printed the penultimate draft her dementia had gotten the better of her ability to concentrate. However, she always asked how the writing was going and frequently reminded me, "Your grandmother said that a real artist leaves the dishes in the sink!" On her deathbed she blurted out in her ever roughening timbre, "How are your students?!"—the last thing I thought she'd have on her mind. She is looking over my shoulder right now, relieved that it is finally done!

My daughters. You are unparalleled sources of delight and surprise. Within our rock and roll ways you demand honesty, better behavior, modernity. Your care, laughter, and best wishes bring new meaning … hold me afloat. This is unconditional love.

Index